Family
Cookbook
Treasury

Family Cookbook Treasury

CRESCENT BOOKS

New York

Recipes created by Rosemary Wadey (Soups and Starters) Julia
Roles (Casserole Cookery) Diana Jaggar (Dinner and Supper
Parties) Moya Maynard (Quick Dishes and Freezer Cookery)
Jill Spencer (Mixer and Blender Cookery)

Photography by John Lee
Front jacket photograph by Paul Williams
Line drawings by John Scott Martin

China kindly loaned by David Mellor, Denby Tableware Limited,
Josiah Wedgwood and Sons Limited, Pointerware (UK) Limited,
Royal Doulton Tableware Limited, Southern Electricity Board
(Hounslow).
Foil products by Alcan Foil

This material originally published in 1977 by
The Hamlyn Publishing Group Limited under the following titles:
The Hamlyn All-Colour Books of *Soups and Starters, Casserole
Cookery, Dinner and Supper Parties, Quick Dishes, Mixer and Blender
Cookery, Freezer Cookery.*

Copyright © 1977, 1980 by The Hamlyn Publishing Group Limited

This 1982 edition published by Crescent Books,
distributed by Crown Publishers, Inc.
Originally published in Great Britain by
The Hamlyn Publishing Group Limited under the title
Your Favourite Cookbook.

Printed in Czechoslovakia

Library of Congress Cataloging in Publication Data

Your favourite cookbook.
   Family cookbook treasury.
   Reprint. Originally published: Your favourite
cookbook. London; New York : Hamlyn, 1980.
   Includes index.
   1. Cookery. I. Title.
TX651.Y68   1982   641.5   82-8103
ISBN 0-517-39127-9   AACR2

h g f e d c b a

Contents

Introduction

Once you have become acquainted with the wide selection of dishes in this book, you will quickly discover the enormous advantages of having every recipe illustrated in colour. By simply looking at the illustrations you can choose dishes which will balance each other when served together in one menu and provide an interesting contrast of colours.

Make the best of fresh vegetables, salads and fruit to make the meal as eye-catching as it is appetising. The same applies to the choice of dishes for cooking and serving. The illustrations show how to use your crockery to the best advantage, using the dish to complement the food.

The illustrations will give you super ideas for garnishes and decorations too – you will soon recognise the extras which are always useful to have around. Grow your own parsley, always keep a spare lemon and a stock of spices, olives, almonds and glacé cherries; in fact start a store of ingredients which, as the illustrations show, can make any dish special.

If you have just bought a freezer, you will find the information for packing and storing in the freezer invaluable. The illustrations show the use of foil, waxed cartons, trays and other containers and the recipes explain the best ways to freeze, store and thaw the dishes. If you have owned a freezer for some time, there will still be new ideas for emergency meals and for dishes to freeze uncooked.

This collection will not only make cooking and menu choosing easier and more interesting, but will ensure that every meal will be enthusiastically received by both family and friends alike.

Useful facts and figures

Notes on metrication

In this book quantities are given in metric and Imperial measures. Exact conversion from Imperial to metric measures does not usually give very convenient working quantities and so the metric measures have been rounded off into units of 25 grams. The table below shows the recommended equivalents.

Ounces	Approx g to nearest whole figure	Recommended conversion to nearest unit of 25
1	28	25
2	57	50
3	85	75
4	113	100
5	142	150
6	170	175
7	198	200
8	227	225
9	255	250
10	283	275
11	312	300
12	340	350
13	368	375
14	396	400
15	425	425
16 (1 lb)	454	450
17	482	475
18	510	500
19	539	550
20 (1¼ lb)	567	575

Note: When converting quantities over 20 oz first add the appropriate figures in the centre column, then adjust to the nearest unit of 25. As a general guide, 1 kg (1000 g) equals 2.2 lb or about 2 lb 3 oz. This method of conversion gives good results in nearly all cases, although in certain pastry and cake recipes a more accurate conversion is necessary to produce a balanced recipe.

Liquid measures The millilitre has been used in this book and the following table gives a few examples.

Imperial	Approx ml to nearest whole figure	Recommended ml
¼ pint	142	150 ml
½ pint	283	300 ml
¾ pint	425	450 ml
1 pint	567	600 ml
1½ pints	851	900 ml
1¾ pints	992	1000 ml (1 litre)

Spoon measures All spoon measures given in this book are level unless otherwise stated.
Can sizes At present, cans are marked with the exact (usually to the nearest whole number) metric equivalent of the Imperial weight of the contents, so we have followed this practice when giving can sizes.

Oven temperatures

The table below gives recommended equivalents.

	°C	°F	Gas Mark
Very cool	110	225	¼
	120	250	½
Cool	140	275	1
	150	300	2
Moderate	160	325	3
	180	350	4
Moderately hot	190	375	5
	200	400	6
Hot	220	425	7
	230	450	8
Very hot	240	475	9

Notes for American and Australian users

In America the 8-oz measuring cup is used. In Australia metric measures are now used in conjunction with the standard 250-ml measuring cup. The Imperial pint, used in Britain and Australia, is 20 fl oz, while the American pint is 16 fl oz. It is important to remember that the Australian tablespoon differs from both the British and American tablespoons; the table below gives a comparison. The British standard tablespoon, which has been used throughout this book, holds 17.7 ml, the American 14.2 ml, and the Australian 20 ml. A teaspoon holds approximately 5 ml in all three countries.

British	American	Australian
1 teaspoon	1 teaspoon	1 teaspoon
1 tablespoon	1 tablespoon	1 tablespoon
2 tablespoons	3 tablespoons	2 tablespoons
3½ tablespoons	4 tablespoons	3 tablespoons
4 tablespoons	5 tablespoons	3½ tablespoons

An Imperial/American guide to solid and liquid measures

Solid measures

Imperial	American
1 lb butter or margarine	2 cups
1 lb flour	4 cups
1 lb granulated or castor sugar	2 cups
1 lb icing sugar	3 cups
8 oz rice	1 cup

Liquid measures

Imperial	American
¼ pint liquid	⅔ cup liquid
½ pint	1¼ cups
¾ pint	2 cups
1 pint	2½ cups
1½ pints	3¾ cups
2 pints	5 cups (2½ pints)

Note: When making any of the recipes in this book, only follow one set of measures as they are not interchangeable.

Notes for American users

Although the recipes in this book give American measures, the lists below give some equivalents or substitutes for terms and commodities which may be unfamiliar to American users.

Equipment and terms
BRITISH/AMERICAN

cling film/saran wrap
flan tin/pie pan
greaseproof paper/wax paper
grill/broil
kitchen paper/paper towels
mince/grind

piping bag/pastry bag
polythene/plastic
sandwich tin/layer cake pan
stoned/pitted
tartlet tins/patty tins
top and tail/stem and end

Ingredients
BRITISH/AMERICAN

aubergine/eggplant
belly of pork/salt pork
bicarbonate of soda/baking soda
biscuit/cookie
black treacle/molasses
chicory/Belgian endive
chipolatas/link sausages
courgettes/zucchini
cream, single, double/light, heavy
digestive biscuit/graham cracker
gherkin/sweet dill pickle
glacé cherry/candied cherry

golden syrup/maple syrup
haricot beans/navy beans
lard/shortening
marrow/squash
plain flour/all-purpose flour
scampi/jumbo shrimp
self-raising flour/all-purpose flour sifted with baking powder
shortcrust pastry/basic pie dough
spring onions/scallions
sultanas/seedless white raisins
topside of beef/top round of beef

Soups and Starters

It is often difficult to be imaginative when choosing a starter to complement a main meal, but this wide variety of recipes with their interesting flavour combinations will ensure that you will never be at a loss.

There are hot and chilled soups, pâtés, salads, fruit cocktails, vegetable dishes, egg, cheese and fish dishes. Almost all the dishes can be frozen except those using salad vegetables or whole eggs; freeze soups for four to six months, remembering that in the case of recipes containing cream, egg yolks or garnishes, these ingredients should be added at the reheating stage.

Try to make full use of seasonal vegetables and fruit for maximum flavour and colour and also select the starter carefully to balance the main course – a hearty soup or pâté with a light main dish or a fruit cocktail with a substantial casserole or roast.

Hot soups

What could be more warming on a cold winter's day than a bowl of hot soup? Home-made soup is a good choice for a starter to a light main course; soup can also be served with slices of hot crusty French bread as a midday snack or late supper dish.

Minestrone soup

METRIC/IMPERIAL/AMERICAN
50 g/2 oz/⅓ cup haricot beans
1.75 litres/3 pints/7½ cups stock
2 carrots, chopped
1 large onion, chopped
1 clove garlic, crushed
2 leeks, trimmed, thinly sliced and washed
3 tablespoons/3 tablespoons/¼ cup oil
25 g/1 oz/2 tablespoons butter
1 (396-g/14-oz/14-oz) can peeled tomatoes
1 tablespoon tomato purée
bouquet garni
salt and pepper
50 g/2 oz/¼ cup spaghetti, broken up
Parmesan cheese

Soak the beans in 600 ml/1 pint/2½ cups of the stock overnight. The following day add a further 600 ml/1 pint/2½ cups stock and simmer gently for 1 hour.

Fry the carrot, onion, garlic and leeks in a mixture of oil and butter until soft – about 5 minutes – and until just beginning to colour. Add the remaining ingredients (except the spaghetti and cheese), the beans, all the stock and bring to the boil. Cover and simmer gently for 1 hour or until tender. Add the spaghetti and continue cooking for 10–15 minutes until tender. Discard the bouquet garni, adjust the seasoning and serve sprinkled with Parmesan cheese.

Serves 4–6

Cream of onion soup

METRIC/IMPERIAL/AMERICAN

50 g/2 oz/¼ cup butter
350 g/12 oz/3 cups onions, finely chopped
2 sticks celery, finely chopped
900 ml/1½ pints/3¾ cups chicken stock
1 blade mace
1 bay leaf
salt and pepper
25 g/1 oz/¼ cup flour
150 ml/¼ pint/⅔ cup milk
150 ml/¼ pint/⅔ cup single or double cream
GARNISH:
fried croûtons
chopped fresh mixed herbs

Melt the butter in a pan and fry the onion and celery for 5 minutes without browning. Add the stock, mace, bay leaf and seasoning. Bring to the boil, cover and simmer for about 45 minutes or until tender. Remove the bay leaf and mace. The soup can be sieved or liquidised if a smooth soup is preferred.

Blend the flour with the milk and whisk gradually into the soup. Return to the boil, stirring continuously, and simmer for 5 minutes. Adjust the seasoning, stir in the cream and reheat before serving. Dip the hot fried croûtons into finely chopped mixed herbs and float them on top of the soup.

Serves 4–6

Consommé

METRIC/IMPERIAL/AMERICAN

generous litre/2 pints/5 cups good beef stock
175 g/6 oz/¾ cup lean beef, minced
2 tablespoons/2 tablespoons/3 tablespoons tomato pulp
   (optional)
1 carrot, chopped
1 small onion, quartered
bouquet garni
whites and shells of 2 eggs
salt and pepper
1 tablespoon sherry (optional)
few julienne strips of cooked carrot

Place the stock in a pan with the beef and leave to soak for 1 hour. Add the tomato, carrot, onion, bouquet garni, unbeaten egg whites, crushed shells and plenty of seasoning. Whisk until nearly boiling then bring to the boil. Simmer very gently for 1 hour, taking care not to break the frothy layer on top.

Pour through a jelly bag or scalded cloth, keeping the froth back until last. Then pour through the filter of egg in the cloth again. Return to the pan, adjusting the seasoning if necessary but take care not to cloud the soup. A little sherry can be added, if liked. Place the cooked julienne strips of carrot into the consommé. Serve with breadsticks.

Serves 4

Mixed fish chowder

METRIC/IMPERIAL/AMERICAN
2 rashers lean bacon, derinded and chopped
1 onion, finely sliced
25 g/1 oz/2 tablespoons butter
1 (396-g/14-oz/14-oz) can peeled tomatoes
750 ml/1¼ pints/3 cups fish stock
1 bay leaf
salt and pepper
50 g/2 oz/⅓ cup long-grain rice
225 g/8 oz/½ lb cooked haddock or cod, flaked
100 g/4 oz/⅔ cup peeled prawns
1 tablespoon chopped parsley
2 tablespoons/2 tablespoons/3 tablespoons cream
few whole prawns to garnish

Fry the bacon and onion in the butter until beginning to colour. Add the tomatoes, stock, bay leaf, seasoning and rice. Bring to the boil, cover and simmer for 20 minutes or until the rice is cooked, stirring occasionally. Add the fish and prawns and continue cooking for 10 minutes. Remove the bay leaf. Adjust the seasoning, stir in the parsley and cream, and serve garnished with the whole prawns.

Serves 4–6

Oatmeal and vegetable soup

METRIC/IMPERIAL/AMERICAN
50 g/2 oz/¼ cup dripping or butter
1 large onion, finely chopped
1 turnip, finely chopped
2 large carrots, chopped
1 large leek, trimmed, thinly sliced and washed
25 g/1 oz/⅓ cup medium oatmeal
900 ml/1½ pints/3¾ cups stock
salt and black pepper
450 ml/¾ pint/2 cups milk

Melt the fat in a pan and sauté all the vegetables for about 5 minutes without browning. Stir in the oatmeal and continue cooking for a few minutes, stirring frequently. Add the stock and seasoning, and bring to the boil. Cover and simmer for about 1 hour or until all the vegetables are tender.

Add the milk, adjust the seasoning and bring back to the boil for 3–4 minutes. Serve piping hot.

Serves 4–6

Mussel and onion soup

METRIC/IMPERIAL/AMERICAN
2.25 litres/4 pints/5 pints mussels
½ bottle dry white wine
2 large onions, finely chopped
50 g/2 oz/¼ cup butter
50 g/2 oz/½ cup flour
1 litre/1¾ pints/4¼ cups milk
salt and pepper
1 tablespoon lemon juice
2 tablespoons/2 tablespoons/3 tablespoons chopped
   parsley
150 ml/¼ pint/⅔ cup cream

Wash and scrub the mussels thoroughly, discarding any that are open or that do not close when given a sharp tap. Place in a pan with the wine and onions. Bring to the boil, cover and simmer very gently for about 10 minutes until all the mussels are open. Remove the mussels and take most of them out of their shells, reserving a few mussels in half shells to garnish.

Melt the butter in a pan and stir in the flour. Cook for 1 minute then gradually add the mussel liquor followed by the milk. Bring to the boil, stirring frequently, season to taste and sharpen with lemon juice. Simmer for 5 minutes. Add the mussels and continue cooking for 2–3 minutes. Stir in the parsley and cream, and reheat without boiling. Garnish with the reserved mussels. Serve with hot crusty French bread.

Serves 6

Giblet soup

METRIC/IMPERIAL/AMERICAN
0.5 kg/1 lb/1 lb giblets
2 onions, chopped
2 sticks celery, chopped
2 carrots, chopped
salt and pepper
1.5 litres/2½ pints/6¼ cups stock or water
1 bay leaf
25–50 g/1–2 oz/about ⅓ cup long-grain rice
2 carrots, coarsely grated
GARNISH:
chopped parsley
fried croûtons

Wash the giblets thoroughly, discarding any yellow parts on the gizzard and liver. Place in a pan with the onion, celery, carrot, seasoning, stock and bay leaf. Bring to the boil. Skim, cover and simmer for 2 hours.

Strain and return the soup to the pan with the rice, grated carrot and some of the finely chopped giblet meat. The cooked vegetables can be sieved or liquidised and added to the soup. Simmer for a further 20 minutes, adjust the seasoning and garnish with the parsley and fried croûtons of bread.

Serves 6

Borscht

METRIC/IMPERIAL/AMERICAN
0.5 kg/1 lb/1 lb raw beetroot, grated
2 carrots, chopped
1 onion, chopped
1 bay leaf
generous litre/2 pints/5 cups chicken stock
salt and pepper
lemon juice
150 ml/¼ pint/⅔ cup soured cream

Put the beetroot into a saucepan with the carrots, onion, bay leaf, stock and seasoning. Bring to the boil, cover and simmer for about 45 minutes. Strain the soup and return to the pan. Adjust the seasoning and sharpen with lemon juice. Bring back to the boil and serve each portion with a spoonful of soured cream.
Note: This soup can also be served chilled with the cream addition as above.

Serves 6

Oxtail soup

METRIC/IMPERIAL/AMERICAN
1 oxtail, jointed
15 g/½ oz/1 tablespoon dripping
2 onions, finely chopped
1 carrot, finely chopped
2 sticks celery, finely chopped
½ leek, finely chopped
2 litres/3½ pints/9 cups beef stock
bouquet garni
salt and pepper
25 g/1 oz/¼ cup flour
1 tablespoon lemon juice
sherry (optional)
chopped parsley to garnish

Wash and dry the oxtail, removing any fat. Fry in the dripping with all the vegetables for about 10 minutes or until evenly browned. Add the stock, bouquet garni and seasoning, and bring to the boil. Cover and simmer for 3–4 hours until the meat is tender. Skim the fat from the pan occasionally.

Remove the meat from the pan and discard the bouquet garni. Sieve or liquidise the soup and return to the pan. Blend the flour with the lemon juice and a little water and whisk into the soup. Bring to the boil and adjust the seasoning. Chop the meat from the bones and return to the pan. Add sherry to taste and simmer for 3–4 minutes. Garnish with the parsley.

Serves 6–8

Cheese soup

METRIC/IMPERIAL/AMERICAN
40 g/1½ oz/3 tablespoons butter
2 onions, chopped
1 carrot, chopped
1 stick celery, chopped (optional)
25 g/1 oz/¼ cup flour
1 litre/1¾ pints/4¼ cups beef stock
salt and pepper
paprika
175 g/6 oz/1½ cups mature Cheddar cheese, finely grated
1 tablespoon chopped parsley

Melt the butter and fry the vegetables until soft and just beginning to colour. Stir in the flour, then gradually add the stock and bring to the boil. Season with salt, pepper and paprika. Cover and simmer for 20 minutes.

Sieve or liquidise the soup and return to the pan. Adjust the seasoning, bring back to the boil, then remove from the heat. Stir in 100 g/4 oz/1 cup of the cheese until melted, then add the parsley. Reheat gently and serve in bowls sprinkled with the remaining cheese.

Serves 4–6

Cream of cauliflower soup

METRIC/IMPERIAL/AMERICAN
1 large onion, chopped
50 g/2 oz/¼ cup butter
1 small cauliflower, trimmed and roughly chopped
600 ml/1 pint/2½ cups chicken stock
600 ml/1 pint/2½ cups milk
salt and pepper
1 bay leaf
2 blades mace
150 ml/¼ pint/⅔ cup cream
chopped parsley to garnish

Fry the onion in the butter until soft. Reserve a few florets of cauliflower for garnish. Add the remaining cauliflower to the onion and continue cooking gently for 5 minutes. Add the stock and milk and bring to the boil. Season, add the bay leaf and mace. Cover and simmer for 30–40 minutes until tender. Discard the bay leaf and mace.

Sieve or liquidise the soup and return to the pan. Adjust the seasoning and add the cream. Reheat without boiling and add the reserved florets of cauliflower. Sprinkle with parsley and serve with Melba toast.

Serves 6

Cauliflower and mushroom soup

METRIC/IMPERIAL/AMERICAN
225 g/8 oz/2 cups mushrooms, chopped
1 onion, chopped
50 g/2 oz/¼ cup butter
1 tablespoon flour
generous litre/2 pints/5 cups chicken stock
225 g/8 oz/½ lb raw cauliflower
salt and pepper
about 300 ml/½ pint/1¼ cups milk
mint sprigs to garnish

Fry the mushrooms and onion gently in the butter until soft but not coloured. Add the flour and mix thoroughly. Gradually add the stock and bring to the boil, stirring. Cut the cauliflower into florets and add to the pan with plenty of seasoning. Cover and simmer for 25–30 minutes.

Sieve or liquidise the soup and return to the pan with sufficient milk to give the desired consistency. Adjust the seasoning, bring back to the boil for 2 minutes and serve garnished with mint sprigs.

Serves 6

Spinach soup

METRIC/IMPERIAL/AMERICAN
25 g/1 oz/2 tablespoons butter
1 onion, finely chopped
1 clove garlic, crushed
4 rashers lean bacon, derinded and finely chopped
1 (227-g/8-oz/½-lb) packet frozen chopped spinach
2 tablespoons/2 tablespoons/3 tablespoons flour
900 ml/1½ pints/3¾ cups chicken stock
salt and pepper
ground nutmeg
25 g/1 oz/¼ cup Cheddar cheese, finely grated

Melt the butter and fry the onion, garlic and bacon gently for 5 minutes. Add the spinach and cook gently until the spinach has thawed out, stirring frequently. Stir in the flour then whisk in the stock. Bring to the boil and season with salt, pepper and nutmeg. Cover and simmer for 25–30 minutes.

Either leave the soup as it is, or sieve or liquidise if a smooth soup is preferred. Return to the pan, bring back to the boil and adjust the seasoning. Serve sprinkled with cheese.

Serves 4–6

Chilli beef chowder

METRIC/IMPERIAL/AMERICAN
25 g/1 oz/2 tablespoons butter
15 g/½ oz/1 tablespoon dripping
1 large onion, finely sliced
225 g/8 oz/1 cup raw beef, finely minced
2 tablespoons/2 tablespoons/3 tablespoons flour
1–2 teaspoons chilli powder
600 ml/1 pint/2½ cups beef stock
1–2 teaspoons tomato purée
3–4 tomatoes, peeled and chopped
1 (198-g/7-oz/7-oz) can red kidney beans, drained
salt and pepper

Melt the butter and dripping in a pan and fry the onion slowly until soft. Stir in the minced beef and cook slowly for 10 minutes, stirring frequently. Add the flour and chilli powder and cook for 1 minute. Gradually add the stock and tomato purée, and bring to the boil. Cover and simmer for 25 minutes, then stir in the tomatoes and beans. Season well and simmer for a further 10 minutes. Adjust the seasoning and serve with crusty French bread and butter.

Serves 4

Cream of pheasant soup

METRIC/IMPERIAL/AMERICAN
40 g/1½ oz/3 tablespoons butter
1 onion, very finely chopped
40 g/1½ oz/6 tablespoons flour
generous litre/2 pints/5 cups good pheasant stock
salt and pepper
ground mace
celery salt
25 g/1 oz/3 tablespoons long-grain rice (optional)
50–75 g/2–3 oz/⅓ cup cooked pheasant meat, chopped
4–6 tablespoons/4–6 tablespoons/⅓–½ cup single cream
GARNISH:
chopped parsley
fried croûtons

Melt the butter and fry the onion until softened. Stir in the flour then gradually add the stock and bring to the boil. Season with salt, pepper, mace and celery salt. Add the rice and simmer for 20 minutes, stirring occasionally. Sieve or liquidise if liked. Add the pheasant and cream, and continue cooking gently for 3–4 minutes. Adjust the seasoning and garnish with parsley and fried croûtons.

Serves 4–6

Chilled soups

Cold soups are ideal to serve on a warm summer's day. As soups freeze so well, they can be made in advance to save time when preparing a lunch or dinner party. When freezing soups, do not add cream or egg yolks until the soup is thawed. Refreshing chilled soups make good picnic fare and can be transported in a vacuum flask.

Cucumber soup

METRIC/IMPERIAL/AMERICAN

1 large cucumber, diced
900 ml/1½ pints/3¾ cups chicken stock
2 tablespoons/2 tablespoons/3 tablespoons finely chopped
   onion
25 g/1 oz/2 tablespoons butter
20 g/¾ oz/3 tablespoons flour
salt and pepper
little lemon juice
green food colouring (optional)
2 egg yolks
4 tablespoons/4 tablespoons/⅓ cup single cream
GARNISH:
mint sprigs
cucumber slices

Place the cucumber in a saucepan with the stock and onion. Bring to the boil, cover and simmer for about 20 minutes until the cucumber is tender. Cool then sieve or liquidise.

Melt the butter in a pan, stir in the flour and cook for 1 minute, then gradually add the cucumber purée. Bring to the boil, stirring frequently, simmer for 2 minutes then season to taste with salt, pepper and lemon juice. Add a little green food colouring, if liked. Blend the egg yolks into the cream then whisk in a little of the soup. Return this mixture to the pan and reheat gently, whisking continuously, to just below boiling point. Cool then chill thoroughly. Serve garnished with mint sprigs on cucumber slices.

Serves 6

Gazpacho

METRIC/IMPERIAL/AMERICAN

600 ml/1 pint/2½ cups canned tomato juice, well chilled
2 teaspoons wine vinegar
2 tablespoons/2 tablespoons/3 tablespoons lemon juice
½ teaspoon Worcestershire sauce
2 cloves garlic, crushed
salt and freshly ground black pepper
225 g/8 oz/1⅓ cups tomatoes, peeled and chopped
½ small onion, peeled and grated
1 (5-cm/2-inch/2-inch) piece cucumber, coarsely grated
½ green pepper, deseeded and finely chopped
ice cubes
chopped parsley to garnish

Place the tomato juice in a bowl with the vinegar, lemon juice, Worcestershire sauce, garlic and seasoning to taste. Add the tomatoes, onion, cucumber and pepper, and mix well. Sieve or liquidise, if liked. Cover the bowl and chill thoroughly.

Place in bowls with 2–3 ice cubes in each and garnish with parsley. Serve this soup with a dish of chopped cucumber, green pepper and tomato wedges.

Serves 4

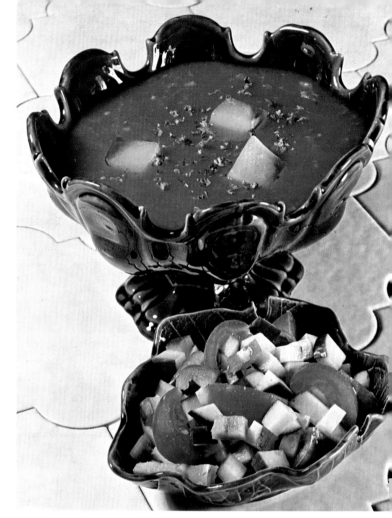

Vichyssoise

METRIC/IMPERIAL/AMERICAN

3 leeks
40 g/1½ oz/3 tablespoons butter
1 onion, thinly sliced
0.5 kg/1 lb/1 lb potatoes, peeled and chopped
900 ml/1½ pints/3¾ cups chicken or veal stock
salt and pepper
pinch ground nutmeg
1 egg yolk
150 ml/¼ pint/⅔ cup single cream
snipped chives to garnish

Clean the leeks, removing most of the green part. Finely slice the remainder. Melt the butter in a pan and sauté the leeks and onion for 5 minutes without browning. Add the potatoes, stock, seasoning and nutmeg, and bring to the boil. Cover and simmer for about 30 minutes or until all the vegetables are soft.

Sieve or liquidise the soup and return to the pan. Blend the egg yolk into the cream, whisk into the soup and reheat gently without boiling. Adjust the seasoning, cool and chill thoroughly. Serve sprinkled with the chives.

Serves 4–6

Chilled avocado soup

METRIC/IMPERIAL/AMERICAN

2 tablespoons/2 tablespoons/3 tablespoons finely chopped
   onion
40 g/1½ oz/3 tablespoons butter
25 g/1 oz/¼ cup flour
750 ml/1¼ pints/3 cups chicken stock
2 medium ripe avocados
1–2 teaspoons lemon juice
salt and pepper
150 ml/¼ pint/⅔ cup milk
150 ml/¼ pint/⅔ cup cream
slices of avocado to garnish

Fry the onion gently in the butter for 3–5 minutes without
colouring. Add the flour and cook for 1 minute. Gradually add
the stock and bring to the boil. Simmer for 5 minutes. Quarter
the avocados, remove the stones and peel. (Reserve a few slices
to garnish.) Roughly chop the avocado flesh and add to the
soup with the lemon juice and seasoning. Simmer for 3–4
minutes.

   Sieve or liquidise, stir in the milk and cream, and adjust the
seasoning. Cool then chill thoroughly. Serve garnished with the
slices of avocado.

Serves 4

Curried prawn soup

METRIC/IMPERIAL/AMERICAN

50 g/2 oz/¼ cup butter
1 onion, chopped
2 carrots, chopped
2 sticks celery, chopped
1–1½ teaspoons curry powder
2 tablespoons/2 tablespoons/3 tablespoons flour
600 ml/1 pint/2½ cups fish stock (or chicken stock)
175 g/6 oz/1 cup peeled prawns
salt and pepper
dash Tabasco sauce
1 tablespoon lemon juice
about 450 ml/¾ pint/2 cups creamy milk
GARNISH:
chopped parsley
whole unshelled prawns

Melt the butter and fry the vegetables until soft and just
beginning to colour. Stir in the curry powder and flour, then
add the stock and bring to the boil. Add 100 g/4 oz/⅔ cup
prawns, seasoning, Tabasco sauce and lemon juice. Cover and
simmer for 30 minutes.

   Sieve or liquidise the soup and return to the pan with
sufficient milk to give the required consistency. Adjust the
seasoning. Roughly chop the remaining prawns and add to the
soup. Cool, then chill thoroughly. Serve garnished with the
parsley and whole unshelled prawns.

Serves 4–6

Iced lemon soup

METRIC/IMPERIAL/AMERICAN
1 onion, chopped
1 clove garlic, crushed (optional)
40 g/1½ oz/3 tablespoons butter
25 g/1 oz/¼ cup flour
900 ml/1½ pints/3¾ cups good chicken stock
grated rind and juice of 1 large lemon
salt and pepper
1 bay leaf
300 ml/½ pint/1¼ cups single cream
GARNISH:
thin slices of lemon
mint sprigs

Fry the onion and garlic in the butter until soft but not coloured. Stir in the flour then gradually add the stock and bring to the boil. Add the lemon rind and juice, seasoning and bay leaf. Cover and simmer for 20 minutes.

Remove the bay leaf, sieve or liquidise the soup and place in a bowl. Stir in the cream and adjust the seasoning. Cool then chill thoroughly. Garnish with thin slices of lemon floating on each portion and a sprig of mint. Serve with breadsticks.

Serves 6

Jellied consommé

METRIC/IMPERIAL/AMERICAN
1 recipe hot consommé (see page 11)
2–3 teaspoons powdered gelatine (see method)
1 tablespoon chopped mixed herbs
julienne strips of orange rind to garnish

If you use a good enough stock which jellies by itself you will not need to add gelatine, but if you use stock cubes or a weak stock then dissolve the gelatine in 3 tablespoons/3 table-spoons/¼ cup consommé in a bowl over a pan of hot water. Add this to the consommé. Stir in the mixed herbs, then chill until set. Serve roughly chopped in soup bowls and garnish with the orange rind, which has been boiled until tender. Serve with Melba toast.

Serves 6

Pâtés

A pâté makes an impressive start to a meal. It can be smooth or coarse textured and is usually served with thin slices of toast or crackers. The recipes in this chapter include ones for both meat and fish pâtés. Pâtés may also be served as a main course with an accompanying salad.

Rosie's pâté

METRIC/IMPERIAL/AMERICAN
2 large onions, chopped
2–3 cloves garlic, crushed
225 g/8 oz/1 cup streaky bacon, derinded and chopped
2 tablespoons/2 tablespoons/3 tablespoons oil
225 g/8 oz/1 cup belly pork, derinded and chopped
0.5 kg/1 lb/1 lb pig's liver, roughly chopped
150 ml/¼ pint/⅔ cup red wine
150 ml/¼ pint/⅔ cup beef stock
2 bay leaves
salt and black pepper
1 teaspoon Worcestershire sauce
GARNISH:
mustard and cress
slices of cucumber
lemon butterflies

Fry the onion, garlic and bacon in the oil until soft. Add the pork and liver and continue cooking for 5–10 minutes. Add all other ingredients. Bring to the boil, cover and simmer for about 40 minutes.

Remove the bay leaves, cool slightly then mince finely. Adjust the seasoning. Pack into a greased 1-kg/2-lb/2-lb loaf tin and stand in a roasting tin containing a 2.5-cm/1-inch depth of water. Cook in a moderately hot oven (180°C, 350°F, Gas Mark 4) for 1 hour. Cool, place a weight on top and chill before turning out. Garnish and serve with toast.

Serves 10

Chicken liver pâté

METRIC/IMPERIAL/AMERICAN
1 onion, very finely chopped
1–2 cloves garlic, crushed
50 g/2 oz/¼ cup butter
0.5 kg/1 lb/1 lb chicken livers
salt and black pepper
2 tablespoons/2 tablespoons/3 tablespoons double cream
2 tablespoons/2 tablespoons/3 tablespoons red wine
melted butter
GARNISH:
capers
bay leaves

Fry the onion and garlic in the butter until soft but not coloured. Wash and drain the chicken livers thoroughly, add to the pan and cook gently for 10 minutes, stirring occasionally to prevent sticking. Remove from the heat and beat in the seasoning, cream and wine.

Sieve or liquidise the pâté, adjust the seasoning and pack into 6 individual dishes. Cover the tops with melted butter and chill thoroughly. Garnish with capers and a bay leaf. The garnish may be put on before pouring over the melted butter.

Serves 6

Farmhouse pâté

METRIC/IMPERIAL/AMERICAN
175 g/6 oz/6 oz pig's liver
175 g/6 oz/6 oz stewing steak
175 g/6 oz/6 oz lean belly pork
1 large onion
1–2 cloves garlic, crushed
25 g/1 oz/½ cup fresh breadcrumbs
1 large egg, beaten
salt and pepper
good pinch ground nutmeg
3–4 tablespoons/3–4 tablespoons/¼–⅓ cup red or white
    wine
175 g/6 oz/6 oz streaky bacon rashers, derinded
GARNISH:
chopped red pepper
chopped cucumber

Coarsely mince the liver, steak, pork and onion. Add the garlic, breadcrumbs, egg, seasoning, nutmeg and wine, and mix very thoroughly. Line a 0.5-kg/1-lb/1-lb loaf tin with the streaky bacon (stretched with the back of a knife) and spoon in the pâté mixture. Press down evenly and fold over the ends of the bacon. Stand the pâté in a roasting tin containing a 2.5-cm/1-inch depth of water. Cook in a moderately hot oven (180°C, 350°F, Gas Mark 4) for 1½–2 hours. Cool with a weight on top. Serve in slices garnished with chopped red pepper and cucumber, and with hot toast and butter.

Serves 6–8

Liver and bacon pâté

METRIC/IMPERIAL/AMERICAN
0.75 kg/1½ lb/1½ lb pig's liver
1 onion
2 cloves garlic, crushed
350 g/12 oz/¾ lb streaky bacon rashers, derinded
25 g/1 oz/½ cup fresh breadcrumbs
salt and pepper
2 tablespoons/2 tablespoons/3 tablespoons brandy or red wine
1 egg, beaten
3 bay leaves
slices of celery to garnish

Put half the liver in a saucepan, cover with water and simmer for 5 minutes. Drain. Mince together finely with the remaining raw liver, onion, garlic and half the bacon. Mix in the breadcrumbs, seasoning, brandy and egg.

Lay the bay leaves in the base of a 0.5-kg/1-lb/1-lb loaf tin. Stretch the remaining rashers with the back of a knife and use to line the inside of the tin. Fill with the liver mixture and fold over the ends of the bacon. Stand the pâté in a roasting tin containing a 2.5-cm/1-inch depth of water. Cook in a moderately hot oven (180°C, 350°F, Gas Mark 4) for 1½–2 hours. Cool, cover with a weighted plate and chill before turning out. Garnish with the celery slices and serve with Melba or hot buttered toast.

Serves 10

Sardine pâté

METRIC/IMPERIAL/AMERICAN
2 (120-g/4¼-oz/4¼-oz) cans sardines in oil, drained
75 g/3 oz/6 tablespoons cream cheese (Philadelphia)
½ teaspoon grated lemon rind
1 tablespoon very finely chopped onion
1 hard-boiled egg, mashed
1–2 tablespoons/1–2 tablespoons/1–3 tablespoons lemon juice
2 tablespoons/2 tablespoons/3 tablespoons cream or natural yogurt
salt and black pepper
garlic powder
GARNISH:
slices of tomato
chopped green pepper
parsley sprigs

Mash the sardines thoroughly. Soften the cream cheese and beat into the sardines with the lemon rind, onion and mashed egg. Add the lemon juice and cream, and mix to give a smooth consistency. Season to taste with salt, pepper and garlic powder. Either serve in individual ramekin dishes or a larger dish garnished with tomato slices, chopped green pepper and parsley sprigs. Hand fingers of hot brown toast separately.

Serves 4–6

24

Smoked mackerel pâté

METRIC/IMPERIAL/AMERICAN
225 g/8 oz/½ lb smoked mackerel
50 g/2 oz/1 cup fresh white breadcrumbs
grated rind of ½ lemon
2 tablespoons/2 tablespoons/3 tablespoons lemon juice
salt and pepper
little garlic powder
2 teaspoons finely chopped onion
50 g/2 oz/¼ cup butter, melted
4–6 tablespoons/4–6 tablespoons/⅓–½ cup cream
GARNISH:
slices of tomato
slices of cucumber
parsley sprigs

Remove the skin and bones from the fish and mash thoroughly. Add the breadcrumbs, lemon rind and juice, seasoning, garlic powder, onion and melted butter, mix very thoroughly. Add sufficient cream to give a softish consistency and divide between 4–6 ramekin dishes or plates. Chill thoroughly and garnish with the tomato and cucumber slices, parsley sprigs and serve with toast.

Serves 4–6

Kipper pâté

METRIC/IMPERIAL/AMERICAN
5–8 frozen kipper fillets
2 tablespoons/2 tablespoons/3 tablespoons finely chopped
  onion
50 g/2 oz/¼ cup butter
½ teaspoon finely grated lemon rind
about 2 teaspoons lemon juice
salt and pepper
little garlic powder (optional)
2 tablespoons/2 tablespoons/3 tablespoons cream
GARNISH:
lettuce leaves
watercress
slices of lemon
tomato wedges

Cook the kippers according to the instructions on the packet. Cool, remove the skin and bones, and flake the flesh. Fry the onion in the butter until soft then beat into the kippers with the lemon rind and juice. Season with a little salt, plenty of pepper and a pinch of garlic powder, if liked. Beat in the cream until the pâté is smooth. Sharpen with more lemon juice, if necessary. Pile on to individual dishes or one large dish and chill. Garnish with the lettuce, watercress, lemon slices and tomato. Serve with plenty of hot toast and butter, or Melba toast.

Serves 6

Salads

Salads make interesting starters with their attractive colours, varying textures and flavours. When purchasing salad vegetables reject ones that are not fresh and crisp, as stale vegetables will not do justice to any finished dish. If adding a dressing either serve separately or pour it over just before serving, to retain the crispness of the dish.

Salad niçoise

METRIC/IMPERIAL/AMERICAN
lettuce leaves
1 (198-g/7-oz/7-oz) can tuna, drained and flaked
1 green pepper, deseeded and sliced
1 tablespoon finely chopped onion
3 large tomatoes, each cut into six
175 g/6 oz/6 oz French beans, cooked
1 tablespoon capers
6 tablespoons/6 tablespoons/½ cup French dressing
GARNISH:
3 hard-boiled eggs
½ (50-g/1¾-oz/1¾-oz) can anchovy fillets, drained
black olives

Arrange the lettuce leaves on 6 small plates or dishes. Lightly toss together the tuna, green pepper, onion, tomatoes, beans, capers and dressing. Spoon over the lettuce leaves. Garnish with quarters of hard-boiled egg, anchovy fillets and black olives. Serve with French bread.

Serves 6

Tuna bean salad

METRIC/IMPERIAL/AMERICAN
2 green eating apples, cored and chopped
1 tablespoon lemon juice
1 (198-g/7-oz/7-oz) can tuna, flaked
1 tablespoon finely chopped onion
3 sticks celery, sliced
1 (425-g/15-oz/15-oz) can red kidney beans, drained
salt and pepper
4–5 tablespoons/4–5 tablespoons/5–6 tablespoons French
    dressing
watercress to garnish

Dip the apple in the lemon juice, then place in a bowl with the
tuna, onion, celery and red kidney beans. Season well, add the
dressing and toss thoroughly. Leave to stand for about 30
minutes before serving on small plates. Garnish with watercress
and serve with French bread and butter.

Serves 4–6

Victorian cocktail

METRIC/IMPERIAL/AMERICAN
3 grapefruit
2 ripe avocados
4 tablespoons/4 tablespoons/$\frac{1}{3}$ cup French dressing
mint sprigs to garnish

Using a sharp knife, cut the top and bottom off each grapefruit.
Stand the grapefruit on one end and cut away all the peel and
pith together in a downward movement. Cut between the
membranes and ease out the segments. Place the segments in a
bowl with any juice.
    Cut the avocados into quarters lengthways, then remove the
stones and peel carefully. Cut the flesh into cubes and add to the
grapefruit. Toss thoroughly in the grapefruit juice. Chill. Spoon
into 4 individual dishes with a little grapefruit juice in each. Add
1 tablespoon French dressing to each dish, garnish with a mint
sprig and serve.

Serves 4

Hidden peaches

METRIC/IMPERIAL/AMERICAN
1 (425-g/15-oz/16-oz) can white peach halves
40 g/1½ oz/½ cup blue cheese, crumbled
15 g/½ oz/1 tablespoon butter, softened
150 ml/¼ pint/⅔ cup single cream
salt and pepper
paprika
1 small lettuce
75 g/3 oz/6 tablespoons soft cream cheese

Drain 4 peach halves. Mash the blue cheese and mix with the butter, 1 tablespoon of the cream, seasoning and paprika to taste. Use to fill the stone cavities of the peaches.

Arrange the lettuce on 4 small plates and place a peach on each with the rounded side upwards. Soften the cream cheese then beat in sufficient cream to give a coating consistency. Spoon carefully over the peaches until completely masked. Sprinkle with paprika and serve with triangles of toast.

Serves 4

Fennel salad

METRIC/IMPERIAL/AMERICAN
1 bulb Florence fennel, chopped
1 tablespoon finely chopped onion
2 carrots, coarsely grated
1 (50-g/1¾-oz/1¾-oz) can anchovy fillets, drained
few black olives, stoned
6 tablespoons/6 tablespoons/½ cup French dressing
salt and pepper
1 small lettuce
50 g/2 oz/2 oz Emmenthal cheese, cut into julienne strips

Place the fennel in a bowl with the onion and grated carrot. Cut the anchovy fillets into 2.5-cm/1-inch lengths and add to the salad with a few black olives. Add the dressing and seasoning, and leave to stand for about 20 minutes. Arrange lettuce leaves in 4 small dishes and spoon the salad on top. Place cheese strips over the salad and top each with an olive.

Serves 4

Dressed French beans

METRIC/IMPERIAL/AMERICAN
0.5 kg/1 lb/1 lb French beans, trimmed
salt and pepper
150 ml/$\frac{1}{4}$ pint/$\frac{2}{3}$ cup French dressing
1 clove garlic, crushed
GARNISH:
4 tomatoes, sliced
2 hard-boiled eggs, chopped

Cook the beans in boiling salted water until just tender – do not overcook. Drain well and place in a bowl. Add the dressing, garlic and seasoning to the hot beans and mix lightly. Cool then chill.

Arrange the beans on small plates, garnish with the sliced tomatoes round the edge and sprinkle with the chopped hard-boiled egg. Serve with brown bread and butter, if liked.

Serves 4

Minted tomato salad

METRIC/IMPERIAL/AMERICAN
0.5 kg/1 lb/1 lb tomatoes
salt and pepper
freshly chopped mint
6 tablespoons/6 tablespoons/$\frac{1}{2}$ cup soured cream
good pinch sugar
$\frac{1}{4}$ teaspoon grated lemon rind
1 tablespoon lemon juice
crisp lettuce leaves
mint sprigs to garnish

Peel the tomatoes, quarter and remove the pips. Sprinkle lightly with salt and pepper and 1 teaspoon chopped mint. Season the cream, adding the pinch of sugar, lemon rind and juice and 1 tablespoon chopped mint.

Arrange crisp lettuce in 4 small dishes, lay the tomatoes on top and spoon the creamy dressing over them. Garnish with the sprigs of mint and serve with Melba or French toast.

Serves 4

Chicory and apple cocktail

METRIC/IMPERIAL/AMERICAN
2 red-skinned apples
1 green-skinned apple
1 tablespoon lemon juice
3 tablespoons/3 tablespoons/$\frac{1}{4}$ cup French dressing
salt and pepper
2 heads chicory, sliced
2 carrots, coarsely grated
watercress sprigs to garnish

Quarter, core and chop 1 red and the green apple. Dip in the lemon juice then add the dressing and seasoning. Add the chicory and grated carrots, and toss thoroughly. Arrange on 4 small plates. Slice the remaining apple and use to garnish the starter together with the watercress.

Serves 4

Artichokes niçoise

METRIC/IMPERIAL/AMERICAN
1 (425-g/15-oz/16-oz) can artichoke hearts, drained
2 tablespoons/2 tablespoons/3 tablespoons chopped onion
150 ml/$\frac{1}{4}$ pint/$\frac{2}{3}$ cup French dressing
salt and black pepper
1 (50-g/1$\frac{3}{4}$-oz/1$\frac{3}{4}$-oz) can anchovy fillets, drained
12 black olives
watercress to garnish

Cut the artichoke hearts into halves or quarters, depending on size, and place in a bowl with the onion, dressing and seasoning. Cut the anchovies into 2.5-cm/1-inch lengths and add to the bowl with the olives. Toss lightly and leave to stand for about 20 minutes. Arrange the salad in 4 small dishes and garnish with watercress.

Serves 4

Vegetable and fruit starters

These, like salads, are seasonal starters. Make sure the vegetables and fruits are fresh and sound. Some vegetables and fruit may be combined in a dish to make an interesting and unusual starter – see the recipe on page 33 for leek and pineapple cocktails.

Stuffed aubergines

METRIC/IMPERIAL/AMERICAN
1 onion, finely chopped
2 lean rashers bacon, derinded and chopped
25 g/1 oz/2 tablespoons butter
2 medium aubergines
175 g/6 oz/1 cup tomatoes, peeled and chopped
1 teaspoon tomato purée
salt and pepper
good pinch garlic powder
75 g/3 oz/¾ cup Emmenthal cheese, grated
parsley sprigs to garnish

Fry the onion and bacon in the butter until just beginning to colour. Cut the aubergines in half lengthways and scoop out the flesh, leaving a thin layer inside the skin. Chop the flesh and add to the pan with the tomatoes, tomato purée, seasoning and garlic powder. Cook gently for about 5 minutes. Remove from the heat and stir in 50 g/2 oz/½ cup of the cheese. Spoon into the aubergine shells, place in an ovenproof dish and sprinkle with the remaining cheese. Bake in a moderately hot oven (200°C, 400°F, Gas Mark 6) for 30–40 minutes until the aubergine is tender and the cheese brown and bubbling. Serve hot, garnished with the parsley.

Serves 4

Mushrooms in garlic butter

METRIC/IMPERIAL/AMERICAN
75 g/3 oz/6 tablespoons butter
1 tablespoon oil
2–3 large cloves garlic, crushed
2 tablespoons/2 tablespoons/3 tablespoons grated onion
350–450 g/¾–1 lb/3–4 cups button mushrooms, trimmed
salt and freshly ground black pepper
GARNISH:
1 tablespoon freshly chopped parsley
1 tablespoon grated Parmesan cheese

Heat the butter and oil in a pan. Add the garlic and onion and
fry gently for 2–3 minutes. If the mushrooms are too large, cut
into halves or quarters, otherwise leave whole. Add to the pan
and fry gently for about 5 minutes, stirring frequently. Season
well with salt and pepper. Spoon into warmed individual dishes
and sprinkle each with a mixture of the parsley and Parmesan
cheese. Serve hot with Melba toast.

Serves 4

Ratatouille

METRIC/IMPERIAL/AMERICAN
1 large onion, sliced
2 cloves garlic, crushed
25 g/1 oz/2 tablespoons butter
2 tablespoons/2 tablespoons/3 tablespoons oil
1 large aubergine, roughly chopped
2 courgettes, trimmed and sliced
1 small red or green pepper, deseeded and sliced
4 tomatoes, peeled and roughly chopped
salt and pepper
dash Worcestershire sauce
2 tablespoons/2 tablespoons/3 tablespoons water
chopped parsley to garnish

Fry the onion and garlic until soft in a mixture of the butter and
oil. Add the aubergine, courgettes, pepper and tomatoes. Mix
well and cook gently for 5–10 minutes, stirring frequently. Add
the seasoning, Worcestershire sauce and water.

Cover the pan and simmer very gently for 45 minutes–1 hour,
stirring occasionally. Adjust the seasoning, cool and chill. Serve
on individual plates and garnish with parsley.
Note: The ratatouille may also be served hot.

Serves 4

Leek and pineapple cocktails

METRIC/IMPERIAL/AMERICAN
2 medium young leeks
4 rings canned pineapple, chopped
1 tablespoon finely chopped onion
4–6 tablespoons/4–6 tablespoons/$\frac{1}{3}$–$\frac{1}{2}$ cup French
  dressing
salt and pepper
100 g/4 oz/$\frac{1}{2}$ cup streaky bacon rashers, derinded and
  chopped

Trim the coarse green parts and root from the leeks, then finely slice the remainder. Wash very thoroughly. Blanch in boiling water for 2 minutes, rinse in cold water and drain very thoroughly. Add the pineapple, onion, dressing and seasoning. Toss well and leave to stand for 15 minutes.

Meanwhile, fry the bacon in its own fat until crispy, drain well and cool. Just before serving, sprinkle with the bacon and serve with hot crusty bread and parsley butter.

Serves 4

Avocado mousse

METRIC/IMPERIAL/AMERICAN
2 ripe avocados
75 g/3 oz/6 tablespoons soft cream cheese (Philadelphia)
1 clove garlic, crushed (optional)
4 tablespoons/4 tablespoons/$\frac{1}{3}$ cup single cream or top
  of the milk
1 teaspoon lemon juice
salt and pepper
1 teaspoon powdered gelatine
1 tablespoon water
watercress sprigs to garnish

Halve the avocados, remove the stones and peel. Mash the flesh until smooth. Beat in the softened cream cheese until completely blended then add the garlic, cream, lemon juice and seasoning to taste.

Dissolve the gelatine in the water in a basin over a pan of hot water, stir this evenly into the avocado mixture. Spoon into 4 individual dishes and chill for up to 2 hours until set. (Do not leave longer or the mousse may begin to discolour.) Garnish with the watercress and serve with toast.

Serves 4

Jellied tomato ring

METRIC/IMPERIAL/AMERICAN
600 ml/1 pint/2½ cups tomato juice
3 tablespoons/3 tablespoons/¼ cup wine vinegar
1 teaspoon Worcestershire sauce
1 tablespoon finely chopped onion
1 tablespoon powdered gelatine
350 g/12 oz/2 cups tomatoes, peeled, deseeded and
   chopped
GARNISH:
watercress
slices of stuffed olive

Blend the tomato juice with the vinegar, Worcestershire sauce
and onion. Dissolve the gelatine in 3 tablespoons/3 table-
spoons/¼ cup of the tomato liquid in a basin over a pan of hot
water. Return to the rest of the liquid, mix well and add the
chopped tomatoes. Turn into a 1-litre/1½-pint/2-pint ring
mould or six 150-ml/¼-pint/⅔-cup individual ring moulds and
chill until set. To serve, turn out and garnish the centre with
watercress and place slices of olive on the ring.

Serves 6

Mushrooms à la grecque

METRIC/IMPERIAL/AMERICAN
1 onion, chopped
2 carrots, diced
3 tablespoons/3 tablespoons/¼ cup oil
150 ml/¼ pint/⅔ cup dry white wine
1 bay leaf
1 clove garlic, crushed
salt and pepper
350 g/12 oz/3 cups button mushrooms
225 g/8 oz/½ lb tomatoes, peeled
chopped parsley to garnish

Sauté the onion and carrot in the oil until soft but not coloured.
Add the wine, bay leaf, garlic and seasoning, and bring to the
boil. Trim the mushrooms and halve or quarter if too large;
then add to the pan. Cover and cook gently for 5–6 minutes.
   Cut the tomatoes into quarters and remove the seeds.
Remove the pan from the heat, take out the bay leaf and add the
tomatoes. Cool then chill thoroughly. Serve in small shallow
dishes and sprinkle with the chopped parsley.

Serves 4

Melon and black grape cocktail

METRIC/IMPERIAL/AMERICAN
225 g/8 oz/½ lb black grapes
1 melon, firm but ripe
fresh mint leaves (optional)
egg white
1 tablespoon castor sugar
mint sprigs to garnish

Halve and depip the grapes, and place in a bowl. Cut the melon in half or quarters and remove the seeds. Either using a melon baller, scoop out as many melon balls as possible and add to the grapes with any juice; or cut the melon flesh into neat cubes. Crush a few mint leaves and mix into the fruit, if liked. Chill.

Before serving, dip the rims of 4 serving glasses into lightly beaten egg white then into castor sugar to give a frosted effect. Spoon in the melon and grape cocktail and garnish with mint sprigs.

Note: Fresh mint leaves or sprigs can also be given a frosted effect by dipping first into egg white and then castor sugar.

Serves 4

Ham and asparagus rolls

METRIC/IMPERIAL/AMERICAN
1 (227-g/8-oz/½-lb) packet frozen asparagus
salt
150 ml/¼ pint/⅔ cup thick mayonnaise
1–2 cloves garlic, crushed
1–2 tablespoons/1–2 tablespoons/1–3 tablespoons top of the milk
½ teaspoon grated lemon rind (optional)
6 slices cooked ham
paprika to garnish

Cook the asparagus in salted water until tender, drain and cool. Combine the mayonnaise, garlic to taste, sufficient top of the milk to give a coating consistency and lemon rind, if used.

Divide the asparagus between the slices of ham and roll up. Put the ham rolls on a serving dish or 6 small plates. Spoon the mayonnaise mixture over the ham and sprinkle with paprika. Serve with brown bread and butter.

Serves 6

Courgettes provençal

METRIC/IMPERIAL/AMERICAN
1 large onion, thinly sliced
1 clove garlic, crushed
50 g/2 oz/¼ cup butter
0.5 kg/1 lb/1 lb courgettes, trimmed
350 g/12 oz/¾ lb tomatoes, peeled and sliced
1 tablespoon tomato purée
salt and pepper
2 tablespoons/2 tablespoons/3 tablespoons water
2–3 tablespoons/2–3 tablespoons/3–4 tablespoons double
  cream
50 g/2 oz/½ cup Cheddar cheese, grated
25 g/1 oz/½ cup fresh breadcrumbs

Fry the onion and garlic in the butter until soft. Slice the
courgettes and add to the onion mixture. Cook gently for
10 minutes, stirring occasionally. Add the tomatoes, tomato
purée, seasoning and water. Cook gently for 10–15 minutes,
stirring occasionally. Adjust the seasoning and stir in the cream.

Spoon into one large or 6 small ovenproof dishes. Combine
the cheese and breadcrumbs, and sprinkle over the courgette
mixture. Place under a moderate grill until golden brown. Serve
hot with granary bread and butter, if liked.

Serves 6

Spinach tartlets

METRIC/IMPERIAL/AMERICAN
100 g/4 oz/1 cup plain flour
salt and pepper
25 g/1 oz/2 tablespoons margarine
25 g/1 oz/2 tablespoons lard or white fat
225 g/8 oz/1 cup cooked spinach, chopped
¼ teaspoon ground nutmeg
1 large egg, beaten
3 tablespoons/3 tablespoons/¼ cup single cream
75 g/3 oz/¾ cup mature Cheddar cheese, grated
slices of tomato to garnish

Sieve the flour into a bowl with a pinch of salt. Rub in the fats
until the mixture resembles fine breadcrumbs. Add sufficient
water to mix to a pliable dough. Roll out the dough and use to
line 4 individual Yorkshire pudding or fluted flan tins.

Combine the spinach, nutmeg, egg, cream, cheese and plenty
of seasoning. Spoon into the uncooked pastry cases. Bake in a
moderately hot oven (200°C, 400°F, Gas Mark 6) for about 30
minutes, until firm to the touch and the pastry is cooked
through. Serve hot, warm or cold. Garnish with sliced
tomatoes, cut into quarters.

Serves 4

Baked mushrooms

METRIC/IMPERIAL/AMERICAN
4 very large flat mushrooms (or 8 medium)
150 ml/¼ pint/⅔ cup stock
1 small onion, finely chopped
50 g/2 oz/¼ cup bacon, derinded and finely chopped
25 g/1 oz/2 tablespoons butter
225 g/8 oz/1 cup cottage cheese
salt and pepper
1 teaspoon dried oregano
parsley sprigs to garnish

Trim the stalks of the mushrooms then dip each mushroom in boiling stock for ½–1 minute. Drain and place on a grill rack, stem upwards.

Fry the onion and bacon in the butter until golden brown. Cool slightly, then mix into the cottage cheese with the seasoning and oregano. Almost cover the dark surface of the mushrooms with the cheese mixture. Place under a moderate grill for about 5 minutes or until the cheese is lightly tinged brown. Serve hot on a croûte of toast and garnish with the parsley.

Serves 4

Apple cocktails

METRIC/IMPERIAL/AMERICAN
2 large (or 4 small) green eating apples
3 tablespoons/3 tablespoons/¼ cup thick mayonnaise
1 tablespoon lemon juice
salt and pepper
good pinch curry powder
8 stuffed olives
50–75 g/2–3 oz/about ½ cup peeled prawns or shrimps
1 tablespoon chopped chives
50 g/2 oz/½ cup Cheddar cheese, finely diced
watercress sprigs to garnish

Cut the apples in half, scoop out the flesh and core, leaving a firm shell inside the peel. (If using whole apples, cut a slice off the top and then scoop out the flesh and core.)

Combine the mayonnaise, lemon juice, seasoning and curry powder. Remove the core from the apple flesh, chop the remaining flesh and add to the mayonnaise together with the sliced olives, halved prawns, chives and cheese. Mix thoroughly then spoon back into the apple shells. Arrange on small plates, garnish with the watercress and serve at once.

Serves 4

Fish starters

These starters make a welcome change and you will see from the recipes in this chapter that prawn cocktail is not the only fish starter! A variety of frozen fish is available and this is a good buy particularly if you do not have a reliable wet fish shop in your area.

Smoked haddock mousse

METRIC/IMPERIAL/AMERICAN
350 g/12 oz/$\frac{3}{4}$ lb smoked haddock fillet
about 150 ml/$\frac{1}{4}$ pint/$\frac{2}{3}$ cup milk
25 g/1 oz/2 tablespoons butter
1 tablespoon flour
salt and pepper
good pinch ground mace
2 eggs, separated
1$\frac{1}{2}$ teaspoons powdered gelatine
1 tablespoon water
150 ml/$\frac{1}{4}$ pint/$\frac{2}{3}$ cup soured cream
300 ml/$\frac{1}{2}$ pint/1$\frac{1}{4}$ cups liquid aspic jelly
GARNISH:
slices of hard-boiled egg
parsley sprigs

Cook the fish in the milk until tender. Drain, reserving 150 ml/$\frac{1}{4}$ pint/$\frac{2}{3}$ cup cooking liquor, made up with more milk if necessary. Cool the fish, remove skin and bones, and flake.

Melt the butter in a pan, stir in the flour and cook for 1 minute then gradually add the reserved milk. Bring to the boil for 1 minute then add salt, pepper and mace. Beat in yolks.

Dissolve the gelatine in the water in a basin over a pan of hot water. Stir into the sauce, then add the soured cream. Add the fish and mix thoroughly. Whisk the egg whites until stiff and fold into the mixture. Pour into a large or 6 individual dishes and chill until set. Pour a layer of liquid aspic over the surface and leave to set. Garnish with the egg slices and parsley.

Serves 6

Sardine-stuffed lemons

METRIC/IMPERIAL/AMERICAN
4 lemons
2 tablespoons/2 tablespoons/3 tablespoons soured cream
1 (120-g/4¼-oz/4¼-oz) can sardines, drained and mashed
2 tablespoons/2 tablespoons/3 tablespoons finely chopped
   cucumber
1 tablespoon chopped capers
salt and pepper
dash Tabasco sauce
1 small lettuce

Cut the tops off the lemons and a small piece from the base so
they stand firmly. Scoop out the lemon flesh and squeeze
1 tablespoon juice from the flesh.

Mix together the soured cream, lemon juice, mashed
sardines, cucumber and capers. Season to taste with salt, pepper
and Tabasco. Spoon the mixture into the lemon shells, chill
thoroughly and serve on lettuce leaves with fingers of toast.

Serves 4

Tuna creams

METRIC/IMPERIAL/AMERICAN
150 ml/¼ pint/⅔ cup natural yogurt
4 tablespoons/4 tablespoons/⅓ cup thick mayonnaise
1 tablespoon lemon juice
salt and pepper
2 teaspoons powdered gelatine
2 tablespoons/2 tablespoons/3 tablespoons water
4 spring onions, finely sliced
1 hard-boiled egg, chopped
2 gherkins, chopped
1 tablespoon capers, chopped
1 (198-g/7-oz/7-oz) can tuna, drained and flaked
GARNISH:
slices of cucumber
slices of lemon

Combine the yogurt, mayonnaise and lemon juice, and season
well. Dissolve the gelatine in the water in a basin over a pan of
hot water. Stir into the yogurt mixture.

Mix together the onions, hard-boiled egg, gherkins, capers
and tuna, and fold into the yogurt mixture. Spoon into
4 individual dishes and chill until set. Serve garnished with a
twist of cucumber and lemon.

Serves 4

Taramasalata

METRIC/IMPERIAL/AMERICAN
175–225 g/6–8 oz/$\frac{1}{3}$–$\frac{1}{2}$ lb smoked cod's roe
3 slices white bread
1 teaspoon finely chopped onion
1–2 cloves garlic, crushed
about 4 tablespoons/4 tablespoons/$\frac{1}{3}$ cup oil
juice of 1 lemon
2 teaspoons chopped parsley
salt and black pepper
1 small lettuce
GARNISH:
watercress sprigs
black olives

Remove and discard the skin from the cod's roe, mash until smooth. Remove the crusts from the bread then soak in cold water; squeeze almost dry and crumble into the cod's roe. Add the onion and garlic, and pound to a paste. Gradually beat in sufficient oil and lemon juice until the mixture becomes thick and creamy. Beat in the chopped parsley and season to taste. Place the taramasalata on lettuce leaves and garnish with watercress sprigs and black olives. Serve with fingers of hot toast and butter.

Serves 4

Chalford cocktail

METRIC/IMPERIAL/AMERICAN
2 avocados
2 grapefruit
2 tablespoons/2 tablespoons/3 tablespoons thick
    mayonnaise
1 tablespoon tomato ketchup
1 tablespoon cream
dash Tabasco sauce
dash Worcestershire sauce
salt and pepper
100 g/4 oz/$\frac{2}{3}$ cup peeled prawns
twists of cucumber to garnish

Halve the avocados and remove the stones. Prepare the grapefruit segments as for Victorian cocktail (see page 27). Rub the cut surface of the avocados with grapefruit juice.

Combine the mayonnaise, ketchup, cream, Tabasco, Worcestershire sauce and seasoning. Fold in the prawns and grapefruit segments, spoon into the avocado stone cavities. Garnish with the twists of cucumber.

Serves 4

Creamed scallops

METRIC/IMPERIAL/AMERICAN
6 scallops
150 ml/¼ pint/⅔ cup dry white wine
150 ml/¼ pint/⅔ cup water
½ teaspoon grated lemon rind
1 tablespoon lemon juice
salt and pepper
25 g/1 oz/2 tablespoons butter
1 onion, finely chopped
2 tablespoons/2 tablespoons/3 tablespoons flour
4 tablespoons/4 tablespoons/⅓ cup cream
40 g/1½ oz/¾ cup fresh breadcrumbs
40 g/1½ oz/3 tablespoons Cheddar cheese, finely grated
watercress to garnish

Loosen the scallops from their shells and wash well. Cut the flesh into cubes and place in a saucepan with the wine, water, lemon rind and juice, and seasoning. Bring to the boil, cover and simmer for 10 minutes until the scallops are tender. Strain and reserve 200 ml/⅓ pint/¾ cup cooking liquor for the sauce.

Melt the butter and sauté the onion until soft. Stir in the flour and cook for 1 minute. Gradually add the cooking liquor and bring to the boil. Season, replace the scallops and simmer for 2 minutes. Remove from the heat, stir in the cream and spoon into 4 deep scallop shells or individual flameproof dishes. Sprinkle with a mixture of the breadcrumbs and cheese, and brown under a moderate grill. Garnish with watercress and serve with brown bread and butter.

Serves 4

Smoked trout mousse

METRIC/IMPERIAL/AMERICAN
15 g/½ oz/1 tablespoon butter
15 g/½ oz/2 tablespoons flour
150 ml/¼ pint/⅔ cup milk
salt and pepper
150 ml/¼ pint/⅔ cup soured cream
1 tablespoon lemon juice
½ teaspoon creamed horseradish
1 (175–225 g/6–8 oz/6–8 oz) smoked trout
1½ teaspoons powdered gelatine
1½ tablespoons/1½ tablespoons/2 tablespoons water
GARNISH:
slices of tomato
lemon butterflies
mustard and cress

Melt the butter in a pan, stir in the flour and cook for 1 minute. Gradually add the milk and bring to the boil. Simmer for 2 minutes, stirring. Remove from the heat, season to taste and beat in the soured cream, lemon juice and horseradish.

Remove the skin and bones from the trout and either mash very finely and mix into the sauce or place the fish and sauce in a liquidiser and blend until smooth.

Dissolve the gelatine in the water in a small basin over hot water, then stir evenly into the mousse. Pour into 4 individual ramekin dishes, a larger dish or into a lightly greased small mould and chill until set. Garnish with the tomato slices, lemon butterflies and mustard and cress.

Serves 4

Marinated kipper fillets

METRIC/IMPERIAL/AMERICAN
175 g/6 oz/6 oz frozen kipper fillets in a boilable bag
2 tablespoons/2 tablespoons/3 tablespoons wine vinegar
2 tablespoons/2 tablespoons/3 tablespoons oil
1 tablespoon lemon juice
salt and pepper
pinch garlic powder
1 small onion, finely sliced
parsley sprigs to garnish

Put the kippers in the bag in a pan of cold water. Bring to the boil and simmer for 2 minutes only. Remove from the water and turn the kippers into a shallow dish.

Combine the vinegar, oil, lemon juice, seasoning and garlic powder, and pour over kippers. Add the onion and allow to become cold. Turn the kippers occasionally, then cover and chill for 12–24 hours. Serve pieces of drained kipper on individual plates with a few pieces of the onion on top and garnished with parsley. Serve with brown bread and butter.

Serves 3–4

Danish style herring salad

METRIC/IMPERIAL/AMERICAN
1 tablespoon tomato purée
2 tablespoons/2 tablespoons/3 tablespoons tomato ketchup
2 tablespoons/2 tablespoons/3 tablespoons wine vinegar
1 teaspoon French mustard
good dash Worcestershire sauce
1 tablespoon lemon juice
salt and black pepper
4 pickled herrings, drained
1 onion, finely chopped
mustard and cress to garnish

Whisk together the tomato purée, ketchup, vinegar, mustard, Worcestershire sauce, lemon juice and seasoning. Slice the herrings thickly and arrange rolled up in 4 small bowls or a larger dish, scattering the chopped onion over. Spoon the tomato mixture over the fish, cover and chill for several hours or preferably overnight. Garnish with mustard and cress.

Serves 4

Moules marinière

METRIC/IMPERIAL/AMERICAN
about 3.5 litres/6 pints/7 pints fresh mussels
50 g/2 oz/¼ cup butter
1 medium onion, very finely chopped
½ bottle dry white wine
bouquet garni
salt and pepper
2 teaspoons flour
chopped parsley to garnish

Thoroughly wash and scrub the mussels, removing any barnacles, mud, etc. Discard any which do not close when given a sharp tap.

Melt 40 g/1½ oz/3 tablespoons of the butter in a pan and sauté the onion until soft but not coloured. Add the wine, bouquet garni and seasoning. Cover and simmer gently for 5 minutes. Add the mussels a few at a time, cover the pan and simmer gently for about 5 minutes, shaking the pan frequently until all the mussels are open.

Place the mussels in soup bowls and keep warm. Cream the remaining butter with the flour and whisk into the juices, discarding the bouquet garni. Bring to the boil for 3–4 minutes, adjust the seasoning and pour over the mussels. Sprinkle with the parsley and serve with plenty of hot crusty French bread.

Serves 4–6

Crab au gratin

METRIC/IMPERIAL/AMERICAN
225 g/8 oz/½ lb crabmeat
40 g/1½ oz/3 tablespoons butter
1 small onion, finely chopped
25 g/1 oz/¼ cup flour
300 ml/½ pint/1¼ cups milk
salt and pepper
½ teaspoon made mustard
good dash Worcestershire sauce
2 teaspoons lemon juice
25 g/1 oz/½ cup fresh breadcrumbs
50 g/2 oz/½ cup Cheddar cheese, finely grated
paprika
GARNISH:
parsley sprigs
slices of lemon

Flake the crabmeat. If using fresh crab, remove all the meat – brown and white – from the shell and claws.

Melt the butter and fry the onion until soft. Stir in the flour and cook for 1 minute. Add the milk and bring to the boil. Stir in the seasoning, mustard, Worcestershire sauce and lemon juice, and simmer for 2 minutes. Add the crabmeat and heat through thoroughly. Spoon into 4–6 small flameproof dishes or scallop shells. Mix the breadcrumbs with the cheese and a good shake of paprika and spoon over the crab mixture. Place under a moderate grill until the topping is well browned. Garnish with the parsley and quartered lemon slices.

Serves 4–6

Prawns Newburg

METRIC/IMPERIAL/AMERICAN
1 small onion, finely chopped
50 g/2 oz/¼ cup butter
225 g/8 oz/1⅓ cups peeled prawns
2 tablespoons/2 tablespoons/3 tablespoons lemon juice
4 tablespoons/4 tablespoons/⅓ cup sherry or Madeira
salt and pepper
50 g/2 oz/¼ cup long-grain rice, cooked
2 egg yolks
150 ml/¼ pint/⅔ cup single cream
watercress sprigs to garnish

Fry the onion gently in the butter until soft. Add the prawns and cook gently for 5 minutes, shaking frequently. Add the lemon juice, sherry, seasoning and bring to the boil. Add the cooked rice and mix thoroughly.

Beat the egg yolks into the cream and add to the pan. Heat gently, stirring continuously, until just below boiling point. Adjust the seasoning and serve in small dishes. Garnish with the watercress and serve with hot toast.

Serves 4

Baked avocados with crab

METRIC/IMPERIAL/AMERICAN
25 g/1 oz/2 tablespoons butter
1 small onion, finely chopped
100–150 g/4–5 oz/4–5 oz crabmeat
2 tablespoons/2 tablespoons/3 tablespoons fresh
    breadcrumbs
1–2 tablespoons/1–2 tablespoons/1–3 tablespoons cream
salt and pepper
paprika
2 ripe avocados
25 g/1 oz/¼ cup Emmenthal or Cheddar cheese, finely
    grated
parsley sprigs to garnish

Melt the butter in a pan and fry the onion until soft. Add the crabmeat and cook gently for 3–4 minutes, stirring frequently. Stir in the breadcrumbs, cream and season with salt, pepper and paprika.

Halve the avocados and remove the stones. Stand the halves in an ovenproof dish. Spoon the crab mixture into the stone cavities. Sprinkle with the cheese and bake in a moderately hot oven (200°C, 400°F, Gas Mark 6) for 15–20 minutes. Serve hot, garnished with parsley.

Serves 4

Egg and cheese starters

Eggs and cheese are excellent sources of protein which is most important in our daily diet. They make nutritious starters which may also be served when the family want a quick and tasty snack. Stuffed egg mayonnaise is easy to prepare and although surprise cheese soufflés need a little more attention they make an impressive starter to any meal.

Baked eggs

METRIC/IMPERIAL/AMERICAN
100 g/4 oz/½ cup lean bacon rashers, derinded and chopped
50 g/2 oz/½ cup button mushrooms, chopped
15 g/½ oz/1 tablespoon butter
salt and black pepper
4 eggs
150 ml/¼ pint/⅔ cup single or double cream
gherkin fans to garnish

Fry the bacon and mushrooms in the melted butter until the bacon is cooked. Season well with pepper and a little salt. Spoon into the base of 4 lightly greased, individual ovenproof ramekin dishes. Carefully break an egg into each dish. Spoon 2 tablespoons/2 tablespoons/3 tablespoons cream over each egg and stand the dishes on a baking sheet. Bake in a hot oven (220°C, 425°F, Gas Mark 7) for 12–15 minutes until the egg is just set. Garnish with a gherkin fan and serve with crispbread and butter.
Note: Peeled and thinly sliced tomatoes can be used in place of the bacon and mushrooms for a change.

Serves 4

Surprise cheese soufflés

METRIC/IMPERIAL/AMERICAN
50 g/2 oz/¼ cup lean bacon, derinded and chopped
100 g/4 oz/1 cup mushrooms, chopped
50 g/2 oz/¼ cup butter
salt and pepper
25 g/1 oz/¼ cup flour
200 ml/⅓ pint/¾ cup milk
½ teaspoon oregano
¼ teaspoon made mustard
2 eggs, separated
50 g/2 oz/½ cup mature Cheddar cheese, finely grated

Fry the bacon and mushrooms in half the butter until soft. Season. Spoon into the bases of 6 individual soufflé dishes and stand them on a baking sheet.

Melt the remaining butter in a pan. Stir in the flour and cook for 1 minute. Gradually add the milk and bring to the boil. Add the oregano, mustard, seasoning and egg yolks. Simmer for 2 minutes, stirring. Remove from the heat and beat in the cheese until melted. Cool slightly. Stiffly whisk the egg whites and fold evenly into the sauce. Spoon into the dishes. Bake in a moderately hot oven (200°C, 400°F, Gas Mark 6) for about 20 minutes or until well risen and golden brown. Serve immediately.

Serves 6

Chackchouka

METRIC/IMPERIAL/AMERICAN
25 g/1 oz/2 tablespoons butter
3 tablespoons/3 tablespoons/¼ cup oil
3 onions, sliced
0.5 kg/1 lb/1 lb tomatoes, peeled and sliced
1 red pepper, deseeded and sliced
1 green pepper, deseeded and sliced
salt and pepper
6 eggs

Heat the butter and oil in a saucepan, add the onions and fry until soft. Stir in the tomatoes and peppers, cover and simmer gently for about 10 minutes. Season well and place in a shallow ovenproof dish or 6 individual ovenproof dishes. Make wells in the mixture and break an egg into each. Cook in a hot oven (220°C, 425°F, Gas Mark 7) for 10–15 minutes until set. Serve hot.

Serves 6

Cottage cheese pâté

METRIC/IMPERIAL/AMERICAN
2 sticks celery, finely chopped
40 g/1½ oz/⅓ cup shelled walnuts, chopped
1 tablespoon finely chopped onion
1 tablespoon chopped chives
salt and black pepper
good dash Worcestershire sauce
1 clove garlic, crushed
225 g/8 oz/1 cup cottage cheese
40 g/1½ oz/3 tablespoons butter, melted

Put the celery, walnuts, onion, chives, seasoning, Worcestershire sauce, garlic and cottage cheese into a bowl and mix very well, breaking down the cottage cheese. Add the butter and mix in evenly. Spoon into a large dish or 4 small serving dishes. Chill until firm.

Serves 4

Stuffed egg mayonnaise

METRIC/IMPERIAL/AMERICAN
6 hard-boiled eggs
150 ml/¼ pint/⅔ cup thick mayonnaise
1 teaspoon curry powder
salt and pepper
2 teaspoons chopped capers
1 small lettuce
lemon juice
1 (190-g/6½-oz/6½-oz) can pimientos, drained, to garnish

Halve the eggs lengthways, scoop out the yolks and mash thoroughly. Add 1 tablespoon mayonnaise, half the curry powder, seasoning and capers. Spoon back into the egg white halves.

Arrange lettuce on 6 small plates, place 2 egg halves on each, cut side downwards. Beat the remaining curry powder into the mayonnaise, with sufficient lemon juice to give a coating consistency. Spoon over the eggs until completely coated. Cut the pimientos into narrow strips and use to garnish the eggs.
Note: The curry powder can be omitted, if preferred.

Serves 6

Celebration starters

When you are serving a special occasion meal, an exciting new starter will certainly impress your guests. The recipes in this chapter have been created with that in mind, yet do not necessitate the hostess spending hours in the kitchen.

Seafood bouchées

METRIC/IMPERIAL/AMERICAN
1 (369-g/13-oz/13-oz) packet frozen puff pastry, thawed
beaten egg to glaze
40 g/1½ oz/3 tablespoons butter
1 tablespoon finely chopped onion
25 g/1 oz/¼ cup flour
150 ml/¼ pint/⅔ cup milk
4 tablespoons/4 tablespoons/⅓ cup double cream
salt and pepper
100 g/4 oz/⅔ cup peeled prawns
50 g/2 oz/2 oz smoked salmon pieces
1 (170-g/6-oz/6-oz) jar mussels, drained and chopped

Roll out the pastry to 0.5-cm/¼-inch thickness and cut into about ten 5–7.5-cm/2–3-inch plain rounds. Place on a baking sheet and brush with beaten egg. Using a 2.5-cm/1-inch plain round cutter, mark a circle in the centre of each. Chill for 10 minutes then bake in a hot oven (230°C, 450°F, Gas Mark 8) for 15–20 minutes until well risen and golden brown. Transfer to a wire rack and remove the lids and centres.

Melt the butter in a pan and sauté the onion until soft. Stir in the flour, cook for 1 minute then add the milk. Simmer for 2 minutes then beat in the cream and seasoning. Add the prawns, salmon and mussels, and heat. Spoon into the bouchées. Replace the lids and reheat in a moderate oven for about 10 minutes.

Serves 10–12

Salmon mousses

METRIC/IMPERIAL/AMERICAN
25 g/1 oz/2 tablespoons butter
25 g/1 oz/¼ cup flour
about 300 ml/½ pint/1¼ cups milk
¼ teaspoon dry mustard
salt and pepper
1 tablespoon wine vinegar
3 large eggs, separated
300–350 g/10–12 oz/10–12 oz cooked salmon
150 ml/¼ pint/⅔ cup single cream
4 teaspoons powdered gelatine
3 tablespoons/3 tablespoons/¼ cup water
slices of cucumber
slices of stuffed olive
150 ml/¼ pint/⅔ cup liquid aspic jelly

Melt the butter in a pan, stir in the flour and cook for 1 minute. Add the milk and bring to the boil, stirring. Add the mustard, seasoning and vinegar. Simmer gently for 2 minutes, stirring. Beat in the egg yolks and cook for 1 minute.

Skin, bone and flake the salmon. Add to the mixture with the cream. Dissolve the gelatine in the water in a basin over a pan of hot water. Cool slightly then stir into the salmon mixture. Leave until beginning to set then whisk the egg whites stiffly and fold in. Pour into 8 individual ramekin dishes and chill until set. Place cucumber and olive slices on the mousses, then cover with a layer of the jelly. Chill.

Serves 8

Smoked salmon and asparagus quiches

METRIC/IMPERIAL/AMERICAN
225 g/8 oz/2 cups plain flour
salt and pepper
50 g/2 oz/¼ cup margarine
50 g/2 oz/¼ cup lard or white fat
225 g/8 oz/½ lb frozen asparagus, cooked
175 g/6 oz/6 oz smoked salmon pieces
4 eggs
450 ml/¾ pint/2 cups single cream

Sieve the flour with a pinch of salt and rub in the fats until the mixture resembles fine breadcrumbs. Add sufficient cold water to mix to a pliable dough. Wrap in foil and chill for 30 minutes. Roll out the dough and use to line a 25-cm/10-inch fluted flan tin or six or eight 11-cm/4½-inch individual flan cases.

Roughly chop the asparagus and place in the bottom of the uncooked pastry case or cases. Cut the salmon into narrow strips and arrange over the asparagus. Beat the eggs with the seasoning and cream, and spoon over the salmon. Cook in a hot oven (220°C, 425°F, Gas Mark 7) for 10–15 minutes then reduce to 180°C, 350°F, Gas Mark 4 for a further 30–40 minutes for a large quiche or 20–25 minutes for the small quiches until just set and lightly browned. Serve warm.
Note: Well-drained canned or cooked fresh asparagus can be used in place of the frozen variety.

Serves 6–8

Ham and pâté cornets

METRIC/IMPERIAL/AMERICAN
6 large thin slices cooked ham
50 g/2 oz/$\frac{1}{4}$ cup butter
225 g/8 oz/$\frac{1}{2}$ lb soft smooth pâté
1–2 tablespoons/1–2 tablespoons/1–3 tablespoons double
  cream
salt and pepper
1 clove garlic, crushed (optional)
300 ml/$\frac{1}{2}$ pint/1$\frac{1}{4}$ cups liquid aspic jelly
GARNISH:
black olives
mustard and cress

Cut each slice of ham in half diagonally (or use 12 small slices).
Roll each piece round a cream horn tin and press lightly into
another tin. Roll the ham around this tin and place in another.
Continue in this way until all the ham is used, to keep in shape.
Wrap lightly in polythene and chill for 15–20 minutes.

Cream the butter until soft then beat in the pâté and sufficient
cream to give a piping consistency. Season with salt and pepper
and add the garlic, if liked. Place in a piping bag fitted with a
star nozzle. Carefully remove the ham cornets from the tins, one
at a time, and fill with the piped pâté. Place on a wire rack and
chill again. Leave the aspic jelly until on the point of setting and
then spoon over the cornets. Garnish each with a piece of black
olive and chill until set. Serve with fingers of toast and garnish
with mustard and cress.

Serves 6–12

Hors d'oeuvre

Arrange each salad separately in a small dish and serve them all
together, allowing everyone to help themselves.
(a) Tomato salad: Arrange 225 g/8 oz/$\frac{1}{2}$ lb sliced tomatoes in a
dish. Combine 3 tablespoons/3 tablespoons/$\frac{1}{4}$ cup soured cream
and 1 tablespoon lemon juice with salt and pepper, and spoon
over the tomatoes. Sprinkle with chopped chives.
(b) Cucumber and corn salad: Combine a 10-cm/4-inch
piece cucumber, diced, 1 small sliced onion and 1 (198-g/7-
oz/7-oz) can sweetcorn; add 2–3 tablespoons/2–3 table-
spoons/3–4 tablespoons French dressing and seasoning, and
toss well. Put into a dish and arrange canned sardines around
the edge.
(c) Mixed meat salad: Arrange overlapping slices of liver
sausage, salami and garlic sausage (100 g/4 oz/$\frac{1}{4}$ lb each meat)
on a dish and garnish with parsley.
(d) Egg mayonnaise: Cut 4 hard-boiled eggs into quarters and
arrange on a bed of shredded lettuce in a dish. Combine
4 tablespoons/4 tablespoons/$\frac{1}{3}$ cup mayonnaise, $\frac{1}{4}$ teaspoon
curry powder and seasoning, and add sufficient lemon juice to
give a coating consistency. Spoon over the eggs and garnish
with a lattice of anchovy fillets with sliced stuffed olives.
(e) Beetroot and carrot salad: Combine 175 g/6 oz/1 cup finely
diced beetroot and 2 grated carrots. Add 2–3 tablespoons/2–3
tablespoons/3–4 tablespoons French dressing and seasoning.
Spoon into a dish and sprinkle with chopped parsley.

Serves 8

Casserole Cookery

Included in this chapter are casseroles using many types of fish, meat, offal, vegetables and fruit. This method of cooking enables you to choose the less expensive cuts which are improved in flavour and texture by the long, slow cooking. Once prepared, many casseroles can be left to cook in the oven without spoiling, to provide a meal when you come home.

Most casseroles are suitable for freezing, although it is best to avoid freezing dishes containing pieces of potato, cooked pasta or rice as these foods tend to lose texture during freezing. Do not over-season casseroles which

are to be frozen and if garlic, cream or egg yolks are included in the recipe, add these at the reheating stage.

Ideal accompaniments to casseroles include potatoes, rice or pasta plus a seasonable vegetable. Some casseroles can be all-in-one meals with the vegetables cooked together with the meat. This makes maximum use of the oven and also cuts down on the washing up.

Fish casseroles

Many people forget that fish can be cooked in a casserole – in fact it is an ideal method because the full flavour is retained. The preparation is quick and easy as it is not necessary to sauté the fish prior to cooking it. When possible use dry white wine as some or all of the cooking liquid – it greatly enhances the flavour of the finished dish. Use parsley, watercress, anchovy fillets, olives or lemon slices as a garnish.

Cod à la provençale

METRIC/IMPERIAL/AMERICAN
0.5 kg/1 lb/2 cups tomatoes, peeled and chopped
1 rosemary sprig, chopped
2 thyme sprigs, chopped
salt and pepper
2 tablespoons/2 tablespoons/3 tablespoons white wine or
    water
3 shallots, chopped
2 cloves garlic, crushed
2 tablespoons/2 tablespoons/3 tablespoons olive oil
0.75 kg/1½ lb/1½ lb cod fillets
few drops anchovy essence (optional)
chopped parsley to garnish

Place the tomatoes in a saucepan with the herbs, seasoning and wine or water. Bring to the boil, then cover and simmer gently for about 15 minutes until soft and pulpy.

Meanwhile, sauté the shallots and garlic in the olive oil until softened.

Lay the fish in the bottom of a casserole and season lightly. Arrange the shallots on top. Add a few drops of anchovy essence to the tomato sauce, if liked, and pour over the fish. Cover and cook in a moderate oven (180°C, 350°F, Gas Mark 4) for 30 minutes. Garnish with chopped parsley and serve with French bread.

Serves 4

Mackerel in mustard sauce

METRIC/IMPERIAL/AMERICAN
4 medium mackerel or herrings
salt and freshly ground pepper
1 tablespoon cornflour
3–4 tablespoons/3–4 tablespoons/4–5 tablespoons made
    mustard
4 tablespoons/4 tablespoons/⅓ cup white wine
1 tablespoon lemon juice
GARNISH:
watercress sprigs
tomato waterlilies

Cut the heads and tails off the fish, gut them and remove the
backbones. Lay the fish, skin side down, in a casserole, season
with salt and pepper. Mix together the cornflour and mustard,
then gradually blend in the wine and lemon juice.

Pour the sauce over the fish, cover and cook in a moderate
oven (160°C, 325°F, Gas Mark 3) for 30 minutes. Garnish with
watercress and tomato waterlilies, serve with crusty brown
bread.

Serves 4

Curried haddock

METRIC/IMPERIAL/AMERICAN
0.75 kg/1½ lb/1½ lb haddock fillets
50 g/2 oz/¼ cup butter
2 onions, finely chopped
1 clove garlic, crushed
1 apple, peeled and sliced
1–1½ tablespoons curry powder
1 tablespoon flour
300 ml/½ pint/1¼ cups chicken stock
225 g/8 oz/1 cup tomatoes, peeled and chopped
2 tablespoons/2 tablespoons/3 tablespoons tomato purée
1 tablespoon lemon juice
1 (2.5-cm/1-inch/1-inch) piece root ginger, chopped
salt and pepper
lemon wedges and watercress sprigs to garnish

Cut the fish into 2.5-cm/1-inch pieces and place in a casserole.
Melt the butter in a saucepan and sauté the onions and garlic for
3 minutes. Add the apple and cook for 2 minutes. Mix together
the curry powder and flour and sprinkle into the pan. Cook,
stirring, for 2 minutes. Remove from the heat and stir in the
stock, tomatoes, tomato purée, lemon juice, ginger and
seasoning. Bring to the boil, stirring, then pour over the fish.
Mix well, cover and place in a moderate oven (160°C, 325°F,
Gas Mark 3) for 30 minutes. Garnish and serve with boiled rice.

Serves 4

Sole with prawns

METRIC/IMPERIAL/AMERICAN
0.5 kg/1 lb/1 lb sole fillets
flour for coating
3 tablespoons/3 tablespoons/¼ cup olive oil
2 onions, finely chopped
2 cloves garlic, crushed
225 g/8 oz/½ lb frozen prawns, thawed
3 tomatoes, peeled and roughly chopped
1 teaspoon chopped fresh thyme
½ teaspoon cayenne pepper
300 ml/½ pint/1¼ cups white wine
2 tablespoons/2 tablespoons/3 tablespoons tomato purée
1 tablespoon lemon juice
salt and pepper
1 egg yolk
3 tablespoons/3 tablespoons/¼ cup cream
slices of lemon and parsley sprig to garnish

Cut the sole into pieces and coat with flour. Heat the oil in a flameproof casserole and sauté the onions and garlic for 2–3 minutes. Add the prawns and sole and continue cooking until the onion is soft. Stir in the tomatoes, thyme, cayenne, white wine, tomato purée and lemon juice. Season. Bring to the boil, then cover and simmer for 15–20 minutes, or cook in a moderate oven (160°C, 325°F, Gas Mark 3). Beat together the egg yolk and cream and stir into the wine sauce, off the heat. Warm through only. Garnish and serve with boiled rice.

Serves 6

Sole véronique

METRIC/IMPERIAL/AMERICAN
1 small onion, finely chopped
15 g/½ oz/1 tablespoon butter
0.75 kg/1½ lb/1½ lb sole or plaice fillets
salt and pepper
juice of ½ lemon
150 ml/¼ pint/⅔ cup white wine
1 bay leaf
175 g/6 oz/6 oz white grapes, peeled and deseeded
25 g/1 oz/2 tablespoons butter
25 g/1 oz/¼ cup flour
150 ml/¼ pint/⅔ cup double cream

Sprinkle the onion over the bottom of a buttered casserole. Fold the sole fillets in half and place on top of the onion. Season and add the lemon juice, wine, bay leaf and enough water to cover. Cover and cook in a moderate oven (180°C, 350°F, Gas Mark 4) for 15 minutes. Reserve a few grapes for garnishing and add the remaining grapes to the dish. Return to the oven to heat. Remove the fish and grapes and keep warm. Discard bay leaf.

Melt the butter in a saucepan, blend in the flour and cook for 1 minute. Remove from the heat and strain in the cooking liquid, made up to 300 ml/½ pint/1¼ cups with extra wine or water. Bring to the boil, stirring. Cook until thick. Remove from the heat and add the cream. Heat through only.

Return the fish and grapes to the casserole or arrange on a serving dish, and pour the sauce over. Garnish with watercress.

Serves 4

Savoury topped fish

METRIC/IMPERIAL/AMERICAN
4 (175-g/6-oz/6-oz) white fish fillets (cod, whiting or
  haddock)
50 g/2 oz/¼ cup butter, melted
salt and pepper
4 tomatoes, sliced
2 shallots, finely chopped
1 small green pepper, deseeded and chopped
25 g/1 oz/½ cup fresh white breadcrumbs
50 g/2 oz/½ cup Cheddar cheese, grated
½ teaspoon Worcestershire sauce
1 teaspoon mixed dried herbs
1 lemon or orange
GARNISH:
twist of lemon or orange
parsley sprig

Place the fish in a well-greased casserole and spoon over half the
melted butter. Season and arrange the tomato slices on top.

Sauté the shallots and green pepper in the remaining butter
until softened. Mix in the breadcrumbs, cheese, Worcestershire
sauce, herbs and the juice and grated rind of the lemon or
orange. Season to taste and spread over the fish and tomatoes.
Bake in a moderate oven (180°C, 350°F, Gas Mark 4) for 30
minutes. Garnish with a twist of lemon or orange and a sprig of
parsley. Serve with minted peas and new potatoes.

Serves 4

Smoked haddock à la russe

METRIC/IMPERIAL/AMERICAN
0.75 kg/1½ lb/1½ lb smoked haddock fillets
300 ml/½ pint/1¼ cups white wine
freshly ground black pepper and salt
25 g/1 oz/2 tablespoons butter
25 g/1 oz/¼ cup flour
½ small green pepper, deseeded and chopped
150 ml/¼ pint/⅔ cup soured cream
GARNISH:
croûtes of bread cut into star shapes
parsley sprig

Place the haddock in a large frying pan and add the wine. Add
enough water to cover. Season with pepper. Bring to the boil,
skim the surface then lower the heat and simmer for 5 minutes.
Remove the fish, drain reserving the cooking liquor, and cut
into squares. Place in a casserole.

Melt the butter in a saucepan and stir in the flour. Cook,
stirring, for 1 minute then remove from the heat and gradually
blend in 300 ml/½ pint/1¼ cups of the strained cooking liquor.
Return to the heat and bring to the boil, stirring continuously.
When the sauce is thick and glossy, add the chopped pepper and
season to taste. Pour the sauce over the fish and mix well. Cover
and cook in a moderate oven (180°C, 350°F, Gas Mark 4) for 20
minutes. Stir in the soured cream and return to the oven to heat
through. Garnish and serve with buttered new potatoes.

Serves 4–6

Beef casseroles

Beef casseroles are always popular and they need never become boring. The changes can be rung by the addition of herbs and different vegetables; stock, wine or ale may be part or all of the cooking liquid. The cuts of beef to choose for casseroles range from chuck, skirt and minced beef to joints of brisket and topside which may be pot-roasted.

Beef Brazilian style

METRIC/IMPERIAL/AMERICAN

1 kg/2 lb/2 lb skirt steak
3 tablespoons/3 tablespoons/$\frac{1}{4}$ cup oil
3 onions, sliced into rings
1 clove garlic, crushed
25 g/1 oz/$\frac{1}{4}$ cup flour
150 ml/$\frac{1}{4}$ pint/$\frac{2}{3}$ cup black coffee (1$\frac{1}{2}$–2 teaspoons instant coffee dissolved in 150 ml/$\frac{1}{4}$ pint/$\frac{2}{3}$ cup boiling water)
150 ml/$\frac{1}{4}$ pint/$\frac{2}{3}$ cup beef stock or red wine
1 (396-g/14-oz/14-oz) can tomatoes
salt and pepper
pinch nutmeg
2 teaspoons soft brown sugar

Cut the meat into strips and fry quickly in the oil. Lower the heat and add the onions and garlic. Cook until softened. Sprinkle in the flour and continue to cook, stirring, for a further minute. Gradually mix in the coffee and stock or wine, then add the tomatoes. Season with salt, pepper, nutmeg and the soft brown sugar. Bring to simmering point, cover and cook in a moderate oven (160°C, 325°F, Gas Mark 3) for 2 hours. Serve with buttered noodles and a green salad.

Serves 4

Braised brisket

METRIC/IMPERIAL/AMERICAN
2 large onions, sliced
2 large carrots, sliced
2 cloves garlic
6–8 peppercorns
6 tablespoons/6 tablespoons/$\frac{1}{2}$ cup olive oil
bouquet garni
300 ml/$\frac{1}{2}$ pint/$1\frac{1}{4}$ cups red wine
1 tablespoon tomato purée
1.25–1.5 kg/$2\frac{1}{2}$–3 lb/$2\frac{1}{2}$–3 lb brisket
1 tablespoon chopped fresh herbs
$1\frac{1}{2}$ tablespoons/$1\frac{1}{2}$ tablespoons/2 tablespoons flour
450 ml/$\frac{3}{4}$ pint/2 cups beef stock

Place half the onion and carrot in a saucepan with 1 chopped
clove garlic, peppercorns, a third of the olive oil, bouquet garni,
wine and tomato purée. Bring to the boil and simmer for 2
minutes. Cool and pour over the meat. Marinate for 24 hours.
Reserve the marinade. Push the herbs into the brisket. Rub the
meat with garlic. Season. Heat the oil in a flameproof casserole
and brown the meat. Remove. Sauté the remaining onion and
carrot. Return the meat and pour the marinade over. Cover and
cook in a moderate oven (160°C, 325°F, Gas Mark 3) for about
2–$2\frac{1}{2}$ hours. Mix the flour and stock. Bring to the boil and
simmer for 15–20 minutes. Remove the meat. Strain juices and
skim. Add to the stock and boil until thick. Carve the meat and
pour the sauce over. Garnish with watercress.

Serves 6–8

Mediterranean pot roast

METRIC/IMPERIAL/AMERICAN
2 tablespoons/2 tablespoons/3 tablespoons olive oil
1.25 kg/$2\frac{1}{2}$ lb/$2\frac{1}{2}$ lb boned and rolled rib of beef
6 shallots
2 carrots, sliced
1 clove garlic, crushed
bouquet garni
salt and pepper
pinch nutmeg
200 ml/$\frac{1}{3}$ pint/$\frac{3}{4}$ cup red wine or beef stock
100 g/4 oz/$\frac{3}{4}$ cup green or black olives, stoned
BEURRE MANIÉ:
15 g/$\frac{1}{2}$ oz/1 tablespoon butter
15 g/$\frac{1}{2}$ oz/2 tablespoons flour

Heat the oil in a flameproof casserole and brown the meat on all
sides over a low heat. Drain off excess fat.

Add the shallots, carrots, garlic, bouquet garni, salt, pepper
and nutmeg. Pour the wine or stock over the meat and cover
with a tight-fitting lid. Cook in a moderate oven (160°C, 325°F,
Gas Mark 3) for 2 hours.

Add the olives to the casserole. Adjust seasoning. Return to
the oven for a further 30 minutes or until tender.

Discard the bouquet garni. Slice the meat and keep warm.
Blend the butter and flour together and add to the cooking
liquid, a little at a time. Warm through to thicken. Pour over the
meat.

Serves 6

Boeuf à la provençale

METRIC/IMPERIAL/AMERICAN
1 kg/2 lb/2 lb lean braising or stewing steak
3 tablespoons/3 tablespoons/¼ cup olive oil
175 g/6 oz/6 oz streaky bacon, chopped
225 g/8 oz/½ lb button onions
225 g/8 oz/1½ cups carrots, sliced
2 tablespoons/2 tablespoons/3 tablespoons tomato purée
3 cloves garlic, crushed
300 ml/½ pint/1¼ cups red wine
300 ml/½ pint/1¼ cups beef stock
bouquet garni
pinch dried thyme, salt and pepper
0.5 kg/1 lb/2 cups tomatoes, peeled and chopped
100 g/4 oz/¾ cup black olives, stoned
25 g/1 oz/2 tablespoons butter
25 g/1 oz/¼ cup flour
chopped parsley and triangles of fried bread to garnish

Cut the beef into 2.5-cm/1-inch squares. Heat the oil in a flameproof casserole and fry the beef until brown. Remove. Add the bacon, onions and carrot and sauté for 5 minutes. Stir in the tomato purée, garlic, wine, stock, bouquet garni, thyme and seasoning. Bring to the boil. Return the meat to the casserole, cover and cook in a cool oven (150°C, 300°F, Gas Mark 2) for 1½ hours. Add the tomatoes and olives and cook for 1 hour. Blend the butter into the flour. Add to the casserole a little at a time. Heat through but do not boil. Garnish.

Serves 4–6

Daube de boeuf

METRIC/IMPERIAL/AMERICAN
0.75–1 kg/1½–2 lb/1½–2 lb topside
flour for coating
3 tablespoons/3 tablespoons/¼ cup olive oil
50 g/2 oz/2 oz streaky bacon, chopped
225 g/8 oz/½ lb button onions
2 tomatoes, peeled and sliced
1 clove garlic, crushed
50 g/2 oz/⅓ cup raisins
25 g/1 oz/1 oz dried apricots, soaked and halved
1 teaspoon dried mixed herbs
2 bay leaves
300 ml/½ pint/1¼ cups red wine
150 ml/¼ pint/⅔ cup beef stock
salt and pepper

Cut the meat into 1-cm/½-inch slices and coat well with the flour. Heat the oil in a flameproof casserole and fry the meat until lightly browned all over. Remove and reserve. Sauté the bacon and onions in the fat in the pan for 3–4 minutes, then return the meat and add the remaining ingredients. Bring to simmering point then cover and place in a cool oven (150°C, 300°F, Gas Mark 2) for 2–2½ hours or until the meat is very tender. Discard the bay leaves. Serve with buttered new potatoes and a good red wine.

Serves 4–6

Boeuf à la bourguignonne

METRIC/IMPERIAL/AMERICAN
1 kg/2 lb/2 lb chuck steak
3 tablespoons/3 tablespoons/¼ cup oil
175 g/6 oz/6 oz streaky bacon, diced
1–1½ tablespoons flour
450 ml/¾ pint/2 cups red wine
150 ml/¼ pint/⅔ cup beef stock
bouquet garni
2 cloves garlic, crushed
salt and pepper
20 button onions
25 g/1 oz/2 tablespoons butter
175 g/6 oz/1½ cups button mushrooms
parsley sprig to garnish

Cut the meat into 5-cm/2-inch squares. Heat the oil in a flameproof casserole and brown the meat. Remove the meat and keep warm. Add the bacon to the casserole and sauté until golden. Sprinkle in the flour. Cook for 1 minute, stirring, then remove from the heat and pour in the wine and stock. Add the bouquet garni and garlic and season. Bring to simmering point, stirring. Return the meat to the casserole, cover and place in a cool oven (150°C, 300°F, Gas Mark 2) for 2 hours.

Meanwhile, blanch the onions for 1 minute in boiling water, then sauté them gently in the butter. Add the onions and mushrooms to the casserole and cook for a further 30 minutes. Discard the bouquet garni. Garnish.

Serves 4–6

Hungarian goulash

METRIC/IMPERIAL/AMERICAN
0.75–1 kg/1½–2 lb/1½–2 lb skirt steak, cubed
3 tablespoons/3 tablespoons/¼ cup oil
3 onions, sliced
1 red pepper, deseeded and chopped
25 g/1 oz/¼ cup flour
2 tablespoons/2 tablespoons/3 tablespoons paprika pepper
0.5 kg/1 lb/2 cups tomatoes, peeled and chopped
600 ml/1 pint/2½ cups beef stock
bouquet garni
1 teaspoon dried thyme
salt
150 ml/¼ pint/⅔ cup soured cream
parsley sprig to garnish

Sauté the meat in the oil in a flameproof casserole; remove.

Lower the heat and sauté the onions and red pepper in the fat remaining in the casserole. When they are softened sprinkle in the flour and paprika pepper. Cook, stirring, for 1 minute. Add the tomatoes and stock and bring to simmering point, stirring continuously. Return the meat to the casserole and add the bouquet garni and thyme. Season with salt to taste. Cover and place in a moderate oven (160°C, 325°F, Gas Mark 3) for 2½–3 hours. Remove the bouquet garni. Spoon a little of the soured cream on top of the goulash to garnish with the parsley, and serve the remainder separately.

Serves 4

Dijon beef

METRIC/IMPERIAL/AMERICAN
1.25 kg/2½ lb/2½ lb topside
3 tablespoons/3 tablespoons/¼ cup Dijon mustard
2 tablespoons/2 tablespoons/3 tablespoons flour
5 tablespoons/5 tablespoons/6 tablespoons olive oil
0.5 kg/1 lb/1 lb onions, sliced
salt and pepper
1 bay leaf
1 teaspoon chopped fresh thyme
450 ml/¾ pint/2 cups beef stock or stock and red wine
chopped parsley to garnish

Cut the beef into 5-mm/¼-inch slices, removing any fat. Spread both sides of the slices liberally with mustard, cover and keep in the refrigerator overnight. Coat in flour and brown the slices lightly in the olive oil. This will probably have to be done in 2 or 3 batches. Arrange alternate layers of meat and onion in a casserole, lightly seasoning each meat layer and finishing with a layer of onion. Add the bay leaf, thyme and stock. Cover and cook in a moderate oven (160°C, 325°F, Gas Mark 3) for 2–2½ hours. Discard the bay leaf. Garnish with chopped parsley.

Serves 6

Beef hotpot with herb dumplings

METRIC/IMPERIAL/AMERICAN
0.75–1 kg/1½–2 lb/1½–2 lb braising steak, cubed
seasoned flour
3 tablespoons/3 tablespoons/¼ cup oil
2 onions, sliced
4 leeks, trimmed and sliced
6 carrots, sliced
1 (396-g/14-oz/14-oz) can tomatoes
450 ml/¾ pint/2 cups stock or red wine
100 g/4 oz/1 cup self-raising flour
50 g/2 oz/½ cup shredded suet
2 teaspoons chopped fresh thyme or 1 teaspoon dried
2 teaspoons chopped fresh sage or 1 teaspoon dried
100 g/4 oz/1 cup mushrooms, sliced

Coat the meat with seasoned flour. Heat the oil in a flameproof casserole and fry the meat quickly to seal. Remove. Fry the onions, leeks and carrots until softened. Add the tomatoes and stock or wine. Bring to the boil, stirring, then return the meat. Season. Cover and cook in a moderate oven (160°C, 325°F, Gas Mark 3) for 2 hours.

Mix the flour and suet, add the herbs and season. Stir in cold water to make an elastic dough and divide into 12 portions. After 2 hours, stir in mushrooms. Place the dumplings around the edge and return to the oven for 15–20 minutes.

Serves 6

Lamb casseroles

The important point to remember about lamb casseroles is that the main cuts which are used – breast, middle, neck and scrag – are fatty and do need to be trimmed of as much fat as possible before cooking. Chump chops and cutlets may be casseroled as a change from grilling and minced lamb is ideal for such favourites as moussaka; a stuffed shoulder of lamb is delicious when braised or pot-roasted.

Lamb chops paprika

METRIC/IMPERIAL/AMERICAN
8 loin or chump chops
salt and pepper
2 tablespoons/2 tablespoons/3 tablespoons flour
25 g/1 oz/2 tablespoons butter
1 onion, chopped
1 green pepper, deseeded and chopped
2 tablespoons/2 tablespoons/3 tablespoons paprika
   pepper
pinch cayenne pepper
1 (396-g/14-oz/14-oz) can tomatoes

Trim any excess fat from the chops and coat in seasoned flour. Heat the butter in a flameproof casserole and brown the chops on both sides. Remove from the casserole. Add the onion and green pepper and continue to sauté until softened. Sprinkle in the paprika pepper and cayenne and cook for 1 minute. Place the chops back in the casserole. Pour in the tomatoes with their juice and adjust seasoning, if necessary. Cover and cook in a moderate oven (160°C, 325°F, Gas Mark 3) for 1–1½ hours. Skim well before serving. Serve with peas.

Serves 4

Navarin of lamb

METRIC/IMPERIAL/AMERICAN
25 g/1 oz/2 tablespoons dripping or butter
1 kg/2 lb/2 lb best end of neck lamb cutlets
225 g/8 oz/½ lb young carrots
225 g/8 oz/½ lb button onions
2 young turnips, quartered
1 tablespoon sugar
1 tablespoon flour
600 ml/1 pint/2½ cups stock
salt and pepper
bouquet garni
8 small new potatoes
chopped parsley to garnish

Heat the dripping or butter in a flameproof casserole and brown the cutlets on both sides. Remove from the casserole. Add the carrots, onions and turnips to the casserole and sprinkle with the sugar. Sauté gently until browned, then stir in the flour. Cook for 1 minute. Gradually add the stock and season well. Bring to the boil, stirring continuously. Return the meat to the casserole, add the bouquet garni, cover and place in a moderate oven (160°C, 325°F, Gas Mark 3) for 45 minutes.

Scrape the potatoes and add to the casserole. Return to the oven for a further 45 minutes. Discard the bouquet garni and garnish with parsley. Serve with crusty French bread, if liked.

Serves 4

Lamb in yogurt and mint sauce

METRIC/IMPERIAL/AMERICAN
3 tablespoons/3 tablespoons/¼ cup oil
0.75–1 kg/1½–2 lb/1½–2 lb lean lamb, cubed
2 onions, sliced
1 tablespoon flour
300 ml/½ pint/1¼ cups white wine
bouquet garni
2 cloves garlic, crushed
salt and pepper
pinch nutmeg
2 tablespoons/2 tablespoons/3 tablespoons chopped mint
150 ml/¼ pint/⅔ cup natural yogurt
mint sprig to garnish

Heat the oil in a flameproof casserole and brown the meat. Remove the lamb and gently sauté the onions until softened. Sprinkle in the flour. Cook, stirring, for 1 minute, then pour in the wine. Bring to the boil, stirring continuously, then lower the heat. Replace the meat, add the bouquet garni, garlic, salt, pepper and nutmeg. Cover and place in a moderate oven (160°C, 325°F, Gas Mark 3) for 1–1½ hours or until the meat is tender.

Mix the chopped mint into the yogurt and stir the yogurt into the casserole. Reheat gently but do not boil. Garnish and serve with boiled rice.

Serves 4

Moussaka

METRIC/IMPERIAL/AMERICAN
2–3 aubergines, sliced
salt and pepper
olive oil for shallow frying
4–5 onions, sliced
0.5 kg/1 lb/1 lb lamb, minced
1 (140-g/5-oz/5-oz) can tomato purée
150 ml/$\frac{1}{4}$ pint/$\frac{2}{3}$ cup stock
$\frac{1}{2}$ teaspoon garlic salt
2 eggs
150 ml/$\frac{1}{4}$ pint/$\frac{2}{3}$ cup natural yogurt, single cream or
    creamy milk
parsley sprig to garnish

Sprinkle the aubergines with salt and leave for 30 minutes. Rinse the slices and dry. Fry in oil until golden, then drain on absorbent paper. Sauté the onions in oil for 5 minutes. Fry the lamb in a dry pan to lightly brown, then drain.

Line the bottom of an ovenproof dish with half the aubergine slices. Cover with a layer of half the onions, then half the lamb. Season and repeat.

Mix the tomato purée with the stock and the garlic salt. Spread this sauce over the top layer of lamb and place in a moderate oven (180°C, 350°F, Gas Mark 4) for 30 minutes. Beat together the eggs and yogurt, season well and pour over the moussaka. Return to the oven for about 15–20 minutes. Garnish.

Serves 4

Lamb with lentils

METRIC/IMPERIAL/AMERICAN
175 g/6 oz/$\frac{3}{4}$ cup lentils
1 kg/2 lb/2 lb boned shoulder of lamb
2 tablespoons/2 tablespoons/3 tablespoons oil
2 carrots, sliced
2 onions, chopped
1–2 cloves garlic, crushed
2 bay leaves
bouquet garni
good pinch nutmeg
salt and pepper
450 ml/$\frac{3}{4}$ pint/2 cups chicken or beef stock
chopped parsley to garnish

Soak the lentils in cold water for 2 hours.

Meanwhile, cut the meat into 4-cm/1$\frac{1}{2}$-inch pieces, removing any excess fat. Heat the oil in a flameproof casserole and brown the meat on all sides over moderate heat. Remove from the casserole. Sauté the carrots and onions until softened then return the meat to the casserole. Add the garlic, bay leaves, bouquet garni, nutmeg and seasoning. Pour over the stock, bring to the boil, cover and place in a moderate oven (180°C, 350°F, Gas Mark 4) for 30 minutes.

Drain the lentils, add to the casserole and return to the oven for a further 45 minutes. Remove the bay leaves and bouquet garni. Serve garnished with chopped parsley.

Serves 4–6

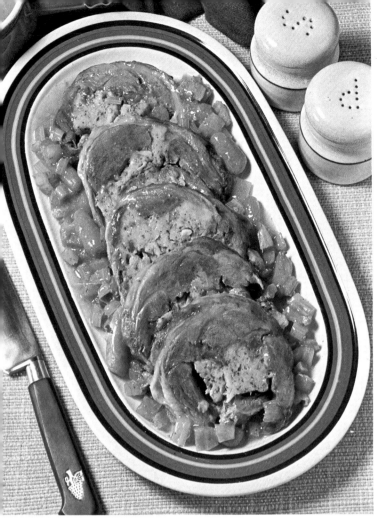

Braised stuffed shoulder of lamb

METRIC/IMPERIAL/AMERICAN
STUFFING:
50 g/2 oz/1 cup fresh breadcrumbs
2 rashers streaky bacon, finely chopped
1 onion, finely chopped
1 clove garlic, crushed
1 tablespoon chopped fresh mint, tarragon and parsley or
    1 teaspoon each dried
grated rind and juice of ½ lemon
salt and pepper
1 egg, beaten

1 (1.5-kg/3½-lb/3½-lb) shoulder of lamb, boned
2 tablespoons/2 tablespoons/3 tablespoons oil
8 small whole carrots
4 sticks celery, chopped
300 ml/½ pint/1¼ cups stock

Mix together all the stuffing ingredients and spread over the boned side of the lamb. Roll up and tie with string. Brown the meat in the oil, drain and place in a flameproof casserole. Sauté carrots and celery and add to meat with stock. Cover and cook in a moderate oven (180°C, 350°F, Gas Mark 4) for 2 hours. Remove meat and vegetables. Thicken the sauce if liked. Slice the meat, add the vegetables and pour the sauce over.

Serves 6–8

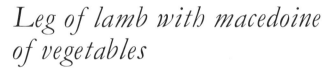

Leg of lamb with macedoine of vegetables

METRIC/IMPERIAL/AMERICAN
1 (1.5-kg/3½-lb/3½-lb) leg of lamb
2 tablespoons/2 tablespoons/3 tablespoons oil
2 onions
4 carrots, diced
2 leeks, sliced
2 tablespoons/2 tablespoons/3 tablespoons tomato purée
1 (396-g/14-oz/14-oz) can tomatoes
1 clove garlic, crushed
bouquet garni
salt and pepper

Brown the meat on all sides in the oil. Drain well and place in a large casserole. Arrange the onions, carrots and leeks around the meat and pour over the tomato purée mixed with the tomatoes and their juice. Add the garlic, bouquet garni and seasoning. Cover and cook in a moderate oven (180°C, 350°F, Gas Mark 4) for 1¼–1½ hours. Discard the bouquet garni and serve the lamb surrounded by the vegetables.

Serves 6–8

Shoulder of lamb boulangère

METRIC/IMPERIAL/AMERICAN
1 (1.5-kg/3½-lb/3½-lb) shoulder of lamb, boned and rolled
2 cloves garlic, sliced
0.75 kg/1½ lb/1½ lb potatoes, sliced
1 teaspoon fresh chopped thyme or ½ teaspoon dried
   thyme
1 large fresh rosemary sprig, chopped, or ½ teaspoon
   dried rosemary
salt and pepper
75 g/3 oz/6 tablespoons butter
watercress to garnish

Make several small cuts in the skin of the lamb and insert the
garlic slices. Arrange a layer of potato slices in the bottom of a
large lightly greased casserole. Sprinkle with half the herbs and
place the lamb on top. Arrange the remaining potato slices
around the lamb and sprinkle with the rest of the herbs. Season
and dot with the butter. Cover with a lid or foil and place in a
moderately hot oven (180°C, 350°F, Gas Mark 4) for 1 hour.
Uncover and increase the oven temperature to 200°C, 400°F,
Gas Mark 6 for 15–30 minutes to brown the meat and potatoes.
Garnish with watercress.

Serves 6

Lamb stew with prunes and apricots

METRIC/IMPERIAL/AMERICAN
1.75 kg/2½ lb/2½ lb middle neck lamb chops
25 g/1 oz/2 tablespoons butter
2 onions, sliced
1½ tablespoons/1½ tablespoons/2 tablespoons flour
300 ml/½ pint/1¼ cups chicken stock
300 ml/½ pint/1¼ cups red wine
bouquet garni
1 clove garlic, crushed
100 g/4 oz/⅔ cup prunes, soaked overnight
50 g/2 oz/⅓ cup dried apricots, soaked overnight
salt and pepper
1 teaspoon soft brown sugar

Brown the meat in the butter in a flameproof casserole. Remove
and add the onions to the casserole and sauté until softened.
Sprinkle in the flour and cook, stirring, over a low heat until the
flour begins to brown. Gradually blend in the stock and wine
and add the bouquet garni and garlic. Bring to the boil, stirring
continuously, then reduce the heat, return the meat to the
casserole and add the drained prunes and apricots. Season with
salt, pepper and sugar. Cover and place in a moderate oven
(180°C, 350°F, Gas Mark 4) for 1½ hours. Skim well before
serving.

Serves 6

Lamb curry

METRIC/IMPERIAL/AMERICAN
1 kg/2 lb/2 lb lean shoulder of lamb
50 g/2 oz/¼ cup ghee or butter
2 onions, sliced
2 cloves garlic, crushed
25 g/1 oz/¼ cup flour
1-cm/½-inch/½-inch piece root ginger, finely chopped
1 teaspoon ground coriander
1½ teaspoons garam masala
300 ml/½ pint/1¼ cups chicken stock
salt and pepper
pinch chilli powder
150 ml/¼ pint/⅔ cup natural yogurt
flaked almonds and chopped parsley to garnish

Cut the meat into 2.5-cm/1-inch pieces. Heat the ghee or butter in a saucepan or flameproof casserole and sauté the lamb until evenly brown. Remove the meat and reserve. Sauté the onions and garlic in the remaining fat until softened, then sprinkle in the flour and cook for 1 minute. Return the meat to the pan and sprinkle in the ginger, coriander and garam masala. Mix well and cook for 2 minutes before pouring in the stock. Bring to the boil and season to taste with salt, pepper and chilli powder. Cover and simmer on top of the cooker or in a moderate oven (160°C, 325°F, Gas Mark 3) for 1–1½ hours until the meat is tender and the flavours have blended. Stir in the yogurt and heat through but do not allow to boil. Garnish.

Serves 4–6

Lancashire hotpot

METRIC/IMPERIAL/AMERICAN
1 kg/2 lb/2 lb middle neck lamb chops
1 kg/2 lb/2 lb potatoes
0.5 kg/1 lb/1 lb onions
salt and pepper
300–450 ml/½–¾ pint/1¼–2 cups light stock

Trim any excess fat from the lamb. Peel and slice the potatoes and onions. Place a layer of half the onions in the bottom of a saucepan or flameproof casserole, then half the chops and half the potatoes, seasoning each layer. Repeat. Pour over almost enough stock to cover. Bring to the boil, cover and simmer on the top of the cooker or place in a moderate oven (180°C, 350°F, Gas Mark 4) for 2½ hours.

Serves 4–6

Pork casseroles

*Any lean boneless piece of pork is suitable for casseroles –
it may be cut from the belly, shoulder, leg or fillet – chump
or loin chops or spare rib cutlets may also be casseroled.
Many herbs go naturally with pork – try rosemary, sage,
thyme, basil or marjoram. Use dry cider as some or all of
the cooking liquid in pork casseroles as it makes a delicious
change. Included in this section are recipes using bacon joints.*

Pork fillet au porto

METRIC/IMPERIAL/AMERICAN
0.75 kg/1½ lb/1½ lb pork fillet
salt and pepper
25 g/1 oz/¼ cup flour
25 g/1 oz/2 tablespoons butter
2 onions, chopped
1 tablespoon Worcestershire sauce
1 tablespoon mushroom ketchup
2 tablespoons/2 tablespoons/3 tablespoons redcurrant
   jelly
2 tablespoons/2 tablespoons/3 tablespoons tomato purée
4 tablespoons/4 tablespoons/⅓ cup port
4 tablespoons/4 tablespoons/⅓ cup double cream
chopped parsley to garnish

Remove the outer skin from the pork fillet and cut into 2.5-cm/
1-inch slices. Coat with seasoned flour and sauté in the
butter until golden. Transfer the meat to a casserole. Sauté the
onions until softened in the butter remaining in the pan then
transfer to the casserole with the meat. Mix together the
remaining ingredients, except the cream, and pour over the
pork and onions. Cover and cook in a moderate oven (180°C,
350°F, Gas Mark 4) for 30–40 minutes or until the meat is
tender. Spoon the cream over the meat and return, uncovered,
to the oven for 5 minutes to heat through. Sprinkle with
chopped parsley.

Serves 4

Pork and beans

METRIC/IMPERIAL/AMERICAN
225 g/8 oz/1 cup haricot or butter beans
salt
3 tablespoons/3 tablespoons/$\frac{1}{4}$ cup olive oil
1 kg/2 lb/2 lb lean pork, cubed
25 g/1 oz/$\frac{1}{4}$ cup flour
pepper
0.5 kg/1 lb/1 lb onions, sliced
2–3 cloves garlic, sliced
600 ml/1 pint/2$\frac{1}{2}$ cups beef stock
4 tablespoons/4 tablespoons/$\frac{1}{3}$ cup tomato purée
1 tablespoon Worcestershire sauce

Soak the beans in cold water overnight. Drain and place in a large saucepan with enough fresh cold water to cover. Add a little salt and bring to the boil. Simmer for 1 hour.

Meanwhile, heat the oil in a large flameproof casserole. Coat the meat in seasoned flour and brown on all sides over a moderate heat. Drain off any excess fat and arrange the onions and garlic on top of the meat. Pour in the stock with the tomato purée and Worcestershire sauce. Bring to the boil, cover and place in a moderate oven (160°C, 325°F, Gas Mark 3) for 1 hour.

Drain the haricot or butter beans and add to the casserole. Adjust seasoning if necessary. Re-cover and return to the oven for a further hour or until the meat is tender and the beans are cooked.

Serves 6

Pork ragoût

METRIC/IMPERIAL/AMERICAN
1 kg/2 lb/2 lb boned belly of pork
2 onions, sliced
225 g/8 oz/$\frac{1}{2}$ lb baby carrots
1 bay leaf
2 teaspoons chopped fresh sage or 1 teaspoon dried sage
1 tablespoon flour
150 ml/$\frac{1}{4}$ pint/$\frac{2}{3}$ cup chicken stock
1 (396-g/14-oz/14-oz) can tomatoes
salt and pepper
0.5 kg/1 lb/1 lb fresh peas, shelled
6 medium potatoes, peeled and quartered
1 teaspoon sugar

Cut the meat into strips, removing excess fat. Fry in a dry pan until brown. Drain and place in a large casserole. Sauté the onions in the pork fat until soft, then add to the casserole, together with the carrots and herbs. Sprinkle the flour into the fat remaining in the pan and cook for 1 minute, stirring. Gradually blend in the stock and tomatoes and bring to the boil, stirring. Season to taste, then pour over the meat and vegetables. Cover and place in a moderate oven (160°C, 325°F, Gas Mark 3) for 1$\frac{1}{4}$ hours.

Add the peas, potatoes and sugar. Re-cover and return to the oven for a further 45 minutes or until the peas and potatoes are tender. Remove the bay leaf before serving.

Serves 6

Normandy pork

METRIC/IMPERIAL/AMERICAN
1 kg/2 lb/2 lb boned shoulder of pork, cubed
3 tablespoons/3 tablespoons/¼ cup oil
2 large onions, sliced
1 clove garlic, crushed
3 tablespoons/3 tablespoons/¼ cup flour
300 ml/½ pint/1¼ cups chicken stock
300 ml/½ pint/1¼ cups dry cider
½ teaspoon dried basil
½ teaspoon dried marjoram
salt and pepper
2 eating apples
3 tablespoons/3 tablespoons/¼ cup double cream
chopped parsley to garnish

Heat the oil in a flameproof casserole and sauté the pork over a moderate heat until golden. Remove the meat and add the onions and garlic to the casserole. Sauté gently until beginning to colour. Sprinkle in the flour, mix well and cook for 1 minute. Gradually blend in the stock and cider and bring to the boil, stirring constantly. Return the pork to the casserole, add the herbs and season to taste. Cover and place in a moderate oven (180°C, 350°F, Gas Mark 4) for 45 minutes. Peel, core and slice the apples, reserving some slices for garnish, and add to the casserole. Return to the oven for a further 45 minutes or until the meat is tender. Stir the cream into the casserole before serving. Garnish with parsley and reserved slices of apple.

Serves 4–6

Pork chops with ham

METRIC/IMPERIAL/AMERICAN
25 g/1 oz/2 tablespoons butter
4 lean pork loin chops
4 shallots, finely chopped
1 (225-g/8-oz/½-lb) piece ham or gammon, diced
300 ml/½ pint/1¼ cups dry white wine or wine and
    chicken stock
bouquet garni
salt and pepper
1 tablespoon cornflour
watercress to garnish

Heat the butter in a flameproof casserole and brown the chops gently on both sides. Add the shallots to soften, then add the diced ham. Pour in the wine, add the bouquet garni and season to taste. Cover and place in a moderate oven (180°C, 350°F, Gas Mark 4) for 1 hour or until tender.

Remove the meat and keep warm. Discard the bouquet garni. Mix the cornflour with a little water and stir in 2 tablespoons/2 tablespoons/3 tablespoons of the sauce from the casserole. Blend this mixture into the casserole, off the heat. Cook the sauce over a low heat, stirring continuously, until it is smooth and has thickened slightly. Adjust the seasoning if necessary and pour the sauce over the chops and ham on a warmed platter or return the meat to the casserole. Garnish with watercress and serve with ratatouille, if liked.

Serves 4

Pork with lemon

METRIC/IMPERIAL/AMERICAN ·
0.75–1 kg/1½–2 lb/1½–2 lb pork fillet, sliced
salt and pepper
3 tablespoons/3 tablespoons/¼ cup flour
2 onions, sliced
50 g/2 oz/¼ cup butter
1 tablespoon oil
1 (396-g/14-oz/14-oz) can tomatoes
150 ml/¼ pint/⅔ cup chicken stock
2 lemons
1 teaspoon chopped fresh thyme or ½ teaspoon dried
    thyme
1 teaspoon chopped fresh tarragon or ½ teaspoon dried
    tarragon
watercress to garnish

Coat the pork with seasoned flour and sauté with the onions in the butter and oil in a flameproof casserole. When the meat has lightly browned, add the tomatoes with their juice, stock and the juice and grated rind of 1 lemon. Sprinkle in the herbs and adjust the seasoning if necessary. Cover and place in a moderate oven (160°C, 325°F, Gas Mark 3) for 1 hour. Garnish with the remaining lemon cut into wedges and watercress. Serve with rice or noodles.

Serves 4

Indian pork

METRIC/IMPERIAL/AMERICAN
1 kg/2 lb/2 lb lean pork
½ teaspoon cumin seeds
2 cloves garlic
5 peppercorns
½ teaspoon ground turmeric
½ teaspoon ground coriander
6 tablespoons/6 tablespoons/½ cup wine vinegar
2 tablespoons/2 tablespoons/3 tablespoons oil
1 (2.5-cm/1-inch/1-inch) piece root ginger, finely
    chopped
2 fresh chillis, finely chopped
1 onion, chopped
300 ml/½ pint/1¼ cups beef stock
salt and pepper

Cut the pork into cubes. Grind the cumin seeds, garlic and peppercorns in a wooden or plastic bowl, and mix with the turmeric, coriander and vinegar. Coat the pork pieces with this mixture, cover and allow to marinate overnight.

Heat the oil in a flameproof casserole and sauté the ginger, chillis and onion for 5 minutes. Drain off any excess fat and add the pork with the marinade. Pour in the stock, season to taste and bring to the boil. Reduce the heat, cover and simmer gently for 1½ hours or until the pork is tender. Serve with boiled rice.

Serves 4–6

Braised gammon

METRIC/IMPERIAL/AMERICAN
1 (1.25-kg/2½-lb/2½-lb) piece gammon or bacon
6–8 carrots
2 bay leaves
6 cloves
3 onions, finely sliced
2 sticks celery, finely chopped
150 ml/¼ pint/⅔ cup white wine or chicken stock
freshly ground black pepper

Soak the gammon or bacon in cold water overnight. Drain, place in a large saucepan and cover with fresh cold water. Add the carrots, bay leaves and cloves. Bring to the boil slowly, skim well, cover and simmer gently for 35 minutes.

Drain again and place the gammon and carrots in a large casserole. Add the onions and celery. Pour in the wine or stock and season to taste with freshly ground black pepper. Cover and place in a moderate oven (180°C, 350°F, Gas Mark 4) for 35–45 minutes. Serve with courgettes and parsley sauce to which the cooking juices can be added, if liked.

Serves 6–8

Sweet and sour bacon

METRIC/IMPERIAL/AMERICAN
1 (0.75–1-kg/1½–2-lb/1½–2-lb) bacon joint
4 tomatoes, peeled, deseeded and chopped
1 green pepper, deseeded and chopped
1 onion, sliced
1 (425-g/15-oz/15-oz) can pineapple tidbits
1 tablespoon cornflour
2 tablespoons/2 tablespoons/3 tablespoons soy sauce
1 tablespoon soft brown sugar
2 tablespoons/2 tablespoons/3 tablespoons wine vinegar
1 tablespoon clear honey
salt and pepper

Soak the bacon joint in cold water for 6 hours or overnight. Drain well, then cut into 1-cm/½-inch cubes.

Place in a casserole with the tomatoes, pepper and onion. Drain the pineapple, reserving the juice, and add the fruit to the casserole.

Blend a little pineapple juice with the cornflour, then place the remaining pineapple juice, soy sauce, soft brown sugar, vinegar and honey in a small saucepan and bring to boiling point. Then pour on to the blended cornflour. Return to the saucepan and allow to thicken. Pour the sauce over the ingredients in the casserole. Cover and cook in a moderate oven (180°C, 350°F, Gas Mark 4) for 1½ hours. Serve with plain boiled rice, if liked.

Serves 4–6

Veal casseroles

This delicately flavoured meat needs careful cooking to do it justice and is therefore ideal for casseroles. Boned and stuffed shoulder or breast and middle neck of veal may be pot-roasted or braised; boneless pie veal, usually cut from the neck or knuckle, and thick cutlets from the best end of neck are also suitable. Use judicious amounts of seasonings and herbs in veal dishes to avoid masking the delicate flavour of the meat.

Veal and orange casserole

METRIC/IMPERIAL/AMERICAN
1 kg/2 lb/2 lb stewing veal, trimmed and cubed
salt and pepper
flour for coating
25 g/1 oz/2 tablespoons butter
1 tablespoon oil
2 onions, sliced
3 carrots, sliced (optional)
2 cloves garlic, crushed
300 ml/$\frac{1}{2}$ pint/$1\frac{1}{4}$ cups chicken stock
juice of 4 oranges
1 teaspoon lemon juice
1–2 teaspoons arrowroot (optional)
GARNISH:
1 tablespoon grated orange rind
chopped parsley

Coat the meat in seasoned flour. Heat the butter and oil in a flameproof casserole and gently sauté the veal, onions, carrots, if used, and garlic for 5 minutes. Drain off any excess fat and pour in the stock mixed with the orange and lemon juice. Bring to the boil, cover and cook in a moderate oven (180°C, 350°F, Gas Mark 4) for 1$\frac{1}{2}$ hours.

If liked, the liquid can be thickened with the arrowroot mixed to a paste with a little water. Add the blended arrowroot to the casserole and stir over gentle heat until the sauce thickens. Garnish with grated orange rind and chopped parsley.

Serves 4–6

Veal with courgettes

METRIC/IMPERIAL/AMERICAN
3 tablespoons/3 tablespoons/$\frac{1}{4}$ cup oil
1 kg/2 lb/2 lb stewing veal, cubed
2 onions, chopped
1 clove garlic, crushed
1 green pepper, deseeded and chopped
300 ml/$\frac{1}{2}$ pint/$1\frac{1}{4}$ cups dry white wine
300 ml/$\frac{1}{2}$ pint/$1\frac{1}{4}$ cups chicken stock
bouquet garni
$\frac{1}{2}$ teaspoon dried mixed herbs
salt and pepper
0.5 kg/1 lb/1 lb courgettes
25 g/1 oz/2 tablespoons butter
25 g/1 oz/$\frac{1}{4}$ cup flour
chopped parsley and triangles of fried bread to garnish

Heat the oil in a flameproof casserole and gently sauté the meat until golden. Add the onions, garlic and green pepper, and continue to sauté until the vegetables are softened. Drain off any excess oil and pour in the wine and stock. Add the bouquet garni and herbs and season. Bring to the boil, cover and place in a moderate oven (180°C, 350°F, Gas Mark 4) for 1 hour.

Slice the courgettes and add to the casserole. Mix well and return to the oven for a further 30 minutes. Remove the bouquet garni. Blend together the butter and flour and stir into the casserole, a little at a time. Heat through until thickened. Garnish.

Serves 4–6

Cheesy veal chops

METRIC/IMPERIAL/AMERICAN
25 g/1 oz/2 tablespoons butter
6 veal chops
3 onions, finely chopped
2 sticks celery, finely chopped
2 cloves garlic, crushed
1 (396-g/14-oz/14-oz) can tomatoes
1 teaspoon dried oregano
4 tablespoons/4 tablespoons/$\frac{1}{3}$ cup tomato purée
salt and freshly ground black pepper
75 g/3 oz/$\frac{3}{4}$ cup Cheddar cheese, grated

Heat the butter in a saucepan or large frying pan and brown the chops on both sides. Remove and keep warm. Add the onions, celery and garlic to the fat remaining in the pan and sauté gently for 5 minutes until soft but not coloured. Add the tomatoes with their juice, oregano, tomato purée and seasoning. Simmer, covered, for 5 minutes. Place the chops in the bottom of a shallow casserole and pour the tomato sauce over. Cover and cook in a moderate oven (180°C, 350°F, Gas Mark 4) for 45 minutes or until tender. Sprinkle with the grated cheese and either place in a hot oven (220°C, 425°F, Gas Mark 7) or under a preheated grill until golden and bubbling. Serve immediately.

Serves 6

Veal méditerranée

METRIC/IMPERIAL/AMERICAN
1 large aubergine
salt
5 tablespoons/5 tablespoons/6 tablespoons olive oil
1 kg/2 lb/2 lb shoulder of veal, cubed
8 small whole onions
1 green pepper, deseeded and chopped
1 red pepper, deseeded and chopped
0.5 kg/1 lb/1 lb tomatoes, peeled and chopped
2 teaspoons chopped fresh marjoram or 1 teaspoon dried
    marjoram
300 ml/½ pint/1¼ cups white wine
salt and pepper
12 black olives, stoned

Dice the aubergine and sprinkle with salt. Leave to stand for 30 minutes. Rinse and dry. Meanwhile, heat the oil in a flameproof casserole and brown the veal all over. Remove with a slotted spoon. Place the aubergine, onions and peppers in the casserole and sauté gently for 5 minutes. Add the tomatoes and marjoram, cover and simmer for 5 minutes. Return the meat to the casserole, pour in the wine and mix well. Season, cover and cook in a moderate oven (160°C, 325°F, Gas Mark 3) for 1 hour, adding a little more liquid (wine or water) if necessary. Add the olives and return to the oven to heat through.

Serves 6

Blanquette de veau

METRIC/IMPERIAL/AMERICAN
1 kg/2 lb/2 lb pie veal, cubed
2 medium onions, chopped, or 12 button onions
100 g/4 oz/¼ lb baby carrots
bouquet garni
½ teaspoon dried thyme
2 bay leaves
salt and pepper
25 g/1 oz/2 tablespoons butter
25 g/1 oz/¼ cup flour
2 egg yolks
5 tablespoons/5 tablespoons/6 tablespoons cream
GARNISH:
lemon wedges
bacon rolls

Place the meat, onions, carrots, bouquet garni and herbs in a saucepan with just enough water to cover. Season. Bring to the boil and skim well. Cover and simmer gently for 1½ hours. Remove the pan from the heat and discard the bouquet garni and bay leaves.

Blend the butter into the flour to form a smooth paste and whisk this, a piece at a time, into the stew. Stir over gentle heat until thickened.

Beat together the egg yolks and cream and pour into the stew. Heat through but do not boil. Serve garnished with lemon wedges and grilled bacon rolls.

Serves 4–6

Osso buco

METRIC/IMPERIAL/AMERICAN
1.25 kg/2½ lb/2½ lb shin of veal
4 carrots, grated
2 onions, finely chopped
1 stick celery, finely chopped
5 tablespoons/5 tablespoons/6 tablespoons olive oil
1 (396-g/14-oz/14-oz) can tomatoes
bouquet garni
1 fresh basil sprig, chopped, or ½ teaspoon dried basil
3 sage leaves
salt and pepper
flour for coating
300 ml/½ pint/1¼ cups dry white wine or chicken stock
grated rind of ½ lemon mixed with 1 tablespoon chopped
    parsley and 1 crushed clove garlic, to garnish

Ask your butcher to saw the veal into 5-cm/2-inch pieces. Sauté the carrots, onions and celery in 2 tablespoons/2 tablespoons/3 tablespoons oil until beginning to brown. Add the tomatoes, and herbs. Cover and simmer. Coat the veal with seasoned flour and brown gently in the remaining oil. Add to the vegetable mixture. Drain off any excess fat from the meat pan and pour in the wine or stock. Bring to the boil, stirring, then add to the casserole. Adjust seasoning, cover and simmer gently for 1½–2 hours. Discard the bouquet garni and sage leaves. Sprinkle the garnish over the meat. Serve with rice or buttered noodles.

Serves 4–6

Veal aux champignons

METRIC/IMPERIAL/AMERICAN
1 kg/2 lb/2 lb breast of veal
50 g/2 oz/¼ cup butter
2 tablespoons/2 tablespoons/3 tablespoons oil
4 shallots, finely chopped
salt and pepper
2 tablespoons/2 tablespoons/3 tablespoons lemon juice
450 ml/¾ pint/2 cups chicken stock
0.5 kg/1 lb/1 lb button mushrooms
25 g/1 oz/¼ cup flour
150 ml/¼ pint/⅔ cup double cream
parsley sprigs and slices of lemon to garnish

Cut the meat into slices. Heat half the butter with the oil in a flameproof casserole and brown the meat gently. Add the shallots and sauté until soft. Season well and pour in the lemon juice and stock. Cover and place in a moderate oven (160°C, 325°F, Gas Mark 3) for 1 hour. Add the mushrooms and return to the oven for a further 45 minutes or until the meat is tender.

Melt the remaining butter in a saucepan and stir in the flour. Off the heat, strain in 300 ml/½ pint/1¼ cups of the cooking liquid. Return to the heat and bring to the boil, stirring continuously. Remove from the heat again and add the cream. Heat through but do not allow to boil. Pour the sauce over the veal and mushrooms and garnish with parsley and lemon slices.

Serves 4–6

Offal casseroles

Offal, which is very nutritious, easily digestible and generally cheap, is often neglected when it comes to casserole dishes. Sweetbreads, tripe, hearts, kidneys, oxtail and liver all make delicious casseroles. Ideally offal should be cooked on the same day it is purchased. Sweetbreads, kidneys and liver do not require the long, slow cooking generally associated with casserole dishes.

Braised sweetbreads

METRIC/IMPERIAL/AMERICAN
0.5 kg/1 lb/1 lb calves' or lambs' sweetbreads
4 rashers streaky bacon, chopped
1 onion, sliced
1 carrot, sliced
2 sticks celery, sliced
1 clove garlic, crushed
25 g/1 oz/2 tablespoons butter
1 tablespoon flour
450 ml/$\frac{3}{4}$ pint/2 cups chicken stock
salt and pepper
chopped parsley to garnish

Soak the sweetbreads in cold water for about 4 hours, changing the water several times. Drain and place in a saucepan. Cover with cold water and bring to the boil. Take out the sweetbreads and rinse under cold water. Remove the membrane and black veins. Wrap in a cloth and leave to cool between 2 plates, lightly weighted.

Place the sweetbreads in a casserole in a single layer. Gently sauté the bacon, onion, carrot, celery and garlic in the butter for 5 minutes, then remove and place on top of the sweetbreads.

Sprinkle the flour into the fat and cook for 1 minute, stirring. Stir in the stock and bring to the boil. Season and pour into the casserole. Cover and cook in a moderate oven (160°C, 325°F, Gas Mark 3) for 45 minutes. Garnish.

Serves 4

Tripe with onions

METRIC/IMPERIAL/AMERICAN
0.5 kg/1 lb/1 lb dressed tripe
0.5 kg/1 lb/1 lb onions, sliced
300 ml/½ pint/1¼ cups chicken stock
150 ml/¼ pint/⅔ cup white wine
1 bay leaf
bouquet garni
salt and pepper
40 g/1½ oz/3 tablespoons butter
40 g/1½ oz/6 tablespoons flour
150 ml/¼ pint/⅔ cup milk or cream
chopped parsley to garnish

Cut the tripe into 2.5-cm/1-inch pieces and place in the bottom of a casserole. Cover with the onions and pour in the stock and wine. Add the bay leaf and bouquet garni and season to taste. Cover and place in a cool oven (150°C, 300°F, Gas Mark 2) for about 3 hours or until the tripe is tender. Strain off the liquid and reserve. Discard the bay leaf and bouquet garni. Keep the tripe warm in a dish.

Melt the butter in a saucepan and add the flour. Cook, stirring, for 1 minute. Remove from the heat and gradually add the reserved cooking liquid. Return to the heat and bring to the boil, stirring continuously. Add the milk or cream and heat through, but do not boil if using cream. Pour over the tripe.

Serves 4

Casserole of stuffed hearts

METRIC/IMPERIAL/AMERICAN
4 lambs' hearts
3 tablespoons/3 tablespoons/¼ cup oil
2 tablespoons/2 tablespoons/3 tablespoons flour
600 ml/1 pint/2½ cups beef stock
2 onions, sliced
4 carrots, sliced
bouquet garni
watercress to garnish
STUFFING:
1 onion, finely chopped
1 stick celery, finely chopped
grated rind of ½ orange
2 walnuts, chopped
40 g/1½ oz/¾ cup fresh breadcrumbs
1 tablespoon melted butter
½ beaten egg
salt and pepper

Prepare the hearts. Mix all the stuffing ingredients and fill the hearts with the mixture. Sew up.

Heat the oil in a pan, add the hearts and brown. Place in the casserole. Sprinkle the flour into the fat and cook, stirring, for 1 minute. Remove from the heat and add the stock. Bring to the boil, stirring. Season and pour over the hearts. Add the onions, carrots and bouquet garni. Cover and place in a moderate oven (160°C, 325°F, Gas Mark 3) for 3 hours. Garnish.

Serves 4

Liver à l'orange

METRIC/IMPERIAL/AMERICAN

2 oranges
2 tablespoons/2 tablespoons/3 tablespoons oil
1 onion, chopped
1 clove garlic, crushed
0.5 kg/1 lb/1 lb lambs' liver
salt and pepper
2 tablespoons/2 tablespoons/3 tablespoons flour
100 g/4 oz/1 cup mushrooms, whole
1 (64-g/2¼-oz/2¼-oz) packet instant potato
chopped parsley to garnish

Thinly peel one of the oranges. Cut this into thin strips and blanch in 300 ml/½ pint/1¼ cups boiling water for 1 minute. Drain, reserving the peel and the water. Squeeze the juice from both oranges. Heat the oil in a flameproof casserole and sauté the onion and garlic. Slice the liver and coat in seasoned flour. Sauté gently in the oil in the pan. Add the mushrooms and the orange juice made up to 300 ml/½ pint/1¼ cups with the reserved blanching water. Season and bring to the boil, stirring. Cover and lower the heat. Simmer gently for 20 minutes.

Make up the potato and pipe a border around the edge of a dish. Arrange the liver in the centre and garnish with blanched peel and parsley.

Serves 4

Liver à l'italienne

METRIC/IMPERIAL/AMERICAN

0.5 kg/1 lb/1 lb lambs' liver
salt and pepper
25 g/1 oz/¼ cup flour
40 g/1½ oz/3 tablespoons butter
4 onions, sliced into rings
4 tomatoes, peeled and sliced
300 ml/½ pint/1¼ cups chicken stock
2 tablespoons/2 tablespoons/3 tablespoons tomato purée
dash Tabasco sauce
1 clove garlic, crushed
½ teaspoon dried oregano
½ teaspoon dried thyme
150 ml/¼ pint/⅔ cup double cream
chopped red pepper to garnish

Cut the liver into fingers and coat in seasoned flour. Heat the butter in a flameproof casserole and gently sauté the onions until softened. Remove.

Sauté the liver in the butter until lightly browned all over. Return the onions to the pan and add the tomatoes, stock, tomato purée, Tabasco sauce, garlic and herbs. Bring to the boil then cover and place in a moderate oven (180°C, 350°F, Gas Mark 4) for 30 minutes. Stir in the cream and heat through without boiling. Adjust seasoning if necessary. Serve with spaghetti and garnish with chopped red pepper.

Serves 4

Poultry and game casseroles

With the rearing and storage methods of today, most poultry (chicken in particular) benefits from being casseroled rather than roasted. Whole birds or joints may be cooked in a casserole. Many game birds, particularly older ones, are best braised. When using frozen poultry and game it must first be allowed to thaw.

Celebration duck

METRIC/IMPERIAL/AMERICAN
1 (1.75-kg/4-lb/4-lb) duckling
salt and pepper
25 g/1 oz/$\frac{1}{4}$ cup flour
25 g/1 oz/2 tablespoons butter
2 onions, sliced
150 ml/$\frac{1}{4}$ pint/$\frac{2}{3}$ cup medium-sweet sherry
150 ml/$\frac{1}{4}$ pint/$\frac{2}{3}$ cup chicken stock
1 clove garlic, crushed
2 tablespoons/2 tablespoons/3 tablespoons tomato purée
2 teaspoons chilli sauce
2 tablespoons/2 tablespoons/3 tablespoons chopped
    parsley
225 g/8 oz/$\frac{1}{2}$ lb fresh red cherries, stoned, or
    1 (227-g/8-oz/8-oz) can red cherries, drained and stoned
watercress to garnish

Divide the duckling into 4 joints and cut away any excess fat. Coat in seasoned flour. Melt the butter in a flameproof casserole and brown the duck pieces on all sides. Add the onions and cook until softened, then drain off all fat. Mix together the remaining ingredients, except the cherries, and pour over the duck. Cover and place in a moderate oven (180°C, 350°F, Gas Mark 4) for 45–60 minutes. Garnish with cherries and watercress.

Serves 4

Duckling with grapes

METRIC/IMPERIAL/AMERICAN
25 g/1 oz/2 tablespoons butter
1 (1.75-kg/4-lb/4-lb) duckling, trussed
2 onions, sliced
1 clove garlic, crushed
1–2 tablespoons/1–2 tablespoons/1–3 tablespoons flour
150 ml/¼ pint/⅔ cup dry white wine
300 ml/½ pint/1¼ cups chicken stock
salt and pepper
bouquet garni
GARNISH:
225 g/8 oz/½ lb black grapes
watercress

Melt the butter in a large flameproof casserole and brown the duckling on all sides. Remove the duckling and sauté the onions and garlic in the fat remaining in the casserole. Pour off most of the excess fat, leaving about 2 tablespoons/2 tablespoons/3 tablespoons. Sprinkle in the flour and cook, stirring, for 1 minute. Gradually add the wine and stock and bring to the boil, stirring continuously. Season to taste, return the duck to the casserole and add the bouquet garni. Cover and cook in a moderate oven (180°C, 350°F, Gas Mark 4) for 1½–2 hours.

Remove the duckling from the casserole and keep hot. Discard the bouquet garni and skim all fat from the sauce.

To serve, place the duckling on a serving platter. Arrange the grapes around the duck and serve the sauce separately. Garnish.

Serves 4–6

Poule au pot

METRIC/IMPERIAL/AMERICAN
1 (1.5-kg/3½-lb/3½-lb) boiling chicken with giblets
600 ml/1 pint/2½ cups water
salt and freshly ground black pepper
3 onions
50 g/2 oz/¼ cup butter
6 carrots, thickly sliced
3 sticks celery, chopped
2 turnips, quartered
2 bay leaves
25 g/1 oz/¼ cup flour

Place the giblets in a saucepan with the water and 1 teaspoon salt. Bring to the boil then cover and simmer for 30 minutes. Meanwhile, place a large onion inside the chicken and truss as for roasting a chicken. Melt half the butter in a large flameproof casserole and brown the chicken all over. Pour off all fat from the casserole. Quarter the remaining onions and arrange around the chicken with the other vegetables and bay leaves. Strain in the giblet stock and season with pepper. Cover and place in a moderate oven (160°C, 325°F, Gas Mark 3) for 2–2½ hours or until tender. Arrange the chicken and vegetables on a large platter. Keep warm. Skim any fat off the sauce. Blend together the remaining butter and the flour to form a paste. Add to the sauce, a little at a time, and stir over a gentle heat until thickened. Do not boil. Adjust seasoning and serve the sauce separately.

Serves 4–6

Chicken with pineapple

METRIC/IMPERIAL/AMERICAN

4 tablespoons/4 tablespoons/⅓ cup olive oil
4 chicken joints
1 green pepper, deseeded and chopped
2 sticks celery, chopped
1 onion, chopped
1 (198-g/7-oz/7-oz) can pineapple slices
1 tablespoon soy sauce
1 tablespoon lemon juice
1 tablespoon tomato purée
salt and pepper
watercress to garnish

Heat the oil in a large frying pan and fry the chicken joints until golden. Transfer to a casserole. Add the pepper, celery and onion to the pan and sauté until softened. Transfer to the casse
lemc
Seas
350°
pine
the oven for a final 15 minutes. Garnish with watercress and serve with boiled rice and mushrooms.

Serves 4

Coq au vin

METRIC/IMPERIAL/AMERICAN

1 (2-kg/4½-lb/4½-lb) chicken with giblets, jointed
salt and pepper
100 g/4 oz/½ cup bacon, chopped
20 button onions
75 g/3 oz/6 tablespoons butter
4 tablespoons/4 tablespoons/⅓ cup brandy
450 ml/¾ pint/2 cups red wine
225 g/8 oz/½ lb mushrooms, sliced
2 cloves garlic, crushed
2 teaspoons soft brown sugar
bouquet garni
pinch ground nutmeg
40 g/1½ oz/6 tablespoons flour
chopped parsley to garnish

Simmer the giblets for 30 minutes in salted water. In a flameproof casserole, sauté the bacon and onions in half the butter until golden. Remove. Add the chicken joints and brown. Pour the brandy, flaming, over the chicken. Return the bacon and onions and add the wine, 150 ml/¼ pint/⅔ cup strained giblet stock, mushrooms, garlic, sugar, herbs, nutmeg and pepper. Bring to the boil, cover and cook in a moderate oven (180°C, 350°F, Gas Mark 4) for 1 hour.

Remove the chicken pieces and keep warm. Blend together the butter and flour and whisk, little by little, into the sauce. Heat through until thickened. Return chicken and garnish.

Serves 6

Chicken in champagne

METRIC/IMPERIAL/AMERICAN
1 (2-kg/4½-lb/4½-lb) chicken, jointed
75 g/3 oz/6 tablespoons butter
4 shallots, finely chopped
2 tablespoons/2 tablespoons/3 tablespoons brandy
300 ml/½ pint/1¼ cups chicken stock
150 ml/¼ pint/⅔ cup champagne
bouquet garni
salt and pepper
225 g/8 oz/2 cups mushrooms, sliced
25 g/1 oz/¼ cup flour
3 tablespoons/3 tablespoons/¼ cup double cream
parsley sprig to garnish

Sauté the chicken in 50 g/2 oz/¼ cup butter in a flameproof casserole, until golden all over. Add the shallots, sauté lightly then pour in the brandy. Cover, remove from the heat and leave to infuse for 5 minutes. Add the stock, champagne and bouquet garni. Season. Cover and place in a moderate oven (180°C, 350°F, Gas Mark 4) for 30 minutes. Add the mushrooms and cook for a further 30 minutes. Transfer the chicken to a deep serving platter. Keep warm.

Blend the remaining butter and the flour together and add, piece by piece, to the sauce in the casserole. Stir over a low heat until thickened. Do not boil. Stir in the cream. Pour over the chicken and garnish with parsley.

Serves 6

Chicken chasseur

METRIC/IMPERIAL/AMERICAN
1 carrot, chopped
2 onions, chopped
25 g/1 oz/2 tablespoons bacon, diced
25 g/1 oz/2 tablespoons butter
50 g/2 oz/½ cup flour
450 ml/¾ pint/2 cups beef stock
1 tablespoon tomato purée
150 ml/¼ pint/⅔ cup white wine
salt and pepper
4 chicken joints
4 tablespoons/4 tablespoons/⅓ cup olive oil
100 g/4 oz/1 cup button mushrooms
100 g/4 oz/½ cup tomatoes, peeled and chopped
parsley sprig to garnish

Sauté the carrot, 1 onion and the bacon in the butter until the vegetables begin to brown. Stir in half the flour and cook until browning. Gradually add the stock, tomato purée and wine. Season, cover and simmer very gently for 1 hour. Strain and skim. Coat the chicken joints in the remaining flour and sauté in the oil in a flameproof casserole. Remove. Add the remaining onion to the casserole and sauté until softened. Strain off any excess fat, then add the chicken, mushrooms and tomatoes. Pour in the sauce and adjust seasoning if necessary. Cover and cook in a moderate oven (180°C, 350°F, Gas Mark 4) for 1–1½ hour. Garnish with parsley.

Serves 4

Rabbit fricassée

METRIC/IMPERIAL/AMERICAN
1 (1.5-kg/3-lb/3-lb) rabbit, jointed
2 large onions, sliced
2 carrots, sliced
2 sticks celery, chopped
bouquet garni
450 ml/¾ pint/2 cups chicken stock
150 ml/¼ pint/⅔ cup white wine
salt and pepper
100 g/4 oz/1 cup button mushrooms
75 g/3 oz/6 tablespoons butter
100 g/4 oz/¼ lb button onions
25 g/1 oz/¼ cup flour
2 egg yolks
150 ml/¼ pint/⅔ cup double cream
chopped parsley and triangles of fried bread to garnish

Place the rabbit in a casserole with the onions, carrots, celery, bouquet garni, stock, wine and seasoning. Cover and cook in a moderate oven (180°C, 350°F, Gas Mark 4) for 1½ hours. Remove the rabbit and keep warm. Reserve the cooking liquor. Sauté the mushrooms in half the butter and cook the button onions in boiling salted water for 5 minutes. Melt the remaining butter and stir in the flour. Blend in 450 ml/¾ pint/2 cups of the strained rabbit liquid. Bring to the boil, stirring continuously. Add the mushrooms and onions. Stir in the egg yolks beaten with the cream. Warm and pour over the rabbit.

Serves 4

Partridges with cabbage

METRIC/IMPERIAL/AMERICAN
1 green, white or red cabbage, quartered
salt
25 g/1 oz/2 tablespoons bacon fat or butter
2 partridges, plucked, drawn and trussed
8 chipolatas
2 onions, chopped
6 rashers streaky bacon, chopped
½ teaspoon ground cloves
freshly ground black pepper
300 ml/½ pint/1¼ cups red wine or wine and stock
watercress to garnish

Blanch the cabbage for 5 minutes in boiling salted water. Drain.
Melt the bacon fat or butter in a large frying pan and brown the partridges and chipolatas all over. Remove. Sauté the onions in the fat remaining in the pan. Sprinkle the bacon in the base of a casserole.
Shred the cabbage and mix with the onion and ground cloves. Spread half the cabbage mixture over the bacon, season with pepper and place the partridges and chipolatas on top. Cover with the remaining cabbage, season with more pepper and pour over the wine. Cover and cook in a moderate oven (160°C, 325°F, Gas Mark 3) for about 1½ hours or until the birds are tender. The exact time will depend on the age of the birds. Garnish with watercress.

Serves 4

Pigeons in tomato sauce

METRIC/IMPERIAL/AMERICAN
4 pigeons
175 g/6 oz/6 oz belly of pork, cubed
25 g/1 oz/2 tablespoons butter
225 g/8 oz/½ lb button onions
25 g/1 oz/¼ cup flour
300 ml/½ pint/1¼ cups white wine
1 (396-g/14-oz/14-oz) can tomatoes
2 cloves garlic, crushed
bouquet garni
1 teaspoon Worcestershire sauce
225 g/8 oz/½ lb button mushrooms
1 tablespoon chopped parsley

Wash the pigeons thoroughly, discarding the giblets, and dry well. Sauté the pork in the butter until golden. Transfer to a large casserole. Sauté the onions gently in the fat in the pan then transfer to the casserole. Add the pigeons to the pan and carefully brown on all sides. Place on the pork and onions. Stir the flour into the fat in the pan and cook for 1 minute. Add the wine and tomatoes and bring to the boil, stirring continuously. Add the garlic, bouquet garni and Worcestershire sauce. Pour over the pigeons, cover and place in a moderate oven (180°C, 350°F, Gas Mark 4) for 1½ hours. Add the mushrooms and parsley and return to the oven for a further 30 minutes. Remove the bouquet garni.

Serves 4

Venison stew

METRIC/IMPERIAL/AMERICAN
1 kg/2 lb/2 lb shoulder of venison, cubed
300 ml/½ pint/1¼ cups red wine
1 large carrot, sliced
1 onion, sliced
2 cloves garlic
2 tablespoons/2 tablespoons/3 tablespoons olive oil
bouquet garni
salt and pepper
25 g/1 oz/2 tablespoons butter
225 g/8 oz/1 cup bacon, diced
225 g/8 oz/½ lb button onions
2 tablespoons/2 tablespoons/3 tablespoons flour
1 bay leaf

Place the meat in a shallow dish. Mix together the wine, carrot, onion, garlic, oil, bouquet garni and seasoning. Pour over the meat. Marinate for 12 hours. Dry the meat. Reserve the marinade. Heat the butter in a flameproof casserole and sauté the bacon and onions lightly. Remove. Add the meat to the casserole and brown over a high heat. Lower the heat and sprinkle in the flour. Mix well and cook for 1 minute. Strain the marinade liquid (discarding the vegetables) over the meat, adding just enough water to cover. Bring to the boil, stirring continuously, then lower the heat. Add the bacon, onions and bay leaf. Season. Cover and place in a moderate oven (160°C, 325°F, Gas Mark 3) for 1½–2 hours. Remove the bay leaf.

Serves 4–6

Casseroled grouse

METRIC/IMPERIAL/AMERICAN
4 mature grouse, trussed
salt and pepper
25 g/1 oz/2 tablespoons butter
2 tablespoons/2 tablespoons/3 tablespoons olive oil
6 shallots, roughly chopped
2 sticks celery, chopped
2 cloves garlic, crushed
1–1½ tablespoons flour
300 ml/½ pint/1¼ cups beef stock
300 ml/½ pint/1¼ cups red wine
8 juniper berries, crushed
2 teaspoons chopped fresh marjoram or 1 teaspoon dried
  marjoram
225 g/8 oz/½ lb button mushrooms

Season the grouse inside and out, and brown all over in the butter and oil in a large flameproof casserole. Remove. Sauté the shallots, celery and garlic in the fat remaining in the pan, then sprinkle in enough flour to soak up the fat. Cook until the flour is beginning to brown then carefully blend in the stock and wine. Bring to the boil, stirring constantly, then return the grouse to the casserole and add the juniper berries and marjoram. Adjust seasoning, cover and cook in a moderate oven (180°C, 350°F, Gas Mark 4) for 1 hour.

Add the mushrooms and continue cooking for a further 30 minutes or until the birds are tender.

Serves 4

Faisan à la normande

METRIC/IMPERIAL/AMERICAN
1 pheasant, with giblets, jointed
bouquet garni
salt and pepper
4 tablespoons/4 tablespoons/⅓ cup oil
2 onions, sliced
2 sticks celery, chopped
2 tablespoons/2 tablespoons/3 tablespoons brandy
300 ml/½ pint/1¼ cups dry cider
1 bay leaf
225 g/8 oz/½ lb cooking apples
2 egg yolks
150 ml/¼ pint/⅔ cup single cream
finely chopped walnuts to garnish

Place giblets and bouquet garni in a pan with 300 ml/½ pint/1¼ cups salted water. Bring to the boil. Cover and simmer for 30 minutes then boil down by half. Meanwhile, coat pheasant in seasoned flour and brown in the oil. Remove. Sauté the onions and celery for 5 minutes. Return the pheasant to the casserole.

Pour brandy, flaming, over pheasant. Strain in giblet stock and add cider and bay leaf. Bring to the boil, cover and place in a moderate oven (180°C, 350°F, Gas Mark 4) for 30 minutes.

Peel, core and slice apples. Add to casserole and return to the oven for a further 30 minutes. Remove pheasant. Stir yolks beaten with the cream into the sauce. Warm through then return the pheasant and garnish.

Serves 4

Vegetable and dessert casseroles

Vegetables cooked in a small amount of liquid in a covered container in the oven are infinitely better than when boiled in too much water in a pan. The vegetable recipes in this section may be served as a dish on their own for a light meal or as an accompaniment to any main course dish.

Included in this section are recipes for fruit which also benefits from being cooked in the oven – soft fruits in particular.

Leeks à la portugaise

METRIC/IMPERIAL/AMERICAN
1 kg/2 lb/2 lb leeks
salt
1 onion, chopped
2 tablespoons/2 tablespoons/3 tablespoons oil
0.5 kg/1 lb/2 cups tomatoes, peeled and chopped
1 clove garlic, crushed
2 tablespoons/2 tablespoons/3 tablespoons chopped
    parsley
2 tablespoons/2 tablespoons/3 tablespoons dry white
    wine
freshly ground black pepper
chopped parsley to garnish

Cut the roots and leaves off the leeks. Wash thoroughly and blanch in boiling salted water for 5 minutes. Drain well and arrange in an ovenproof dish.

Meanwhile, sauté the onion in the oil until softened, then add the remaining ingredients and cook, covered, for 5 minutes. Pour this sauce over the leeks, cover and cook in a moderate oven (180°C, 350°F, Gas Mark 4) for 45–55 minutes. Garnish with chopped parsley. Delicious hot with fish or cold as a starter.

Serves 4–6

Mushrooms and courgettes in garlic butter

METRIC/IMPERIAL/AMERICAN
225 g/8 oz/½ lb flat mushrooms
225 g/8 oz/½ lb courgettes
salt
100 g/4 oz/½ cup butter
3 cloves garlic, crushed
2 tablespoons/2 tablespoons/3 tablespoons chopped
    parsley
grated rind of 1 lemon

Wipe the mushrooms carefully. Cut the courgettes into 5-mm/ ¼-inch slices and blanch for 1 minute in boiling salted water. Drain well and pat dry.

Arrange the mushrooms and courgettes in the bottom of an ovenproof dish. Melt the butter in a saucepan and add the garlic. Pour the garlic butter over the mushrooms and courgettes and bake, uncovered, in a moderately hot oven (200°C, 400°F, Gas Mark 6) for 15 minutes. Sprinkle the parsley mixed with the lemon rind over the dish and return to the oven for a further 5 minutes. Spoon the garlic butter over the vegetables when serving. This dish is delicious with roast or grilled meat, or alone as a starter.

Serves 4

Potatoes lyonnaise

METRIC/IMPERIAL/AMERICAN
0.75 kg/1½ lb/1½ lb potatoes
salt
100 g/4 oz/½ cup butter
1 clove garlic, crushed
225 g/8 oz/2 cups onions, chopped
1–2 tablespoons/1–2 tablespoons/2–3 tablespoons milk
freshly ground black pepper
3 tablespoons/3 tablespoons/¼ cup chopped fresh parsley
    or 25 g/1 oz/¼ cup Parmesan cheese, grated
GARNISH:
slices of tomato
parsley sprigs

Peel the potatoes and boil them until just tender in salted water.

Meanwhile, melt three-quarters of the butter in a frying pan and sauté the garlic and onions until softened.

Drain the potatoes and mash. Mix in all the contents of the frying pan and enough milk to bind without making the mixture too wet. Season to taste with salt and freshly ground black pepper. Either chopped parsley or grated cheese can be added according to taste.

Spoon the potato mixture into greased individual ovenproof dishes and dot with the remaining butter. Bake, uncovered, in a moderately hot oven (200°C, 400°F, Gas Mark 6) for 20 minutes. Garnish each dish with a slice of tomato and parsley.

This dish is particularly tasty with fish.

Serves 4

Macedoine à la française

METRIC/IMPERIAL/AMERICAN
100 g/4 oz/½ cup streaky bacon, chopped
12 button onions, whole
225 g/8 oz/½ lb young carrots
150 ml/¼ pint/⅔ cup chicken stock
50 g/2 oz/¼ cup butter
1 tablespoon sugar
salt
0.5 kg/1 lb/1 lb fresh peas, shelled or 225 g/8 oz/½ lb
   frozen peas
1 (56-g/2-oz/2-oz) can anchovy fillets, halved
chopped parsley to garnish

Gently sauté the bacon in a saucepan or flameproof casserole
until the fat runs. Add the onions and sauté in the bacon fat until
beginning to colour. Remove the onions and add the carrots
(whole if they are small; otherwise slice), stock, butter, sugar
and salt to taste. Bring to the boil, cover and simmer for
20 minutes. Add the peas after 10 minutes if using fresh. After
20 minutes, uncover and raise the heat. Add frozen peas at this
stage. Cook until the stock has evaporated and the vegetables
and bacon are coated in a buttery glaze. Arrange the anchovy
fillets in a criss-cross pattern on top of the vegetables and place
the reserved onions in between. Reheat for 5 minutes. This dish
is excellent served with a beef casserole.

Serves 4

Cauliflower cheese with bacon and onion

METRIC/IMPERIAL/AMERICAN
1 large cauliflower, broken into florets
salt and pepper
225 g/8 oz/1 cup streaky bacon, chopped
2 onions, chopped
40 g/1½ oz/3 tablespoons butter
25 g/1 oz/¼ cup flour
300 ml/½ pint/1¼ cups milk
2 tablespoons/2 tablespoons/3 tablespoons cream
150 g/5 oz/1¼ cups Cheddar cheese, grated
nutmeg
parsley sprig to garnish

Cook the cauliflower in boiling salted water for 10 minutes.
Drain well. Meanwhile, gently sauté the bacon until golden.
Remove from the pan. Sauté the onions in the bacon fat and
butter until softened. Add the flour and cook, stirring, for
1 minute. Gradually blend in the milk and bring to the boil,
stirring continuously. Remove from the heat and add the cream
and all but 1 tablespoon of the grated cheese. Stir in the reserved
bacon and season with salt, pepper and nutmeg. Pour over the
cauliflower in an ovenproof dish. Sprinkle with the reserved
cheese. Bake in a moderately hot oven (190°C, 375°F, Gas Mark
5) for 30–40 minutes until golden and bubbling. Garnish with
parsley.

Serves 4–6

Braised red cabbage

METRIC/IMPERIAL/AMERICAN

1 red cabbage
100 g/4 oz/½ cup streaky bacon, chopped
1 onion, sliced
2 cooking apples, peeled and chopped
50 g/2 oz/⅓ cup sultanas
2 cloves garlic, crushed
3 tablespoons/3 tablespoons/¼ cup wine vinegar
2 tablespoons/2 tablespoons/3 tablespoons soft brown
   sugar
150 ml/¼ pint/⅔ cup chicken stock
grated rind of ½ lemon
salt and freshly ground black pepper
pinch nutmeg
25 g/1 oz/2 tablespoons butter

Remove the coarse outer leaves from the cabbage, quarter it,
remove the central core and shred the leaves.

Place a flameproof casserole over a low heat and add the
bacon. Sauté gently until the fat runs then turn up the heat and
fry until crisp. Lower the heat, add the shredded cabbage and
mix well. Cover and braise gently for 5 minutes.

Add the onion, apple, sultanas, garlic, wine vinegar, sugar,
stock and lemon rind. Season to taste with salt, pepper and
nutmeg. Mix all the ingredients thoroughly, then cover tightly
and place in a cool oven (150°C, 300°F, Gas Mark 2) for 1½–2
hours, adding a little more stock if necessary. Dot with butter.

Serves 4

Dauphinoise potatoes

METRIC/IMPERIAL/AMERICAN

0.5 kg/1 lb/1 lb potatoes
2 cloves garlic
salt and pepper
175 g/6 oz/1½ cups Leicester cheese, grated
200 ml/⅓ pint/¾ cup single cream
mint sprig to garnish

Peel the potatoes and slice very thinly. Rub a cut clove of garlic
around the inside of a shallow ovenproof dish and line the
bottom of the dish with a layer of half the potato slices. Sprinkle
with salt, pepper and a little crushed garlic. Cover with half the
grated cheese. Repeat. Pour the cream over the top and bake in
the centre of a moderate oven (180°C, 350°F, Gas Mark 4) for
45 minutes–1 hour. Garnish with mint. This dish makes a
delicious accompaniment to roast lamb or beef.

Serves 4

Baked apples in orange

METRIC/IMPERIAL/AMERICAN
4 medium cooking or crisp eating apples
juice of 1 lemon
FILLING:
25 g/1 oz/2 tablespoons butter
25 g/1 oz/¼ cup icing sugar
1 egg yolk
50 g/2 oz/½ cup ground almonds
grated rind of 1 orange

juice of 3 oranges
angelica leaves to decorate

Peel and core the apples, leaving them whole. Brush with lemon juice to prevent discoloration. Arrange upright in an ovenproof dish.

Cream together the filling ingredients and use this mixture to stuff the centres of the apples.

Pour the orange juice around the apples and bake in a moderate oven (180°C, 350°F, Gas Mark 4) for 45 minutes–1 hour, basting frequently with orange juice. The apples should be tender but still hold their shape. Decorate each apple with angelica leaves.

Serves 4

Cherry clafoutis

METRIC/IMPERIAL/AMERICAN
0.5 kg/1 lb/1 lb black cherries or 1 (425-g/15-oz/15-oz) can black cherries
25 g/1 oz/2 tablespoons butter
2 eggs
25 g/1 oz/¼ cup flour
pinch salt
40 g/1½ oz/3 tablespoons castor sugar
300 ml/½ pint/1¼ cups milk
few drops almond essence
1 tablespoon icing sugar

If using fresh cherries, remove the stalks and wash, stone and drain the fruit. If using canned cherries, drain thoroughly and stone. Use half the butter to grease an ovenproof dish and arrange the cherries evenly in the dish.

Beat the eggs together in a bowl, then blend in the flour sifted with the salt. Add the sugar and mix well. Stir in the milk and the almond essence. Melt the remaining butter and beat into the batter. Pour the batter over the cherries and bake just above the centre of a moderately hot oven (190°C, 375°F, Gas Mark 5) for 45 minutes–1 hour until set but still creamy. Sprinkle with icing sugar just before serving lukewarm.

Serves 4

Peaches in sherry and almond sauce

METRIC/IMPERIAL/AMERICAN

6 medium peaches or 1 (539-g/15½-oz/15½-oz) can white peach halves
25 g/1 oz/2 tablespoons soft brown sugar
25 g/1 oz/¼ cup flaked almonds
6 tablespoons/6 tablespoons/½ cup medium-sweet sherry

Nick the skins of the fresh peaches, put them in a basin and cover with boiling water for 30 seconds. Remove with a slotted spoon and cool in cold water. The skins can now be peeled off easily.

Halve the peaches, remove the stones and arrange the peach halves in a casserole. Sprinkle with the sugar and a few flaked almonds, reserving some for decoration, and pour the sherry over.

Cover and place in a moderate oven (160°C, 325°F, Gas Mark 4) for 20 minutes. Serve with whipped cream or ice cream. Sprinkled with the reserved almonds.

Serves 4

Pears and plums in red wine

METRIC/IMPERIAL/AMERICAN

75 g/3 oz/3 oz lump sugar
150 ml/¼ pint/⅔ cup water
150 ml/¼ pint/⅔ cup red wine
small piece cinnamon stick
4 dessert pears
juice of 1 lemon
0.5 kg/1 lb/1 lb plums

Dissolve the sugar in the water over gentle heat. Boil until syrupy, then add the wine and cinnamon. Simmer, covered, for 5 minutes, then strain.

Peel the pears but leave them whole. Brush with lemon juice to prevent discoloration, and place in an ovenproof dish. Wipe the plums and arrange them between the pears.

Pour the wine syrup over the fruit, cover and cook in a moderate oven (160°C, 325°F, Gas Mark 3) for 35–45 minutes.

Serves 4

Danish rhubarb layer pudding

METRIC/IMPERIAL/AMERICAN
0.5 kg/1 lb/1 lb rhubarb
2 teaspoons ground ginger
50 g/2 oz/$\frac{1}{4}$ cup castor sugar
3 tablespoons/3 tablespoons/$\frac{1}{4}$ cup water
50 g/2 oz/$\frac{1}{4}$ cup butter
150 g/5 oz/2$\frac{1}{2}$ cups fresh breadcrumbs
75 g/3 oz/6 tablespoons soft brown sugar

Trim the rhubarb, wash and chop into 2.5-cm/1-inch lengths. Mix with the ginger and castor sugar. Place in a saucepan with the water and cook over gentle heat until just softened.

Meanwhile, melt the butter in a deep frying pan and add the breadcrumbs mixed with the brown sugar. Fry until crisp but do not allow the crumbs to burn.

Arrange a layer of rhubarb in an ovenproof dish and sprinkle with a layer of fried crumbs. Repeat the layers until all the rhubarb and crumbs are used up, finishing with a layer of crumbs. Place in the centre of a moderate oven (180°C, 350°F, Gas Mark 4) for 30 minutes. Serve hot with whipped cream or ice cream. This dish can be made with gooseberries instead of rhubarb, or with a mixture of both.

Serves 4–6

Oranges with raspberries

METRIC/IMPERIAL/AMERICAN
4 oranges
0.5 kg/1 lb/1 lb raspberries
225 g/8 oz/1 cup granulated sugar
150 ml/$\frac{1}{4}$ pint/$\frac{2}{3}$ cup water
2 tablespoons/2 tablespoons/3 tablespoons sherry
25 g/1 oz/2 tablespoons butter

Using a potato peeler, pare the rind from 1 orange, making sure it is free from any pith. Cut the rind into very thin strips and cook in boiling water for 2 minutes. Drain.

Remove the rind, pith and skin from all the oranges and cut across the flesh in slices. Remove any pips. Do this over a plate or bowl and reserve any orange juice. Hull the raspberries.

Arrange the orange slices and raspberries in an ovenproof dish and sprinkle the shredded orange rind over the top.

Dissolve the sugar in the water over low heat, then add the sherry, butter and any orange juice. Bring to the boil and pour over the oranges and raspberries. Place, uncovered, in a moderately hot oven (190°C, 375°F, Gas Mark 5) for 30 minutes. Serve warm with cream.

Serves 4–6

Dinner and Supper Parties

Remember that entertaining should be fun for the hostess too, so make plans for your meal, be it a fork buffet, dinner party or informal supper, and do as much as possible in advance.

The recipes here are exciting and delicious – choose your menu to suit the number of guests, the weather, the space available for entertaining and the type of occasion for which you are catering. Balance the courses so that the foods complement each other, simple flavours contrasted with rich ones, varied textures, shapes and

colours, with no two foods in the one meal alike. Serve fruit, vegetables and game when they are in season to make your menus varied and interesting.

Present all your dishes so that they look appetising; garnishes and decorations are all-important.

Soups and starters

In this chapter you will find an exciting variety of soup and starter recipes to choose from. Plan your starter so it is not too filling or too over-powering. Try to choose foods such as melons and avocados when they are in season.

Soups are always enhanced by garnishes, such as croûtons or swirls of cream for that extra touch of luxury. There are some interesting ideas for cold soups, perfect for those summer dinner parties. The more unusual fish soups are really to be recommended, although it is advisable to make the ones that use shellfish in the summer months when they can be bought fresh.

Prawn bisque

METRIC/IMPERIAL/AMERICAN
scant 1.5 litres/2½ pints/6¼ cups whole prawns
225 g/8 oz/½ lb sole bones and trimmings for stock
pared rind of ½ lemon
1 bay leaf
parsley stalks
few peppercorns
225 g/8 oz/2 cups onion, finely chopped
40 g/1½ oz/3 tablespoons butter
25 g/1 oz/¼ cup plain flour
cayenne pepper
100 ml/4 fl oz/½ cup white wine
½ teaspoon anchovy essence
chopped parsley to garnish

Peel the prawns, reserving 6 for garnish with just the body shell removed. Put the shells in a pan with the sole bones and trimmings, 2.25 litres/4 pints/5 pints water, lemon rind, bay leaf, parsley stalks and peppercorns. Bring to the boil and simmer for 20 minutes. Strain, return to the pan and boil to reduce by half.

Sauté the onion in the butter, add the flour and cook for 1 minute; gradually add the reduced fish stock. Whisk until smooth. Season with salt, pepper and cayenne, bring to the boil and simmer for 15 minutes. Add the wine, anchovy essence and peeled prawns. Garnish each bowl with a prawn and parsley.

Serves 6

Chilled avocado and crab soup

METRIC/IMPERIAL/AMERICAN
2 ripe avocado pears
juice of 1 lemon
100 g/4 oz/¼ lb crabmeat
300 ml/½ pint/1¼ cups chicken stock
450 ml/16 fl oz/2 cups plain yogurt
1 teaspoon Worcestershire sauce
few drops Tabasco sauce
salt and freshly ground pepper

Halve, peel and quarter the avocados. Slice thinly and dip completely in lemon juice reserving a few slices for garnish. Place a little of this mixture in a covered bowl in the refrigerator. Put the remainder, together with the crabmeat, stock and yogurt into a liquidiser and blend until very smooth. Add Worcestershire sauce, Tabasco and seasoning to taste. Chill thoroughly. Before serving, stir the reserved avocado into the soup. Place 1 or 2 ice cubes into each bowl and add the soup. Float the reserved avocado slices on top.
Note: Broken crab claws may be carefully cracked and the whole pieces of crabmeat from each used to garnish the soup for a special occasion.

Serves 6

Iced cherry soup Chantilly

METRIC/IMPERIAL/AMERICAN
1 kg/2¼ lb/2¼ lb fresh black cherries, stalks removed
generous litre/2 pints/5 cups water
pared rind and juice of 1 orange
1 cinnamon stick
225 g/8 oz/1 cup castor sugar
300 ml/½ pint/1¼ cups sweet red wine
3 tablespoons/3 tablespoons/¼ cup arrowroot
GARNISH:
150 ml/¼ pint/⅔ cup soured cream
50 g/2 oz/½ cup flaked almonds

Reserving 100 g/4 oz/¼ lb whole cherries, gently simmer the remainder with the water, orange rind and juice and cinnamon stick for 20 minutes. Strain the juices into a clean pan, pressing the cherries very well. Add the sugar and bring slowly to the boil. Stone the remaining cherries over a basin to reserve the juices. Add these to the pan with the wine. Thicken with the arrowroot blended with a little cold water and bring to the boil for 1 minute. Leave to cool, then chill thoroughly. Serve cold with a spoonful of soured cream on each serving and a few flaked almonds.

Serves 6

Eggs Jacqueline

METRIC/IMPERIAL/AMERICAN

3 hard-boiled eggs, halved lengthwise
25 g/1 oz/2 tablespoons softened butter
100 g/4 oz/⅔ cup peeled prawns
paprika
225 g/8 oz/½ lb asparagus, trimmed, cooked and cut in
    4-cm/1½-inch/1½-inch pieces
25 g/1 oz/¼ cup Parmesan cheese, grated
watercress to garnish
BÉCHAMEL SAUCE:
20 g/¾ oz/1½ tablespoons butter
20 g/¾ oz/3 tablespoons flour
300 ml/½ pint/1¼ cups flavoured milk (infused with slice
    of onion, bay leaf and peppercorns)

Remove the egg yolks and sieve into a bowl. Mix with butter
and 25 g/1 oz/2 tablespoons of chopped prawns. Season with
paprika, salt and pepper. Spoon mixture into the whites and
sandwich. Put the asparagus into the base of 6 ovenproof
ramekin dishes. Place eggs on top and add remaining prawns.

Make béchamel sauce: melt butter in a small pan and stir in
the flour. Cook for 1 minute then gradually add the flavoured
milk and bring to the boil. Simmer for 2 minutes and season to
taste. Spoon over the eggs, sprinkle with cheese and cook in a
moderate oven (180°C, 350°F, Gas Mark 4) for 15–20 minutes
until well browned. Garnish with watercress.

Serves 6

Moules farcies Bretonne

METRIC/IMPERIAL/AMERICAN

generous litre/2 quarts/5 cups large mussels
225 g/8 oz/1 cup unsalted butter
1 large onion, finely chopped
3 cloves garlic, crushed
1 tablespoon chopped parsley
50 g/2 oz/1 cup fresh white breadcrumbs
40 g/1½ oz/⅓ cup grated Parmesan cheese
100 ml/4 fl oz/½ cup dry white wine

Wash and scrub the mussel shells under cold water. Remove
beards and discard any open shells. Place the mussels in a
steamer or colander over a pan of boiling water. Cover with a
lid and steam for 2–3 minutes until the shells just open. Do not
overcook. Stir to ensure all shells are steamed. Remove from
the heat. Break off the empty half of each shell and place the
filled halves on a board.

Cream the butter with the onion, garlic, parsley and pepper.
Spread a little into each shell and arrange close together in 6
individual ovenproof gratin dishes or one large ovenproof dish.
Sprinkle with breadcrumbs and cheese mixed together and
spoon over the wine. Chill.

Place the dish on a baking sheet and cover with foil. Cook for
15–20 minutes at the top of a moderate oven (180°C, 350°F, Gas
Mark 4). Remove the foil and continue cooking for a further
5 minutes to brown. Serve with French bread.

Serves 6

Gratin au fruits de mer

METRIC/IMPERIAL/AMERICAN
350 g/12 oz/¾ lb cod fillet, skinned and cut into strips
100–150 g/4–6 oz/¾–1 cup peeled prawns
6 scallops, cut into quarters
juice of 1 lemon
salt and pepper
1 small onion, finely chopped
50 g/2 oz/¼ cup butter
100 ml/4 fl oz/½ cup white wine
40 g/1½ oz/6 tablespoons plain flour
450 ml/¾ pint/2 cups milk, infused with 1 bay leaf,
  1 blade mace and peppercorns
25 g/1 oz/¼ cup grated Parmesan cheese
parsley sprigs to garnish

Mix the cod strips, prawns and scallops with the lemon juice
and seasoning. Divide between 6 deep scallop shells or
ovenproof dishes. Sauté the onion in the butter then add the
wine and bring to the boil. Simmer until reduced by half before
whisking in the flour. Cook until smooth, stirring continuously.
Strain in the infused milk and bring back to the boil. Simmer for
2–3 minutes. Adjust the seasoning and spoon over the fish to
cover. Sprinkle with cheese. Bake at the top of a moderately hot
oven (190°C, 375°F, Gas Mark 5) for 20–30 minutes until
golden brown on top. Garnish with parsley sprigs.
Note: Scampi, halibut or nuggets of firm white fish mixed with
some sliced mushrooms can be used as an alternative.

Serves 6

Prawn soufflés

METRIC/IMPERIAL/AMERICAN
20 g/¾ oz/1½ tablespoons butter
1 teaspoon paprika
600 ml/1 pint/2½ cups shelled prawns
few drops Tabasco sauce
450 ml/¾ pint/2 cups béchamel sauce (see method)
2 tablespoons/2 tablespoons/3 tablespoons cream
3 egg yolks
4 egg whites
little grated cheese mixed with browned breadcrumbs

Melt the butter in a large pan and add the paprika. Cook for 1
minute then add the prawns, Tabasco, salt and pepper. Add the
prepared béchamel sauce and cream and mix well. For the
béchamel sauce, melt 40 g/1½ oz/3 tablespoons butter in a pan.
Stir in 40 g/1½ oz/6 tablespoons flour and cook for 1 minute.
Gradually add 450 ml/¾ pint/2 cups milk which has been
infused with 1 bay leaf, 1 blade of mace and a slice of onion and
then strained. Bring to the boil for 2 minutes and season to
taste.

Cool slightly then beat in the egg yolks thoroughly, one at a
time. Whisk the egg whites until stiff but not dry and stir
1 tablespoon into the mixture. Carefully fold in the remainder.
Spoon into 6 individual ovenproof soufflé dishes, place on a
baking sheet and sprinkle with the cheese and breadcrumb
mixture. Bake in a moderate oven (180°C, 350°F, Gas Mark 4)
for 20–25 minutes until firm. Serve immediately.

Serves 6

Ogen melon with mint ice

METRIC/IMPERIAL/AMERICAN
MINT ICE:
450 ml/¾ pint/2 cups water
100 g/4 oz/½ cup sugar
pared rind and juice of 2 lemons
large handful of fresh mint
few drops of green food colouring

3 small ogen melons, chilled

Boil the water, sugar and pared lemon rinds for 5 minutes. Remove from the heat and add the mint. Infuse for 10 minutes then add the lemon juice. Strain and add colouring sparingly. Cool, then freeze until firm. Whisk with an electric beater or use a liquidiser. Return to the freezer until firm.

To serve, cut the melons in half, open and discard the seeds. Pile spoonfuls of the mint ice into the centre of each melon and decorate with crystallised mint leaves, if liked. Serve at once.

(To crystallise mint leaves, pick the small tips of the mint only. Brush sparingly with egg white and dip in sugar until completely coated. Lay on a metal sheet and freeze until crisp.)
Note: Mint ice is also delicious served with grapefruit.

Serves 6

Avocado mousse ring

METRIC/IMPERIAL/AMERICAN
3 ripe avocado pears
juice of 1 lemon
2 tablespoons/2 tablespoons/3 tablespoons French
    dressing
25 g/1 oz/2 envelopes powdered gelatine
150 ml/¼ pint/⅔ cup chicken stock
150 ml/¼ pint/⅔ cup dry white wine
150 ml/¼ pint/⅔ cup thick mayonnaise
150 ml/¼ pint/⅔ cup double cream, whipped
1 teaspoon onion juice
2 teaspoons Worcestershire sauce
GARNISH:
600 ml/1 pint/2½ cups whole unshelled prawns
1 bunch watercress, washed and picked into sprigs

Peel and slice the avocado pears. Mix with the lemon juice and French dressing and leave to marinate for 30 minutes. Liquidise or sieve to make 450 ml/¾ pint/2 cups purée. Meanwhile, soak the gelatine in a little of the chicken stock in a basin and dissolve over a pan of hot water. Add the remaining stock and the white wine. Add the mayonnaise and cream to the avocado purée with onion juice and Worcestershire sauce. Stir in gelatine mixture evenly and add salt and pepper. Turn into an oiled 23-cm/9-inch ring mould. Cover with cling film and chill until set. Meanwhile remove the body shells from prawns.

To serve, turn the mousse out on to a flat serving dish. Arrange the prawns around and fill the centre with watercress.

Serves 6

Fish dishes

The following fish recipes can be either served as a fish course after the starter, or as the main course. If you are serving a fish course the quantities need only be small, just enough to tempt the appetite.

When buying fish you must always check that it is really fresh. The flesh must be firm and not flabby, the eyes and any natural markings should be bright.

If you are lucky enough to acquire a salmon trout when they are in season, try serving it hot, with a dill and cucumber sauce.

A fish fondue can be a huge success at a dinner party – everyone is involved in cooking the food at the table. It is also ideal for the hostess as all the preparation can be done in advance, leaving her completely free to enjoy the company of her guests.

Stuffed plaice florentine

METRIC/IMPERIAL/AMERICAN
$\frac{3}{4}$–1 kg/1$\frac{1}{2}$–2 lb/1$\frac{1}{2}$–2 lb fresh spinach, cooked
1 small onion, finely chopped
25 g/1 oz/2 tablespoons butter
2 egg yolks
freshly grated nutmeg
4 large whole fillets of plaice, skinned and trimmed
100 ml/4 fl oz/$\frac{1}{2}$ cup white wine
juice of 1 lemon
25 g/1 oz/2 tablespoons butter
25 g/1 oz/$\frac{1}{4}$ cup plain flour
300 ml/$\frac{1}{2}$ pint/1$\frac{1}{4}$ cups milk
$\frac{1}{2}$ teaspoon French mustard
75 g/3 oz/$\frac{3}{4}$ cup Cheddar cheese, grated
pinch cayenne pepper
2 tablespoons/2 tablespoons/3 tablespoons cream

Chop spinach. Sauté onion in butter, then add spinach and cook for 5 minutes. Add yolks, nutmeg, salt and pepper. Cool.

Divide the spinach mixture between the plaice fillets and roll up from tail to head. Place in a greased ovenproof dish. Pour over the wine and lemon juice and cover. Bake in a moderate oven (180°C, 350°F, Gas Mark 4) for 20 minutes.

Melt the butter, add the flour and stir for 1 minute. Add the milk and bring to the boil. Stir in the mustard, most of the cheese, fish juices, cayenne, salt, pepper and cream; heat gently. Coat fillets with sauce, sprinkle with cheese and brown.

Serves 4

Salmon trout with dill and cucumber sauce

METRIC/IMPERIAL/AMERICAN
$\frac{1}{2}$ bottle white wine
1 medium onion, finely chopped
1 bay leaf
juice of 1 lemon
6 peppercorns
1.25–1.5 kg/2$\frac{1}{2}$–3 lb/2$\frac{1}{2}$–3 lb whole salmon trout
75 g/3 oz/6 tablespoons butter, melted
DILL AND CUCUMBER SAUCE:
4 egg yolks
1 teaspoon chopped dill
175 g/6 oz/$\frac{3}{4}$ cup soft butter
juice of 1 small lemon
150 ml/$\frac{1}{4}$ pint/$\frac{2}{3}$ cup double cream, whipped
$\frac{1}{2}$ cucumber, peeled and finely chopped
1 teaspoon chopped parsley

Heat the wine, 600 ml/1 pint/2$\frac{1}{2}$ cups water, onion, bay leaf, lemon juice and peppercorns in a fish kettle. Simmer for 15 minutes. Add the whole fish and simmer gently for 35–40 minutes without boiling. Drain the fish, remove skin and lift on to a serving dish. Garnish, pour butter over trout and hand sauce separately.

Cream yolks with salt and pepper, dill and a little butter until thick. Add lemon juice and whisk in a bowl over hot water over a gentle heat until thick. Still whisking, add butter. Fold in cream, cucumber and parsley.

Serves 6

Salmon Louise

METRIC/IMPERIAL/AMERICAN
4 salmon steaks
150 ml/$\frac{1}{4}$ pint/$\frac{2}{3}$ cup white wine
juice of 1 lemon
1 slice onion
6 peppercorns
watercress sprigs to garnish
TOMATO SAUCE:
1 bunch spring onions, shredded
25 g/1 oz/2 tablespoons butter
$\frac{1}{2}$ cucumber, peeled, cut into coarse matchsticks,
    blanched and drained
225 g/8 oz/$\frac{1}{2}$ lb tomatoes, skinned and quartered
salt and pepper
chopped parsley

Poach the steaks in the wine with lemon juice, onion and peppercorns added, in a covered dish in a moderate oven (180°C, 350°F, Gas Mark 4) for about 15 minutes, depending on the thickness of the fish, until just cooked. Carefully remove the skin from the salmon.

Meanwhile, prepare the sauce. Sauté the spring onions in melted butter. Add the cucumber sticks and sauté quickly. Stir in the tomatoes and heat through carefully. Season, adding a little parsley.

Spoon the tomato sauce into a dish and place salmon on top. Spoon over tarragon-flavoured hollandaise sauce and garnish.

Serves 4

Fish fondue with sauces

METRIC/IMPERIAL/AMERICAN
225 g/8 oz/½ lb haddock or cod fillet, cooked
40 g/1½ oz/3 tablespoons butter
40 g/1½ oz/6 tablespoons plain flour
150 ml/¼ pint/⅔ cup milk
3 tablespoons/3 tablespoons/¼ cup double cream
lemon juice
salt and cayenne pepper
whitebait, washed
whole prawns
whole button mushrooms, washed

For the fish balls, mix the fish with a white sauce (see page 99), adding curry paste if liked. Add lemon juice and seasoning to taste and beat well. Chill. Form into walnut-sized balls with floured hands and then coat with egg and breadcrumbs.

Place a few fish balls, whitebait, prawns and mushrooms on individual plates for each guest to spear and cook in the fondue pan. Serve with rice, salad and sauces.
Avocado sauce: Mash a ripe avocado pear with lemon juice and French dressing. Add a little mayonnaise, double cream, Worcestershire sauce, diced cucumber and seasoning.
Tomato chilli sauce: Mix together mayonnaise, tomato chutney, finely grated onion, 1–2 teaspoons Tabasco, lemon juice, salt and pepper, and whipped cream.

Serves 4

Mediterranean fish casserole

METRIC/IMPERIAL/AMERICAN
450 g/1 lb/1 lb cod steak, skinned and cut into cubes
450 g/1 lb/1 lb halibut, skinned and cut into cubes
seasoned flour
6 tablespoons/6 tablespoons/½ cup oil
350 g/12 oz/¾ lb onions, peeled, halved and sliced
3 cloves garlic, crushed
350 g/12 oz/¾ lb tomatoes, skinned and quartered
1 teaspoon tomato purée
½ bottle dry white wine
juice of 1 lemon
pinch thyme
½ teaspoon fennel
1 tablespoon chopped parsley
generous litre/1 quart/5 cups mussels, prepared (see page 96)
900 ml/1½ pints/3 cups whole prawns
chopped parsley to garnish

Toss the cubed cod and halibut in seasoned flour. Heat 3–4 tablespoons oil and fry the cubes until browned. Remove. Add remaining oil to the pan and sauté the onions and garlic. Add the tomatoes, tomato purée, white wine, lemon juice and herbs and bring to the boil. Return the fish cubes to the pan and simmer gently, covered, for 10–15 minutes until just cooked. Add the mussels, cover and leave for 3–4 minutes until they open. Discard any that do not open. Add the prawns. Sprinkle with parsley.

Serves 6

Meat dishes

The recipes in this section have all been created to form the main part of the meal, probably the most exciting course on the menu. You can really go to town with these recipes, remembering that the final presentation is very important.

For those that like traditional dishes there is Beef Wellington or a Crown roast, or the more adventurous hostess may like to serve a Carré de porc à l'orange. In fact there is something for every taste, whether it be beef, lamb, pork, veal or offal. Remember to choose suitable vegetables to complement the particular meat you are serving.

Beef Wellington

METRIC/IMPERIAL/AMERICAN
1.25 kg/2½ lb/2½ lb whole fillet of beef (thick end)
2 tablespoons/2 tablespoons/3 tablespoons brandy
1 clove garlic, cut in half
50 g/2 oz/¼ cup butter
225 g/8 oz/2 cups onions, finely chopped
225 g/8 oz/2 cups mushrooms, finely chopped
1 teaspoon chopped parsley
3 slices cooked ham, cut in half
1 (368-g/13-oz/13-oz) packet frozen puff pastry, thawed
beaten egg to glaze

Trim the fillet and marinate in brandy for a few hours. Rub with cut garlic and season with pepper. Melt the butter and brown the fillet all over. Pour over the brandy marinade and ignite, then cool. Add the onions and mushrooms to the pan and fry until soft. Season, add the parsley and cool. Mark the fillet into 6 portions and cut two-thirds through. Fold the ham slices in half and sandwich between the cuts.

Roll the pastry to a rectangle double the size of the fillet. Spread the mushroom mixture over. Lay the fillet on top, cut side down. Fold over the pastry to make a parcel, sealing with water. Lift on to a greaseproof covered baking sheet with the folds underneath and brush with egg. Lightly score the pastry. Use trimmings to make pastry leaves. Bake in a hot oven (230°C, 450°F, Gas Mark 8) for 30–40 minutes until browned. Garnish with watercress.

Serves 6

Pork stroganoff

METRIC/IMPERIAL/AMERICAN
50 g/2 oz/¼ cup butter
1 small onion, chopped
175 g/6 oz/1½ cups button mushrooms, trimmed
1 teaspoon French mustard
1 teaspoon tomato purée
150 ml/¼ pint/⅔ cup soured cream
1 tablespoon oil
0.75–1 kg/1½–2 lb/1½–2 lb pork fillet, cut into thin strips
100 ml/4 fl oz/½ cup vermouth
pinch dried basil and tarragon
juice of ½ lemon
salt and freshly ground pepper
GARNISH:
chopped parsley
lemon wedges

Melt half the butter in a pan and slowly fry the onion and mushrooms until soft. Add the mustard, tomato purée and most of the soured cream then set aside. Heat the oil and remaining butter together and fry the meat over a high heat until well browned. Pour over the vermouth and ignite. Blend in the sauce, adding herbs, lemon juice and seasoning to taste. Simmer gently for 10 minutes, stirring occasionally. Serve with a little soured cream spooned over. Sprinkle with parsley and garnish with lemon wedges. Serve with rice.

Serves 4–6

Carré de porc à l'orange

METRIC/IMPERIAL/AMERICAN
2 small (6 bone) best ends of pork, skinned
1 onion, finely chopped
2 sticks celery, finely chopped
25 g/1 oz/2 tablespoons butter
100 g/4 oz/ 2 cups fresh white breadcrumbs
grated rind and juice of 1 orange
50 g/2 oz/⅓ cup raisins
2 teaspoons chopped parsley
50 g/2 oz/¼ cup soft brown sugar
juice of 1 orange and ½ lemon
1 tablespoon Worcestershire sauce
150 ml/¼ pint/⅔ cup each white wine and stock
2 oranges, sliced and fried in butter to garnish

Ask the butcher to trim the cutlets and make into a guard of honour. Fry the onion and celery in the butter. Add to the breadcrumbs, orange rind, raisins, parsley, salt and pepper and mix well. Bind with the orange juice. Place this stuffing in the middle of the guard of honour in a roasting tin. Bring the sugar, orange and lemon juices and Worcestershire sauce to the boil. Spoon over the meat and roast in a moderately hot oven (190°C, 375°F, Gas Mark 5) for about 2 hours, basting regularly.

Top bones with cutlet frills and place on a serving dish. Remove fat from the juices in the tin then add the wine and stock. Bring to the boil, season and serve with the pork. Arrange fried orange slices around the meat.

Serves 6

Noisettes d'agneau Arlésienne

METRIC/IMPERIAL/AMERICAN
0.75 g/1½ lb/1½ lb joint of best end neck of lamb
salt and freshly ground pepper
1 tablespoon chopped fresh herbs
2 cloves garlic, halved
1 aubergine, cut into 4–5-cm/1½–2-inch cubes
2 tablespoons/2 tablespoons/3 tablespoons oil
225 g/8 oz/½ lb onions, halved and thickly sliced
225 g/8 oz/½ lb tomatoes, skinned and quartered
pinch basil
chopped parsley
50 g/2 oz/¼ cup butter

Bone the lamb. Dust with seasoning and herbs and roll up. Secure with string at 2-cm/¾-inch intervals. Cut between the string into noisettes. Rub garlic over and reserve.

Sprinkle the aubergine with salt and leave for 30 minutes. Rinse, drain and dry the aubergine cubes and quickly brown in the oil in a deep frying pan. Remove from the pan. Fry the onions with reserved garlic cloves, crushed, in the same pan. Return aubergines to pan with tomatoes, basil and some parsley. Season and simmer, covered, for 10 minutes.

Heat butter and sauté noisettes for 5–8 minutes each side. Remove string and arrange on a dish with the vegetables. Sprinkle with parsley and place a pat of savoury butter on each.

Serves 4–6

Veal escalopes italienne

METRIC/IMPERIAL/AMERICAN
50 g/2 oz/¼ cup butter
4 escalopes of veal, beaten flat
2 red peppers, halved, cored, sliced and blanched
1 clove garlic, crushed
175–225 g/6–8 oz/2 cups button mushrooms, sliced
200 ml/8 fl oz/1 cup Marsala
150 ml/¼ pint/⅔ cup stock
lemon juice

Melt the butter in a large deep frying pan and fry the seasoned escalopes briskly for 5–7 minutes on each side until well browned. Remove and fry the peppers and garlic for 2 minutes. Add the mushrooms and fry until just soft. Add Marsala and ignite; then stir in the stock and bring to the boil. Replace the escalopes, season, cover the pan and simmer for 10–12 minutes. Place the escalopes on a serving dish, adding lemon juice to taste. Spoon the sauce over.

Variation: Veal viennoise
Dip the escalopes in seasoned flour, brush with beaten egg and coat with an equal mixture of dry white breadcrumbs and grated Parmesan cheese. Fry in melted butter for 7–10 minutes on each side. Add a little lemon juice. Garnish with anchovy fillets, chopped or sieved egg yolk and chopped egg white (see picture). Surround with cooked asparagus, sliced lemon, tomato and watercress.

Serves 4

Spicy gammon steaks

METRIC/IMPERIAL/AMERICAN
2 teaspoons dry mustard
2 teaspoons powdered cinnamon
100 g/4 oz/½ cup soft brown sugar
4 gammon steaks, 1-cm/½-inch thick
juice of 2 large oranges
1 (454-g/16-oz/16-oz) can peach halves
450 g/1 lb/1 lb cooking apples, peeled, quartered, cored
  and sliced
2 tablespoons/2 tablespoons/3 tablespoons chutney
20 g/¾ oz/3 teaspoons cornflour
watercress sprig to garnish

Mix the mustard, cinnamon and sugar together and spoon half the mixture over the gammon steaks, arranged in an ovenproof dish. Make the orange juice up to 450 ml/¾ pint/2 cups with the juice from the drained peaches and pour round the gammon. Cover with foil and bake in a moderate oven (180°C, 350°F, Gas Mark 4) for 45 minutes. Arrange the apples over the steaks and spoon over the remaining spicy mixture. Baste with juices and return to the oven, uncovered, for a further 30 minutes. Spoon chutney into the peach halves, place in an ovenproof dish and heat through in the oven for 10 minutes. Serve with the gammon.

   Place the gammon steaks on a dish. Thicken the juices with the cornflour blended with a little water. Spoon over the steaks and garnish.

Serves 4

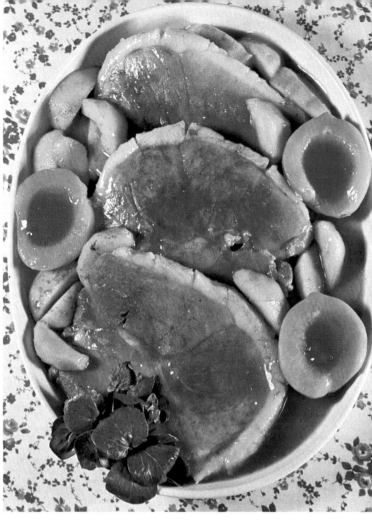

Lambs' kidneys bourguignonne

METRIC/IMPERIAL/AMERICAN
50 g/2 oz/¼ cup butter
8 lambs' kidneys, skinned, halved and cored
200 ml/8 fl oz/1 cup red wine
225 g/8 oz/½ lb button onions, peeled and blanched
1 clove garlic, crushed
225 g/8 oz/2 cups whole button mushrooms, trimmed
45 g/1¾ oz/scant ½ cup plain flour
300 ml/½ pint/1¼ cups stock
1 bay leaf
salt and freshly ground pepper
225 g/8 oz/½ lb tomatoes, skinned, quartered and
  deseeded
chopped parsley to garnish

Melt half the butter in a pan and sauté the kidneys quickly over a high heat until browned. Add the wine and ignite. Transfer to a casserole. Melt the remaining butter in the pan and lightly brown the onions and garlic, add the mushrooms and fry for a further 2–3 minutes. Add to the casserole. Stir the flour into the pan juices then gradually add the stock and bring to the boil for 2 minutes. Add to the kidneys in the casserole with the bay leaf and seasoning. Cover and simmer gently for 20–25 minutes. Add the tomatoes and continue to cook for 5 minutes. Discard bay leaf and garnish. Serve with saffron rice, if liked.

Serves 4–6

Sweetbreads Florentine

METRIC/IMPERIAL/AMERICAN
0.75 kg/1½ lb/1½ lb calves' sweetbreads, soaked in salted
  water overnight
75 g/3 oz/6 tablespoons butter
1 onion, finely chopped
1 clove garlic, crushed
100 ml/4 fl oz/½ cup white wine
1 bay leaf
450 g/1 lb/1 lb cooked leaf spinach
grated nutmeg
75 g/3 oz/¾ cup cheese, grated
300 ml/½ pint/1¼ cups béchamel sauce (see page 96)
cayenne pepper

Drain the sweetbreads. Cover with water and bring to boil.
Refresh with cold water, trim and press between 2 plates. Melt
half the butter, add onion, garlic and sweetbreads and sauté for
10 minutes. Add wine, bay leaf, salt and pepper; simmer for
about 10 minutes.

Meanwhile, toss the spinach in the remaining butter, adding
nutmeg, salt and pepper. Arrange in a hot serving dish. Add 50 g/
2 oz/½ cup cheese to the béchamel sauce (see page 12), together
with 150 ml/¼ pint/⅔ cup cooking liquor from the sweetbreads
and salt and cayenne. Simmer gently. Place the sweetbreads in
the centre of the spinach and cover with sauce. Sprinkle with
cheese and brown in the top of a moderately hot oven (200°C,
400°F, Gas Mark 6) for about 10 minutes.

Serves 4

Cotelettes de veau Foyot

METRIC/IMPERIAL/AMERICAN
4 best end neck of veal cutlets, trimmed
salt and freshly ground pepper
50–75 g/2–3 oz/4–6 tablespoons butter
225 g/8 oz/2 cups onions, chopped
1 clove garlic, crushed
1 tablespoon chopped parsley
40 g/1½ oz/¾ cup fresh white breadcrumbs
50 g/2 oz/½ cup Parmesan cheese, freshly grated
pinch cayenne pepper
300 ml/½ pint/1¼ cups white wine and veal or chicken
  stock mixed

Season the cutlets and brown on each side in 50 g/2 oz/¼ cup of
the butter. Remove. Add the onions and garlic to the pan and
fry gently until lightly coloured. Remove from the heat, add the
parsley and spoon half the mixture into a deep ovenproof dish.
Arrange the cutlets on top. Add the breadcrumbs and cheese to
the remaining onion mixture. Mix well, season, adding cayenne,
and press on top of each cutlet. Melt the remaining butter and
spoon over the topping on the cutlets. Add the wine and stock
to the pan, heat and pour round the cutlets. Cover with a lid or
foil and cook in a moderate oven (160°C, 325°F, Gas Mark 3)
for 45 minutes, basting occasionally. Remove the foil and cook
for a further 30 minutes until the meat is tender and topping
brown.

Serves 4

Poultry and game dishes

For those special dinner and supper parties, here are some exotic recipes for poultry and game. Poultry is always readily available but game is restricted to certain times of the year. If you are looking for an excuse to have a dinner party, have one when game is in season! Serve pheasant cooked in Calvados and wine or with chestnuts, partridge cooked with onions and mushrooms in red wine, barbecued duck and many more delicious dishes.

Included in this section is a recipe for Chicken parisienne. This is an unusual way of serving chicken as the bird is boned and then stuffed. It makes a very attractive dish and easy to serve at the table.

Poussin à l'estragon

METRIC/IMPERIAL/AMERICAN
1 lemon
handful fresh tarragon or 1 tablespoon dried tarragon
3 (0.75-kg/1½–2-lb/1½–2-lb) baby chickens, prepared
175 g/6 oz/¾ cup butter
200 ml/8 fl oz/1 cup white wine
225 g/8 oz/2 cups onions, finely chopped
225 g/8 oz/2 cups button mushrooms, sliced
40 g/1½ oz/6 tablespoons plain flour
300 ml/½ pint/1¼ cups stock
1 tablespoon chopped parsley
watercress sprigs to garnish

Squeeze the lemon juice. Remove leaves from fresh tarragon. Cut up lemon skin and put a piece inside each bird with the tarragon stalks and a knob of butter. Keep 50 g/2 oz/¼ cup of butter and spread the remainder over chickens. Put in a roasting tin, pour over wine and cook in a moderate oven (180°C, 350°F, Gas Mark 4) for 40–50 minutes.

Sauté the onions in the reserved butter, add the mushrooms and sauté. Sprinkle on the flour and cook for 1 minute. Add the stock, bring to boil and add reserved lemon juice, chopped tarragon, parsley, salt and pepper. Simmer for 15 minutes.

When the chickens are cooked, strain the juices into the sauce and cook to a coating consistency. Just before serving, cut each bird in half with poultry scissors. Arrange chicken in a dish. Spoon over sauce, serve with mushrooms and garnish.

Serves 6

Chicken parisienne

METRIC/IMPERIAL/AMERICAN
1 (1.5-kg/3½-lb/3½-lb) roasting chicken, prepared
50 g/2 oz/¼ cup soft butter
150 ml/¼ pint/⅔ cup stock
3 tablespoons/3 tablespoons/¼ cup sherry
watercress to garnish
STUFFING:
1 onion, finely chopped
25 g/1 oz/2 tablespoons butter
225 g/8 oz/1 cup each veal and ham, minced
3 tablespoons/3 tablespoons/¼ cup fresh white
   breadcrumbs
2 teaspoons chopped parsley
1 teaspoon chopped tarragon
grated rind and juice of ½ lemon
1 egg, beaten

Bone the chicken, taking care not to puncture the skin. Spread out skin side downwards on a board and season.

For the stuffing, sauté the onion in the butter. Cool and mix with the minced meats, breadcrumbs, herbs and lemon rind. Bind together with egg and lemon juice, season. Spread over the chicken and sew up.

Spread 50 g/2 oz/¼ cup butter over chicken, place in a roasting tin with stock and sherry. Cook in a moderately hot oven (190°C, 375°F, Gas Mark 5) for 1½ hours, basting well. Slice chicken and serve, if liked, with a mushroom sauce.

Serves 4–6

Poulet aux amandes

METRIC/IMPERIAL/AMERICAN
100 g/4 oz/½ cup butter
1 (1.5-kg/3½-lb/3½-lb) roasting chicken, prepared
sprig tarragon
150 ml/¼ pint/⅔ cup white wine or chicken stock
50 g/2 oz/½ cup almonds, blanched and shredded
225 g/8 oz/½ lb red peppers, halved and sliced
1 onion, chopped
20 g/¾ oz/3 tablespoons plain flour
300 ml/½ pint/1¼ cups stock
pinch mace
150 ml/¼ pint/⅔ cup single cream
parsley to garnish

Put 15 g/½ oz/1 tablespoon butter inside the bird with the tarragon. Spread 40 g/1½ oz/3 tablespoons butter over the bird and roast with the wine in a moderately hot oven (200°C, 400°F, Gas Mark 6) for about 1 hour, basting well.

Melt the remaining butter and fry the almonds until brown. Add the peppers and onion and sauté until soft. Remove. Add the flour to the pan and cook for 1 minute, then add the stock, mace, salt and pepper. Return the almond and pepper mixture with the strained juices from the cooked chicken. Bring back to the boil and add the cream.

To serve, joint the chicken and arrange on a dish. Spoon over the sauce and garnish.

Serves 4–6

Poulet au citron

METRIC/IMPERIAL/AMERICAN
2 tablespoons/2 tablespoons/3 tablespoons oil
50 g/2 oz/¼ cup butter
1 (1.5-kg/3½-lb/3½-lb) roasting chicken, jointed
1 onion, finely chopped
1 clove garlic, crushed
¼ teaspoon powdered saffron
200 ml/8 fl oz/1 cup white wine
300 ml/½ pint/1¼ cups chicken stock
pared rind and juice of 1 lemon
175 g/6 oz/1½ cups button mushrooms, quartered
25 g/1 oz/¼ cup plain flour
2 egg yolks and 150 ml/¼ pint/⅔ cup single cream

Heat the oil in a pan. Add 25 g/1 oz/2 tablespoons butter and brown the chicken pieces. Remove to an ovenproof casserole. Add the onion and garlic to the pan and when softened add the saffron, wine and stock. Bring to the boil, adding lemon juice, salt and pepper and pour over the chicken. Cover and simmer for 45–60 minutes. Cut lemon rind into fine strips, blanch and add most of the strips to the chicken at end of cooking.

For the sauce, melt the remaining butter and sauté the mushrooms. Sprinkle on the flour and cook for 1 minute. When the chicken is cooked, pour the cooking juices into the mushroom mixture. Pour some of this on to the yolks and cream mixed and return to pan. Reheat gently without boiling. Spoon over chicken on a dish. Sprinkle with lemon strips.

Serves 4

Pheasant Vallée d'Auge

METRIC/IMPERIAL/AMERICAN
1 tablespoon oil
50 g/2 oz/¼ cup butter
1 plump pheasant, prepared
100 ml/4 fl oz/½ cup Calvados
1 onion, thinly sliced
2 sticks celery, thinly sliced
225 g/8 oz/2 cups Cox's apples, peeled and sliced
15 g/½ oz/2 tablespoons plain flour
100 ml/4 fl oz/½ cup white wine
300 ml/½ pint/1¼ cups chicken stock
salt and freshly ground pepper
150 ml/¼ pint/⅔ cup double cream
apple rings and watercress to garnish

Heat the oil in a frying pan, add 25 g/1 oz/2 tablespoons butter and brown the pheasant. Add the Calvados and ignite. Place the pheasant in a casserole. Add the remaining butter to the pan and sauté the onion for 5 minutes. Add the celery and apple, cook for 5 minutes then stir in the flour, wine and stock. Bring to the boil, season and pour over the pheasant. Cover and simmer for 45–50 minutes.

To serve, lift the pheasant on to a serving dish and keep warm. Remove the fat from the pan juices then liquidise or sieve. Place in a pan and bring to the boil. Whisk in the cream and cook until thickening. Adjust seasoning and serve with the pheasant separately. Garnish and serve.

Serves 4–6

Pheasant casserole with chestnuts

METRIC/IMPERIAL/AMERICAN
1 tablespoon oil
25 g/1 oz/2 tablespoons butter
1 plump pheasant, prepared
225 g/8 oz/½ lb button onions, skinned
225 g/8 oz/½ lb fresh chestnuts, peeled and skinned
25 g/1 oz/¼ cup plain flour
450 ml/¾ pint/2 cups stock
100 ml/4 fl oz/½ cup red wine
grated rind and juice of 1 orange
2 teaspoons redcurrant jelly
1 bay leaf
salt and freshly ground pepper
chopped parsley to garnish

Heat the oil in a frying pan, add the butter and brown the pheasant all over. Cut into serving pieces and place in a casserole. Add the onions and chestnuts to the pan and cook until golden brown, then transfer to the casserole. Add the flour to the frying pan and cook for 1 minute before whisking in the stock, wine, orange rind and juice and redcurrant jelly. Bring to the boil, add the bay leaf and season to taste. Pour over the pheasant, cover and cook in a moderate oven (160°C, 325°F, Gas Mark 3) for 1½–2 hours until tender. Remove the bay leaf and any fat from the juices. Adjust seasoning and garnish.

Serves 4–6

Partridge bourguignonne

METRIC/IMPERIAL/AMERICAN
50 g/2 oz/¼ cup butter
2 partridges, prepared
175 g/6 oz/6 oz lean bacon, cut in strips and blanched
150 ml/¼ pint/⅔ cup red wine
300 ml/½ pint/1¼ cups chicken stock
1 teaspoon tomato purée
bouquet garni
salt and freshly ground pepper
350 g/12 oz/¾ lb pickling onions, skinned
1 clove garlic, crushed
175 g/6 oz/1½ cups button mushrooms
1 tablespoon chopped parsley

Melt 25 g/1 oz/2 tablespoons butter in a pan and brown the birds. Transfer to a casserole. Brown the bacon in the same pan, add the wine, stock and tomato purée. Bring to the boil. Pour into the casserole adding bouquet garni and seasoning. Cover and cook in a moderate oven (180°C, 350°F, Gas Mark 4) for 1 hour.

Meanwhile, melt the remaining butter in a pan, add the onions and garlic and brown. Add the mushrooms. Add with parsley to casserole 30 minutes before end of cooking time.

To serve, cut each bird in half with poultry scissors. Remove backbone, trim wing and leg bones and place in a deep serving dish. Remove the bouquet garni from the sauce, adjust seasoning and spoon over.

Serves 4

Vegetable dishes and salads

Vegetables and salads do not always get the attention and credit they deserve. They not only add colour and texture to the meal but also provide valuable nutrients to the diet. With this book as your guide, you can create some interesting combinations of vegetable and salad ideas, such as new potatoes with cucumber.

There are also many unusual salads that will make a refreshing accompaniment to any meal.

Braised celery with walnuts

METRIC/IMPERIAL/AMERICAN
1 head celery, trimmed and washed
salt and freshly ground pepper
1 medium onion, finely chopped
50 g/2 oz/¼ cup butter
50 g/2 oz/½ cup broken shelled walnuts
coarsely grated rind of 1 lemon

Cut the celery into 4-cm/1½-inch slanting sticks. Blanch in boiling salted water for 5 minutes. Sauté the onion in 25 g/1 oz/2 tablespoons butter then add the celery and sauté gently for 5–10 minutes until tender but still crisp. Meanwhile, fry the walnuts in the remaining butter for 1–2 minutes until crisp. Stir in the lemon rind then add to the celery and toss well. Season to taste.

Serves 4

Cauliflower amandine

METRIC/IMPERIAL/AMERICAN
1 medium cauliflower
salt and freshly ground pepper
75 g/3 oz/6 tablespoons butter
100 g/4 oz/1 cup whole almonds, blanched and shredded
chopped parsley to garnish

Break the cauliflower into florets then trim, wash and cook in boiling salted water for 10–15 minutes until just cooked but still crisp. Drain. Melt the butter and sauté the almonds until golden brown. Toss gently with the cauliflower and season to taste. Turn into a serving dish and sprinkle with parsley.

Serves 4

Spinach italienne

METRIC/IMPERIAL/AMERICAN
1 kg/2 lb/2 lb fresh leaf spinach, thoroughly washed and shredded
2 tablespoons/2 tablespoons/3 tablespoons oil
75 g/3 oz/6 tablespoons butter
1 clove garlic, roughly chopped
100 g/4 oz/$\frac{1}{4}$ lb back bacon, cut into thin strips
100 g/4 oz/$\frac{1}{4}$ lb Italian salami, cut into thin strips
salt and freshly ground pepper
pinch nutmeg
lemon juice

Blanch the spinach in boiling salted water for 3–5 minutes until tender but not too soft. Drain thoroughly. Heat the oil in a frying pan. Add 50 g/2 oz/$\frac{1}{4}$ cup of the butter and sauté the garlic until brown. Remove and discard. Add the bacon and salami and sauté until crisp. Add the drained spinach and remaining butter. Reheat thoroughly and season to taste, adding nutmeg to bring out the flavour of the spinach and a little lemon juice. Turn into a serving dish.

Serves 4

Fantail potatoes

METRIC/IMPERIAL/AMERICAN
6 medium potatoes, peeled and shaped into even-sized
   ovals
1 slice lemon
50 g/2 oz/¼ cup butter
1 onion, finely chopped
salt and freshly ground pepper
25 g/1 oz/¼ cup Parmesan cheese, grated
25 g/1 oz/¼ cup Cheddar cheese, grated
parsley sprig to garnish

Cut each potato into thin vertical slices but leaving a hinge at
the base. Soak in cold water with a slice of lemon added, until all
are completed. Melt the butter in a pan and fry the onion until
soft. Drain the potatoes and arrange cut side upwards in an
ovenproof dish. Spoon the onion and butter over and season.
Cook at the top of a moderately hot oven (190°C, 375°F, Gas
Mark 5) for 30 minutes, basting occasionally. Mix the cheeses
and sprinkle over the potatoes. Continue cooking for a further
20–30 minutes until crisp and golden brown.

Serves 6

Minty new potatoes with cucumber

METRIC/IMPERIAL/AMERICAN
450 g/1 lb/1 lb small new potatoes, washed and scraped
few mint stems
salt and pepper
½ large cucumber, peeled
50 g/2 oz/¼ cup butter
2 teaspoons chopped fresh mint
150 ml/¼ pint/⅔ cup single cream (optional)

Cook the potatoes with mint stems in boiling salted water for
10–15 minutes until just tender. Quarter the cucumber
lengthwise and cut across into cubes. Melt the butter in a pan
and sauté the cucumber for 5 minutes. Add the drained cooked
potatoes and chopped mint. Season to taste and toss thoroughly. Add the cream, if used, and heat to just below boiling. Turn
into a serving dish.

Serves 4–6

Chinese salad

METRIC/IMPERIAL/AMERICAN
½ cucumber, peeled
225 g/8 oz/4 cups beansprouts, washed and drained
2 red peppers, halved, deseeded and finely sliced
1 (198-g/7-oz/8-oz) can sweetcorn, drained
2 teaspoons chopped parsley
LEMON DRESSING:
2 tablespoons/2 tablespoons/3 tablespoons lemon juice
4 tablespoons/4 tablespoons/⅓ cup olive oil
2 tablespoons/2 tablespoons/3 tablespoons soy sauce
2 tablespoons/2 tablespoons/3 tablespoons single cream
salt and freshly ground pepper
sugar to taste

chopped parsley to garnish

Wipe the cucumber and cut into matchsticks. Mix with the beansprouts, peppers, sweetcorn and parsley. Put all the dressing ingredients into a screw-topped jar and shake well with seasoning and sugar to taste. Add the dressing to the salad and toss well. Serve piled into individual bowls with a little extra parsley sprinkled over. The rind from the lemon may be grated and sprinkled on top, if liked.
Note: Suitable to serve with cold meats and any sweet and sour dishes.

Serves 4–6

Fruit slaw

METRIC/IMPERIAL/AMERICAN
½ medium white cabbage, trimmed, halved and cored
3 tablespoons/3 tablespoons/¼ cup oil
salt and freshly ground pepper
2 Cox's apples, quartered and cored
juice of 1 lemon
225 g/8 oz/½ lb mixed black and white grapes, halved and seeded
½ cucumber, peeled and cut into matchsticks
½ endive, thoroughly washed and drained (optional)
DRESSING:
150 ml/¼ pint/⅔ cup soured cream
2 tablespoons/2 tablespoons/3 tablespoons lemon juice
1 tablespoon castor sugar
salt and pepper
1 tablespoon chopped parsley

Slice the cabbage finely on a mandoline slicer or with a sharp knife. Mix with the oil and seasoning and leave in the refrigerator for 2 hours to soften.

Slice the apples thinly and toss in lemon juice. Add the grapes and cucumber. Mix the dressing ingredients together and add to the salad together with the cabbage. Toss thoroughly. Tear the endive into pieces, if used, and mix into the salad. Spoon the fruit slaw into a salad bowl and serve.

Serves 6

Hot and cold sweets

Care must be taken when selecting a sweet, bearing in mind what has been served previously.

Hot sweets must be timed very carefully, so they are ready when you are! If you have the courage of your convictions, the Grand Marnier soufflé is a must. It will really impress your guests.

The cold sweets have the advantage that they can be made in advance. The summer fruits come into their own in this section. A favourite is the old-fashioned Summer gâteau, sometimes known as a Summer pudding. If you have a freezer it is a good idea to freeze fruit when there is an abundance so that you can enjoy fruits throughout the year.

Grand Marnier soufflé

METRIC/IMPERIAL/AMERICAN
icing sugar or castor sugar
1 packet sponge finger biscuits or sponge cake
6 tablespoons/6 tablespoons/½ cup Grand Marnier
150 ml/¼ pint/⅔ cup milk
75 g/3 oz/6 tablespoons castor sugar
finely grated rind of ½ lemon
thinly pared rind of 1 orange
25 g/1 oz/2 tablespoons butter
25 g/1 oz/¼ cup plain flour
3 eggs, separated

Grease a soufflé dish and dust with the sugar. Line it with the sponge fingers soaked in one-third of the liqueur. Bring the milk, sugar, lemon and orange rinds to the boil over gentle heat. Set aside for 10 minutes. Melt the butter in a large pan. Add the flour and cook for 1 minute before adding the strained milk. Bring slowly to the boil, beating continuously until smooth. Leave to cool, then beat in the egg yolks, one at a time. Add the remaining liqueur.

Whisk the egg whites until stiff but not dry. Stir 1 tablespoon into the soufflé mixture and cut and fold in the rest. Turn into the soufflé dish and smooth the top. Bake in a moderate oven (180°C, 350°F, Gas Mark 4) for 40–45 minutes. Carefully open the door and draw the oven shelf forward. Dust the top of the soufflé with icing sugar then continue cooking for a few minutes to colour. Serve at once.

Serves 4–6

Summer gâteau

METRIC/IMPERIAL/AMERICAN

3 eggs
95 g/3¾ oz/bare ½ cup castor sugar
grated rind of ½ lemon
75 g/3 oz/¾ cup plain flour, sifted with ½ teaspoon ground
    cinnamon and a pinch of salt
1–1.25 kg/2–2½ lb/2–2½ lb mixed soft fruits as available –
    redcurrants, blackcurrants, raspberries, loganberries,
    strawberries (sliced), blackberries
soft brown sugar
50 g/2 oz/½ cup split almonds, toasted
300 ml/½ pint/1¼ cups double cream, whipped
sugar to taste

Whisk the eggs, sugar and lemon rind in a bowl over hot water
until thick. Remove from the heat and whisk until cold. Fold in
the sifted flour and spread the mixture evenly into a Swiss roll
tin lined with greased greaseproof paper. Bake in a moderate
oven (180°C, 350°F, Gas Mark 4) for 15–20 minutes until
cooked. Leave to cool. Turn out and cut the sponge to line a
1.25-litre/2-pint/2½-pint basin, reserving enough for a lid.

Reserve some whole fruit for decoration then mix the
remaining fruits for filling with soft brown sugar to taste. Add
the almonds and pack into the basin right to the top. Press
down well and cover with the sponge lid. Weight down and
chill for 24 hours. Turn out. Sweeten cream. Pipe rosettes over
the sponge. Decorate with reserved fruit.

Serves 6

Stuffed pears with Cointreau and orange sauce

METRIC/IMPERIAL/AMERICAN

200 g/7 oz/scant 1 cup sugar
450 ml/¾ pint/2 cups water
thinly pared rind of 2 oranges, shredded and blanched
juice of 2 oranges
6 William pears
1–2 tablespoons Cointreau
FILLING:
75 g/3 oz/¾ cup ground almonds
50 g/2 oz/½ cup icing sugar
25 g/1 oz/2 tablespoons butter, softened
grated rind and juice of 1 lemon and 1 orange

Bring the sugar, water and orange shreds to the boil and cook
for 5 minutes until a syrup forms. Add orange juice.

Mix together the almonds, sugar, butter and lemon and
orange rinds. Bind with a little orange juice if necessary. Peel
the pears, leaving them whole, then remove core from the base.
Dip in lemon juice and fill with the almond mixture. Stand in an
ovenproof dish and pour the syrup over with any remaining
orange and lemon juice. Cover and bake in a moderate oven
(180°C, 350°F, Gas Mark 4) for 20–25 minutes until tender.
Baste with syrup during cooking. Remove the pears to a
serving dish and keep warm. Boil the syrup until reduced. Add
liqueur and spoon over pears.

Serves 6

Apricot and almond strudel

METRIC/IMPERIAL/AMERICAN
1 packet strudel pastry (2 sheets)
melted butter
450 g/1 lb/1 lb fresh apricots, stoned and sliced
100 g/4 oz/1 cup ground almonds
25 g/1 oz/¼ cup flaked almonds
grated rind of 1 lemon
75 g/3 oz/6 tablespoons castor sugar

Spread one sheet of pastry on a tea towel and brush with melted butter. Place the second sheet on top and brush again. Mix the apricots, almonds, lemon rind and sugar together and spoon over the pastry. Roll up with the help of the tea towel, folding in the ends. Cover a baking sheet with non-stick paper and lift on the strudel, forming into a horseshoe shape. Bake in a moderately hot oven (200°C, 400°F, Gas Mark 6) for 30 minutes until crisp and golden brown. Slide on to a serving dish and dust with icing sugar. Serve hot or cold with cremet.

To make cremet, pour 300 ml/½ pint/1¼ cups milk into a pan, reserving about 2 tablespoons. Bring gently to the boil. Meanwhile, mix 2 heaped teaspoons custard powder with sugar to taste and the reserved milk. Remove the boiled milk from the heat, stir in the custard and return to the heat to thicken, stirring. Leave to cool. Add 150 ml/5 fl oz/⅔ cup natural yogurt and chill before serving.

Serves 4–6

Normandy apple pie

METRIC/IMPERIAL/AMERICAN
2 egg yolks
100 g/4 oz/½ cup castor sugar
40 g/1½ oz/3 tablespoons butter
50 g/2 oz/¼ cup lard
2 tablespoons/2 tablespoons/3 tablespoons water
225 g/8 oz/2 cups plain flour, sifted
¾ teaspoon powdered cinnamon
50 g/2 oz/½ cup walnuts, finely ground
0.5–0.75 kg/1–1½ lb/1–1½ lb Cox's apples, peeled, cored
    and quartered
150 ml/¼ pint/⅔ cup double cream, lightly whipped
Calvados or brandy (optional)

Cream together the egg yolks, sugar, butter, lard and water. Add the flour, cinnamon and walnuts gradually and work together to a paste. Knead until smooth. Wrap and chill in the refrigerator for at least 30 minutes. Roll out two-thirds of the pastry and use to line a 20-cm/8-inch fluted flan ring. Arrange the prepared apples, cut side down, in the flan case. Roll out the remaining pastry to make a lid. Dampen the edges, position and press together. Cut a 7.5-cm/3-inch circle out of the centre of the lid. Brush the pastry with cold water and dust with castor sugar. Bake in a moderate oven (180°C, 350°F, Gas Mark 4) for 35–40 minutes until the pastry is crisp and cooked. Just before serving pipe the whipped cream, flavoured with liqueur and sugar to taste, around the centre.

Serves 6

Raspberry dacquoise

METRIC/IMPERIAL/AMERICAN
175 g/6 oz/1¼ cups whole almonds
7 egg whites
400 g/14 oz/1¾ cups castor sugar
large pinch cream of tartar
0.75 kg/1½ lb/1½ lb raspberries, fresh or frozen
600 ml/1 pint/2½ cups double cream
castor sugar to taste
icing sugar

Blanch the almonds and grind in a mouli grater. Whisk egg whites until stiff. Add 1 tablespoon of measured sugar and whisk for a further 2–3 minutes. Fold in the rest of the sugar with the almonds and cream of tartar. Pipe the mixture into three separate circles on to baking sheets lined with non-stick paper, using a plain 1-cm/½-inch nozzle. Bake in a very cool oven (110°C, 225°F, Gas Mark ¼) for 1–1½ hours until dry. Leave to cool.

Meanwhile, reserve some raspberries for decoration and whip the cream with sugar to taste. Place a meringue circle on a suitable serving dish. Spread one-third of the cream over the base and sprinkle with a few raspberries. Repeat the layers and press the remaining meringue on top. Dust with icing sugar, pipe rosettes of cream around the edge and decorate with the remaining whole raspberries.
Note: This gâteau must not be assembled more than 1–1½ hours before serving or it will become too soft.

Serves 6

Chocolate and orange roulade

METRIC/IMPERIAL/AMERICAN
5 eggs, separated
175 g/6 oz/¾ cup castor sugar
175 g/6 oz/6 squares plain chocolate, melted to a cream
    with 2 tablespoons/2 tablespoons/3 tablespoons water
6 large oranges
450 ml/¾ pint/2 cups double cream

Whisk the egg whites until stiff. In a separate bowl, whisk the egg yolks and sugar until thick and very pale in colour. Add the melted chocolate then fold in the whisked egg whites. Spread evenly in a Swiss roll tin lined with non-stick paper. Bake in a moderate oven (180°C, 350°F, Gas Mark 4) for 20–25 minutes until cooked. Cover with a layer of wet kitchen paper. Wrap in cling film and leave overnight. Carefully turn out on to greaseproof paper well dusted with icing sugar and peel off non-stick paper.

For the filling, finely grate the rind of 1 orange. Cut away peel and pith from all the oranges with a sharp knife and remove the segments over a bowl to catch the juice. Whip the cream with the orange rind and any juice until thick. Add sugar to taste. Reserving some cream for decoration, spread the remainder over the sponge. Keep some orange segments for decoration and scatter the rest along the middle of the sponge. Roll up and turn on to a flat serving dish. Dust with icing sugar. Pipe stars of cream on top, decorate with orange segments and chill.

Serves 6

Galette noisette Normande

METRIC/IMPERIAL/AMERICAN
75 g/3 oz/6 tablespoons butter
65 g/2½ oz/5 tablespoons castor sugar
125 g/4½ oz/1 cup plus 2 tablespoons plain flour, sifted
   with a pinch of salt
75 g/3 oz/⅔ cup hazel nuts, toasted and ground
0.75 kg/1½ lb/1½ lb Cox's apples, peeled and cored
3 cloves
grated rind and juice of 1 lemon
1 tablespoon smooth apricot jam
50 g/2 oz/⅓ cup sultanas or raisins
300 ml/½ pint/1¼ cups double cream
icing sugar and toasted hazel nuts to decorate

Beat together butter and sugar. Add flour and nuts and knead
until smooth. Wrap and chill for at least 30 minutes.
   Slice the apples and cook with the cloves, lemon rind, juice
and jam over low heat until soft. Remove the cloves. Add the
sultanas and cook for 5 minutes longer. Leave to cool.
   Divide the pastry into three. Roll into 20-cm/8-inch circles
on non-stick paper. Place on baking sheets. Bake in a moderate
oven (180°C, 350°F, Gas Mark 4) for 15–20 minutes. While still
warm cut one round into six portions. Whip the cream and
reserve some for decoration. Spread half of the remainder on
one pastry round and cover with half the apple mixture. Repeat
the layers and place cut portions on top. Dust with icing sugar.
Pipe a rosette of cream on to each portion and decorate.

Serves 6

Gâteau Paris Brest

METRIC/IMPERIAL/AMERICAN
150 ml/¼ pint/⅔ cup water
50 g/2 oz/¼ cup butter
65 g/2½ oz/½ cup plus 2 tablespoons plain flour, sifted
   twice with a pinch of salt
2 eggs, lightly whisked
25 g/1 oz/¼ cup flaked almonds
little castor sugar
2 egg whites, stiffly whisked
450 ml/¾ pint/2 cups double cream, whipped
450 g/1 lb/1 lb strawberries, tossed in sugar

Prepare the choux paste by heating the water and butter slowly
until the butter has melted. Bring to the boil, draw aside and
immediately add all the flour. Beat until the mixture becomes
smooth and leaves the sides of the pan. Leave to cool before
beating in the eggs gradually and thoroughly until smooth and
shiny. Using a plain 2.5-cm/1-inch nozzle, pipe on to a greased
baking sheet in a 23-cm/9-inch ring. Sprinkle with almonds and
dust with sugar. Bake in a moderately hot oven (200°C, 400°F,
Gas Mark 6) for 30 minutes. Lower to 180°C, 350°F, Gas Mark
4 and continue until crisp and golden. Remove and cool.
   Split the choux ring in half. Fold the egg whites into the
cream and place in a piping bag. Use two-thirds to fill the base
ring then cover with the strawberries and pipe the rest of the
cream on top. Lightly press the almond-covered ring on top,
dust with icing sugar and serve.

Serves 6

Vacherin Chantilly glacé

METRIC/IMPERIAL/AMERICAN
100 g/4 oz/½ cup granulated sugar
pared rind and juice of 1 medium lemon
225 g/8 oz/½ lb strawberries, fresh or frozen
50 g/2 oz/½ cup icing sugar
juice of 1 large orange
6 egg whites
275 g/10 oz/1¼ cups castor sugar
whipped cream and fresh strawberries to decorate

For the sorbet: simmer sugar, 300 ml/½ pint/1¼ cups water and lemon rind for 5 minutes. Cool and strain. Liquidise the strawberries with the icing sugar, sieve and add the orange and lemon juices and sugar syrup. Freeze in a shallow container. When half-frozen, beat well. Whisk one egg white until stiff and fold in. Freeze until hard.

For the meringue case, whisk the remaining egg whites until stiff. Add 50 g/2 oz/¼ cup of the measured sugar and whisk hard for 3½ minutes. Fold in the remaining sugar. Reserve a quarter of the meringue in the refrigerator and, using a large star nozzle, pipe about two-thirds of the remainder into a 20-cm/8-inch circle on a baking sheet lined with non-stick paper. Pipe the remaining one-third into a second wide border round the edge of the circle. Cook in a very cool oven (110°C, 225°F, Gas Mark ¼) until slightly coloured. Pipe the reserved meringue on top of the second border while the case is still hot. Return to the oven to dry. When cool, pile sorbet into meringue case; decorate.

Serves 6

Bavaroise française

METRIC/IMPERIAL/AMERICAN
pared rind and juice of 1 lemon
300 ml/½ pint/1¼ cups milk
4 egg yolks
50 g/2 oz/¼ cup castor sugar
15 g/½-oz packet/1 envelope powdered gelatine soaked in
    3 tablespoons/3 tablespoons/¼ cup cold water
300 ml/½ pint/1¼ cups double cream, whipped
2 egg whites, whisked
450 g/1 lb/1 lb fresh black cherries
3 tablespoons/3 tablespoons/¼ cup redcurrant jelly

Add the lemon rind to the milk and bring to the boil slowly over a gentle heat. Infuse for 10 minutes. Beat the egg yolks and sugar together until thick. Pour on the milk and return to the rinsed pan. Thicken the custard over a very gentle heat, stirring continuously. Add the soaked gelatine, remove from the heat and stir until the gelatine is dissolved. Strain into a bowl and cool. When the mixture begins to thicken, fold in two-thirds of the cream and then the egg whites and pour into a wetted savarin mould. Chill until set.

Stone the cherries, reserving any juice. Melt the redcurrant jelly with the lemon juice in a pan and add any cherry juice. Cool then add the cherries.

Turn out the bavaroise ring on to a serving dish. Pile some of the prepared cherries in the centre. Decorate with rosettes of the reserved cream and the remaining cherries around the edge.

Serves 6

Charlotte mexicaine

METRIC/IMPERIAL/AMERICAN
225 g/8 oz/8 squares plain chocolate, coarsely grated
450 ml/¾ pint/2 cups strong coffee
3 eggs, separated
50 g/2 oz/¼ cup castor sugar
15 g/½-oz packet/1 envelope powdered gelatine, soaked in
    3 tablespoons/3 tablespoons/¼ cup cold water
300 ml/½ pint/1¼ cups double cream, lightly whipped
300 ml/½ pint/1¼ cups double cream, thickly whipped
langue de chat biscuits
coarsely grated chocolate

Dissolve the chocolate in the coffee. Cream the egg yolks and sugar until thick and pale in colour. Add the chocolate mixture. Return to the rinsed pan and thicken over a gentle heat, without boiling, stirring continuously. Remove the pan from the heat, add the soaked gelatine to the custard and stir until dissolved. Strain into a bowl and cool. Add the lightly whipped cream. Whisk the egg whites until stiff and fold into the mixture. When on the point of setting, pour into a lightly oiled straight-sided 18-cm/7-inch mould or cake tin with a removable base. Leave in the refrigerator to set.

    To serve, turn out and spread a thin layer of whipped cream round the sides. Press the biscuits around. Put the remaining cream into a piping bag and pipe small stars down each biscuit join. Decorate the top with rosettes of thickly whipped cream and grated chocolate.

Serves 6

Strawberry mille feuille

METRIC/IMPERIAL/AMERICAN
350 g/12 oz/¾ lb puff pastry
600 ml/1 pint/2½ cups double cream
sugar to taste
3 tablespoons/3 tablespoons/¼ cup orange liqueur
1 kg/2 lb/2 lb medium strawberries, hulled
icing sugar

Divide the pastry into three. Roll each piece into a strip approximately 13 x 30 cm/5 x 12 inches. Trim the edges evenly with a sharp knife. Place each strip on a wet baking sheet. Prick all over and bake in a hot oven (220°C, 425°F, Gas Mark 7) for 10–15 minutes until golden brown and well risen. Leave to cool on a wire rack.

    Whisk the cream and flavour with sugar and liqueur. Place one pastry sheet on a flat serving dish. Spread with some of the cream and cover with half the prepared strawberries. Repeat the layers and cover with the remaining pastry. Press down lightly. Dredge with sifted icing sugar.

Serves 6

Pineapple soufflé en surprise

METRIC/IMPERIAL/AMERICAN
4 eggs, separated
100 g/4 oz/½ cup castor sugar
150 ml/¼ pint/⅔ cup canned pineapple juice
15 g/½-oz packet/1 envelope powdered gelatine
2 tablespoons/2 tablespoons/3 tablespoons cold water
juice of 1 large lemon
150 ml/¼ pint/⅔ cup double cream, whipped
1 medium fresh pineapple, peeled, cored and cubed
sugar to taste
Kirsch (optional)
whipped cream and angelica leaves to decorate

Surround a 15–18-cm/6–7-inch soufflé dish with double grease-proof paper and secure firmly with string. Place a small well-oiled jar in the centre.

Whisk the egg yolks, sugar and pineapple juice over hot water until thick. Remove from the heat and continue whisking until cold. Soak the gelatine in the water and dissolve over a gentle heat. Add the lemon juice and stir into the mixture. Fold in the cream then the stiffly whisked egg whites. Pour into the soufflé dish and leave to set. Meanwhile, marinate the pineapple with sugar and Kirsch.

When the soufflé is firm, remove the paper surrounding the dish then gently remove the jam jar from the centre. Fill the hole with the pineapple and decorate the top.

Serves 4–6

Caramel oranges with Cointreau

METRIC/IMPERIAL/AMERICAN
6 large seedless oranges
350 g/12 oz/1½ cups granulated sugar
300 ml/½ pint/1¼ cups water
3 tablespoons/3 tablespoons/¼ cup Cointreau
CARAMEL:
175 g/6 oz/¾ cup granulated sugar
4 tablespoons/4 tablespoons/⅓ cup water

Pare the rind thinly from 4 oranges and cut into long julienne strips. Blanch for 15 minutes. Drain and refresh. Bring the sugar and water to the boil, add the orange strips and simmer for 20 minutes. Add Cointreau and cool.

Cut away all skin and pith from the oranges. Slice each orange thinly and reshape, holding together with a cocktail stick. Strain the syrup over the oranges, reserving the orange strips. Chill thoroughly.

Meanwhile, make the caramel by dissolving the sugar in the water. Cook steadily to a rich brown colour, without stirring. Pour immediately on to a well-oiled surface or waxed paper. Leave to harden, then crush in a mortar or with a rolling pin. Sprinkle over the oranges, together with the reserved strips of rind. Serve with cream handed separately.

Serves 6

Fresh peach and almond flan

METRIC/IMPERIAL/AMERICAN
100 g/4 oz/½ cup butter
75 g/3 oz/6 tablespoons castor sugar
grated rind of ½ lemon
1 small egg
1 egg yolk
175 g/6 oz/1½ cups plain flour, sifted
75 g/3 oz/¾ cup ground almonds
3 large ripe peaches, halved
175 g/6 oz/¾ cup granulated sugar dissolved in 300 ml/
    ½ pint/1¼ cups water
175 g/6 oz/¾ cup cream cheese
grated rind of 1 small lemon
2 tablespoons/2 tablespoons/3 tablespoons single cream
25 g/1 oz/2 tablespoons castor sugar
25 g/1 oz/¼ cup ground almonds
whole blanched almonds and angelica to decorate

For the almond pastry, blend the butter, sugar, lemon rind and
eggs until well mixed. Work in the flour and almonds and knead
to a smooth paste. Wrap and chill for at least 1 hour. Line a flan
ring with the pastry. Bake blind in a moderate oven (180°C,
350°F, Gas Mark 4) for 30 minutes. Leave to cool.

Poach the peaches in the sugar syrup, then remove the skins.
Reduce the syrup to a glazing consistency. Cool.

Beat the cream cheese with the lemon rind, cream, sugar and
almonds. Spread over the pastry base. Arrange the peach halves
on top. Brush with syrup glaze and decorate.

Serves 6

Buck's fizz sorbet

METRIC/IMPERIAL/AMERICAN
175 g/6 oz/¾ cup castor sugar
150 ml/¼ pint/⅔ cup water
4 large oranges
finely grated rind and juice of 1 lemon
900 ml/1½ pints/3¾ cups champagne, chilled
2 egg whites, stiffly whisked
2–3 tablespoons/2–3 tablespoons/3–4 tablespoons Grand
    Marnier
50 g/2 oz/2 oz ratafia biscuits
DECORATION:
150 ml/¼ pint/⅔ cup double cream, whipped
orange rind

Bring the sugar and water slowly to the boil. Boil rapidly for
6 minutes to make a syrup. Finely grate the rind of one orange
and add with the lemon rind. Set aside. Cut the remaining
oranges in half lengthwise and scoop out all the flesh. Reserve
the shells. Press the flesh through a nylon sieve into the syrup.
Add the lemon juice and cool. Stir in the champagne and freeze
for 1½–2 hours until frozen round the edges. Whip until smooth
in a mixer or blender. Fold in the egg whites and Grand Marnier
and freeze for at least 3 hours until hard.

Sit each reserved orange shell in a champagne goblet. Divide
the ratafia biscuits between the shells and sprinkle with Grand
Marnier. Keep chilled until ready to serve. Pile the sorbet into
orange shells. Pipe cream on top, decorate with orange rind.

Serves 6

Egg and cheese dishes

These recipes are particularly suitable to serve at supper parties. Eggs and cheese are two basic ingredients most likely to be kept in stock and the recipes in this section show what versatile and imaginative dishes can be prepared.

A slightly more unusual way of serving a Camembert cheese is shown in the Iced wine Camembert. The cheese is sieved and mixed with wine and butter before it is set and chilled.

Smoked salmon quiche

METRIC/IMPERIAL/AMERICAN
PASTRY:
175 g/6 oz/1½ cups plain flour
pinch salt
100 g/4 oz/½ cup butter
1 egg, beaten
FILLING:
3 eggs
300 ml/½ pint/1¼ cups single cream
100–175 g/4–6 oz/4–6 oz smoked salmon, cut into strips
pinch nutmeg
freshly ground pepper
2 teaspoons chopped parsley

To make the pastry, sift the flour and salt into a bowl, then rub in the butter until the mixture resembles breadcrumbs. Bind together with the egg, adding a few drops of cold water if necessary to give a firm dough. Knead lightly, then cover and chill for at least 30 minutes. Roll out and use to line a 20-cm/8-inch flan ring. Prick the base and bake blind in a moderate oven (180°C, 350°F, Gas Mark 4) for 10 minutes.

Beat the eggs with the cream. Add the salmon, nutmeg, pepper to taste and the parsley. Pour into the flan case and return to the oven to cook for 30–35 minutes until set. Serve hot or cold.

Note: Use cheaper ends or off-cuts of smoked salmon.

Serves 4–6

Gruyère roulade

METRIC/IMPERIAL/AMERICAN
40 g/1½ oz/3 tablespoons butter
30 g/1¼ oz/5 tablespoons plain flour
300 ml/½ pint/1¼ cups milk
25 g/1 oz/¼ cup Gruyère cheese, grated
2 tablespoons/2 tablespoons/3 tablespoons cream
350 g/12 oz/¾ lb fresh asparagus, cooked and trimmed
ROULADE:
175 g/6 oz/1½ cups Gruyère cheese, grated
50 g/2 oz/1 cup fresh white breadcrumbs
4 eggs, separated
150 ml/¼ pint/⅔ cup single cream
40 g/1½ oz/6 tablespoons Parmesan cheese, grated

Make a white sauce for the filling with the butter, flour and
milk, adding Gruyère cheese, cream and salt and pepper to
taste. Warm the asparagus through.

For the roulade, mix the cheese and breadcrumbs together,
then work in the egg yolks and cream. Season with salt and
cayenne pepper to taste. Whisk the egg whites stiffly and fold
into the mixture. Spread the mixture evenly into a Swiss roll tin
lined with non-stick paper and sprinkle with a little Parmesan
cheese. Bake in a moderately hot oven (200°C, 400°F, Gas Mark
6) for 10–15 minutes until firm. Turn out on to a sheet of
greaseproof paper sprinkled with the remaining Parmesan
cheese. Spread thickly with the sauce, lay the asparagus along
the middle and roll up.

Serves 6

Gougère de la mer

METRIC/IMPERIAL/AMERICAN
CHOUX PASTRY (SEE PAGE 119)
150 ml/¼ pint/⅔ cup water
50 g/2 oz/¼ cup butter
65 g/2½ oz/½ cup plus 2 tablespoons plain flour
2 eggs, beaten
50 g/2 oz/½ cup Gruyère or Cheddar cheese, finely diced
FILLING:
1 onion, finely sliced
50 g/2 oz/½ cup button mushrooms, sliced
25 g/1 oz/2 tablespoons butter
20 g/¾ oz/3 tablespoons plain flour
150 ml/¼ pint/⅔ cup fish stock or milk
2 tablespoons/2 tablespoons/3 tablespoons single cream
350 g/12 oz/2 cups peeled prawns
½ teaspoon each chopped fennel and parsley
25 g/1 oz/¼ cup each Parmesan and browned crumbs
slices of tomato and parsley to garnish

Make up the choux pastry and fold in the cheese. Pipe or spoon
the mixture around the sides of a well buttered shallow ovenproof dish, leaving a hollow in the centre. Sauté the onion and
mushrooms in the butter, stir in the flour. Add the stock and
bring to the boil. Off the heat, add the cream, prawns, herbs and
salt and pepper. Spoon into the centre of the dish. Dust with the
cheese and breadcrumbs mixed and bake in a moderately hot
oven (200°C, 400°F, Gas Mark 6) for 35–40 minutes. Garnish.

Serves 4–6

Iced cheese soufflés

METRIC/IMPERIAL/AMERICAN
75 g/3 oz/¾ cup fresh Parmesan cheese, grated
50 g/2 oz/½ cup Gruyère cheese, grated
½ teaspoon French mustard
salt and pepper
pinch cayenne pepper
300 ml/½ pint/1¼ cups aspic jelly
2 teaspoons tarragon vinegar
100 g/4 oz/½ cup cream cheese
300 ml/½ pint/1¼ cups double cream, whipped
2 egg whites, stiffly whisked
GARNISH:
dry grated Parmesan cheese, browned under the grill
stuffed olives

Tie a band of greaseproof paper firmly round 6 individual soufflé dishes. Mix the cheeses with the mustard and seasonings. Add the aspic jelly and vinegar and leave to get cold. Whip with an electric mixer until frothy but not set. Add the cream cheese to the whipped cream and fold into the mixture, followed by the egg whites. Spoon into the prepared dishes and level the tops. Chill in the refrigerator for several hours.

To serve: remove the papers carefully and press the browned Parmesan cheese round the sides. Garnish with slices of olive.

Serves 6

Iced wine Camembert

METRIC/IMPERIAL/AMERICAN
1 medium ripe Camembert
100–250 ml/4–8 fl oz/½–1 cup white wine
100 g/4 oz/½ cup soft butter
1 tablespoon fine fresh white breadcrumbs
salt and cayenne pepper
50 g/2 oz/½ cup Parmesan cheese, grated
paprika
white grapes, cut into small bunches, to garnish

Scrape most of the rind from the cheese. Pour the wine over the cheese, cover and leave overnight. Lift out the cheese and sieve. Beat with the butter until smooth, adding 2 tablespoons/2 tablespoons/3 tablespoons of the marinating wine and the breadcrumbs. Season well. Turn into a lightly oiled mould, smooth the top, cover and leave to chill for about 3 hours or until firm. Turn out and coat all over with the Parmesan cheese mixed with a little paprika. Set on a flat board or dish.

Cut a circle of greaseproof paper the diameter of the cheese and cut out a design. Lay on top of the cheese and sprinkle with paprika. Remove the paper, being careful not to ruin the design. Arrange the grapes with pretzels, water biscuits and cheese biscuits around the dish.

Serves 4–6

Savoury pears

METRIC/IMPERIAL/AMERICAN
2 thick slices bread with crusts removed, cut into 5-
   mm/¼-inch dice
25 g/1 oz/2 tablespoons butter
1 bunch watercress, washed and chopped
2 ripe dessert pears, peeled, cored and sliced
100 g/4 oz/¼ lb Stilton cheese, crumbled
4 tablespoons/4 tablespoons/⅓ cup double cream
freshly ground pepper
chopped parsley

Fry the diced bread in melted butter until crisp and golden brown. Place the croûtons in 4 buttered ramekin dishes. Cover with layers of cress, sliced pears and Stilton cheese. Spoon the cream over, then sprinkle with pepper and parsley. Cover with foil and bake in a moderate oven (180°C, 350°F, Gas Mark 4) for 10–12 minutes. Remove the foil and brown for a few minutes more. Serve at once, garnished with chopped parsley.

Serves 4

Cheese straw bundles

METRIC/IMPERIAL/AMERICAN
175 g/6 oz/1½ cups plain flour
salt and cayenne pepper
100 g/4 oz/½ cup butter
100 g/4 oz/1 cup dry Cheddar cheese, finely grated

Sift the flour with the seasonings into a bowl and rub in the butter until the texture of breadcrumbs. Add the cheese, work the mixture together and knead until smooth. Wrap and chill for 30 minutes.

   Roll out on a floured surface into an oblong 5 mm/¼ inch thick. Cut out a few circles 4 cm/1½ inches in diameter with a plain cutter, then using a cutter two sizes smaller, cut out the centres to form rings. Lift carefully on to a baking sheet. Cut the remaining pastry into 13–15-cm/5–6-inch long narrow strips. Lift carefully on to the baking sheet. Cook in a moderately hot oven (190°C, 375°F, Gas Mark 5) for 10–15 minutes until just lightly golden brown. Lift carefully on to a wire cooling rack. When cold, gather the sticks into small bundles and place in each ring. Arrange on a serving dish and serve with peanuts, olives, etc., as cocktail savouries.

Serves 4–6

Fork supper dishes

The busy hostess is always on the look-out for new ideas, and there are plenty to choose from in this section. It is important to incorporate dishes which not only look attractive but also ones that offer a choice of flavours and are easy to eat with a fork.

Fork suppers tend to be for larger gatherings of people, so a good selection of food is important. Offer a couple of cold starters and a choice of hot and cold main dishes. Salads are always popular so serve a variety, making full use of colour and texture.

Salade méditerranée

METRIC/IMPERIAL/AMERICAN
1 large cucumber
4 tomatoes, skinned, deseeded and diced
350 g/12 oz/¾ lb French beans, cooked and cut into
   2.5-cm/1-inch/1-inch pieces
225 g/8 oz/½ lb onions, quartered, sliced and blanched
225 g/8 oz/½ lb green or red peppers, diced
2 (198-g/7-oz/7-oz) cans tuna, drained
French dressing
1 tablespoon chopped fresh herbs – parsley, fennel, basil
1 (56-g/2-oz/2-oz) can anchovy fillets, halved lengthwise
100 g/4 oz/⅔ cup black olives, halved and stoned
oil to glaze

Cut a small piece off the cucumber. Peel the remaining cucumber and keep half of this for garnish. Dice the cucumber and mix with the tomatoes, beans, onions, peppers and tuna. Moisten with French dressing and add the herbs. Leave to marinate for 1 hour.

Drain off any excess liquid then spoon on to a flat serving dish and mould to the shape of a fish. Slice the reserved peeled cucumber thinly and surround the salad with slices. Arrange anchovy halves in a lattice pattern as scales. Peel the reserved end piece of cucumber, slice in half and arrange as a tail. Place an olive in the centre of each lattice. Place a halved stuffed olive for an eye, if liked. Brush with a little oil. Serve chilled with hot garlic bread.

Serves 4–6

Festival chicken

METRIC/IMPERIAL/AMERICAN
1 lemon
50 g/2 oz/¼ cup butter
1 (1.75-kg/4-lb/4-lb) roasting chicken, prepared
100 ml/4 fl oz/½ cup white wine
1 small onion, chopped
1 tablespoon oil
1 tablespoon curry powder
150 ml/¼ pint/⅔ cup chicken stock
1–2 tablespoons mango chutney
2 tablespoons/2 tablespoons/3 tablespoons apricot jam
300 ml/½ pint/1¼ cups double cream
150 ml/¼ pint/⅔ cup thick mayonnaise
150 ml/¼ pint/⅔ cup soured cream
chopped red pepper, grapes and cress to garnish

Squeeze the lemon and place the shells with a knob of butter inside the chicken. Place in a roasting tin, spread the remaining butter over the bird and pour some juice and the wine over. Roast in a moderately hot oven (200°C, 400°F, Gas Mark 6) for 25 minutes per 0.5 kg/1 lb. Baste well. Cool, strain off juices.

Soften the onion in the oil. Add the curry powder and cook for 3–4 minutes. Stir in the chicken juices, stock, chutney and jam. Bring to the boil, simmer for 10 minutes, then liquidise or sieve and cool. Whip the cream, add the mayonnaise, soured cream and curry sauce. Season. Add chopped chicken flesh to the sauce. Pile into a dish lined with lettuce and chill. Garnish.

Serves 6

Vitello tonnato

METRIC/IMPERIAL/AMERICAN
1 (56-g/2-oz/2-oz) can anchovy fillets
2 cloves garlic, crushed
1.25 kg/2½ lb/2½ lb boned breast of veal, rolled
100 ml/4 fl oz/½ cup vermouth
freshly ground pepper
1 (198-g/7-oz/7-oz) can tuna, drained
1 large egg yolk
150 ml/¼ pint/⅔ cup oil
300 ml/½ pint/1¼ cups double cream, whipped
lemon juice
1 tablespoon drained capers
stoned black olives and capers to garnish

Mash 6 anchovy fillets and garlic, spread over the veal. Place on foil in a tin, add vermouth and pepper, and package in the foil. Roast in a moderately hot oven (200°C, 400°F, Gas Mark 6) for 1½ hours. Cool.

Mash the tuna with the remaining anchovy fillets to a smooth paste. Add the egg yolk and beat in the oil, a few drops at a time, with an electric mixer. Add cream and enough strained veal liquid to give a coating consistency. Add lemon juice to taste.

Slice the meat and cut into cubes. Mix with the sauce and place in a dish. Sprinkle with capers. Cover and chill in the refrigerator at least overnight. Garnish before serving.

Serves 6

Seafood pancakes

METRIC/IMPERIAL/AMERICAN
300 ml/½ pint/1¼ cups pancake batter mixture
4 scallops
150 ml/¼ pint/⅔ cup each water and white wine
juice of 1 lemon
225 g/8 oz/1⅓ cups peeled prawns
3 hard-boiled eggs, coarsely chopped
75 g/3 oz/6 tablespoons butter
1 large onion, chopped
175 g/6 oz/1½ cups button mushrooms, quartered
40 g/1½ oz/6 tablespoons plain flour
150 ml/¼ pint/⅔ cup each single and double cream
chopped parsley
25 g/1 oz/¼ cup Parmesan cheese, grated

Make 8–10 thin pancakes and leave to cool; prepare filling.
Poach the scallops in the water, wine and lemon juice for 5 minutes. Strain and reserve the liquid. Quarter the scallops and mix with the prawns and eggs. Melt the butter and fry the onion and mushrooms until soft. Add the flour and cook for 1 minute then stir in the reserved fish stock and bring to the boil, stirring. Add the single cream, cook gently for 5 minutes then stir in 1 tablespoon parsley and season. Place a spoonful of the mixture on each pancake, roll up and arrange in a greased ovenproof dish. Heat the double cream and spoon over. Sprinkle with the cheese and place in the top of a moderately hot oven (200°C, 400°F, Gas Mark 6) for 10 minutes. Garnish with parsley.

Serves 4

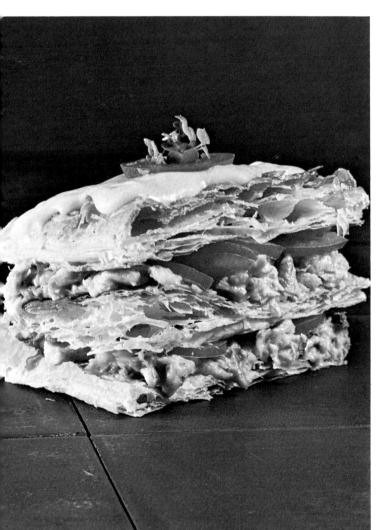

Chicken mille feuille

METRIC/IMPERIAL/AMERICAN
350 g/12 oz/¾ lb puff pastry
BÉCHAMEL SAUCE:
50 g/2 oz/¼ cup butter
50 g/2 oz/½ cup plain flour
450 ml/¾ pint/2 cups flavoured milk
150 ml/¼ pint/⅔ cup single cream
225 g/8 oz/2 cups button mushrooms, sliced
juice of 1 lemon
1 teaspoon dried tarragon
350 g/12 oz/1½ cups cooked chicken, diced
25 g/1 oz/¼ cup Cheddar cheese, grated
tomato slices and cress to garnish

Roll out the pastry thinly and cut into three strips 10 x 30 cm/4 x 12 inches. Lift on to wetted baking sheets, prick and bake in a hot oven (220°C, 425°F, Gas Mark 7) for 15 minutes. Cool.
Make up the béchamel sauce (see page 12) and keep 150 ml/¼ pint/⅔ cup aside. Sauté the mushrooms quickly in the lemon juice with the tarragon. Mix with the chicken and the remaining sauce. Season.
·Place one pastry sheet on an ovenproof dish and spread with half the chicken mixture. Cover with another layer of pastry and chicken mixture and lay the remaining pastry on top. Press down level with a baking sheet. Spoon over the reserved sauce. Sprinkle with the cheese and place in the top of a moderately hot oven (200°C, 400°F, Gas Mark 6) for 10–15 minutes.

Serves 4–6

Quick Dishes

There are times when an appetising meal has to be produced quickly or at short notice. The recipes here have been created to help you do just that.

The ingredients used in many of the recipes are ones which can always be at hand in the store cupboard; rice, pasta, flavourings, herbs, seasonings, sauces and spices, canned fruit, vegetables, soups, fish and meat. Prepared frozen foods can also form the basis of a quick meal.

There are also recipes using the cuts of meat which do not require lengthy cooking, and with these basic ideas

and ingredients you will find it easy to prepare and serve a meal when time is short.

Even when time is at a premium, do not neglect the appearance of the finished dish – a simple garnish of fresh parsley can make all the difference.

Soups and starters

This section gives a selection of exciting first course recipes which should be suitable to serve for a family meal or when entertaining. None of the recipes are lengthy to prepare or cook, yet they will impress your family and guests. By looking at the pictures alongside the recipes you will be able to see how to garnish and present these dishes.

Tomato and corn soup with garlic toast

METRIC/IMPERIAL/AMERICAN
75 g/3 oz/$\frac{3}{4}$ cup onion, chopped
2 teaspoons corn oil
1 (298-g/10$\frac{1}{2}$-oz/10$\frac{1}{2}$-oz) can condensed tomato soup
300 ml/$\frac{1}{2}$ pint/1$\frac{1}{4}$ cups milk
1 tablespoon tomato purée
1 (198-g/7-oz/7-oz) can sweetcorn with peppers
GARLIC TOAST
50 g/2 oz/$\frac{1}{4}$ cup butter
1 large clove garlic, crushed
salt and pepper
4 slices medium sliced bread

Place the onion and oil in a pan and cook very slowly for 5 minutes until soft without browning. Stir in the soup, milk and tomato purée and mix until the ingredients are thoroughly blended. Add the sweetcorn with the liquor and cook gently, uncovered, for 10–15 minutes.

Meanwhile, make the garlic toast by blending the butter, garlic and seasoning together. Spread half the mixture on one side of each piece of bread, and toast under the grill. Spread the remaining butter mixture on the uncooked side and toast. Remove the crusts and cut in half before serving with the soup.

Serves 4

132

Blue cheese and cauliflower soup

METRIC/IMPERIAL/AMERICAN
1 medium cauliflower
225 g/8 oz/2 cups onion, chopped
1 litre/1¾ pints/4¼ cups chicken stock
pepper
40 g/1½ oz/3 tablespoons unsalted butter
25 g/1 oz/¼ cup plain flour
50 g/2 oz/½ cup Danish blue cheese, crumbled
GARNISH:
chopped parsley
fried croûtons

Prepare the cauliflower and break into sprigs. Place in a large pan with the onion, stock and pepper. Cover and cook slowly for 10–15 minutes until the vegetables are tender. Cool slightly, then sieve or liquidise until smooth.

Melt the butter in a saucepan, stir in the flour and cook gently for a few seconds. Gradually stir in the cauliflower purée, bring to the boil and cook for about 3 minutes.

Add the cheese, a little at a time, until completely dissolved. Garnish each bowl of soup with chopped parsley and serve with fried croûtons.

Serves 6

Sweetcorn and cucumber salad

METRIC/IMPERIAL/AMERICAN
½ cucumber, peeled
1 teaspoon salt
1 (198-g/7-oz/7-oz) can sweetcorn
2 teaspoons grated onion
150 ml/¼ pint/⅔ cup soured cream
pepper
mint sprigs to garnish

Coarsely grate the cucumber, put on a plate and sprinkle with salt; leave to stand for at least 30 minutes. Drain off excess water from the cucumber using kitchen paper.

Mix the drained corn and the cucumber together in a bowl with the grated onion. Pour off any excess liquid from the soured cream, then stir into the cucumber mixture with some freshly ground pepper.

Place in serving dishes and garnish with the mint.

Serves 4

Florida cocktail

METRIC/IMPERIAL/AMERICAN
2 large oranges
1 grapefruit
4 tomatoes
salt and pepper
pinch mustard powder
pinch castor sugar
4 tablespoons/4 tablespoons/$\frac{1}{3}$ cup oil
2 tablespoons/2 tablespoons/3 tablespoons white wine
   vinegar
mint sprigs to garnish

Using a sharp knife, remove the rind and pith from the oranges and grapefruit and cut out the segments from in between the membrane. Place in a bowl with the skinned, quartered and deseeded tomatoes.

Place the seasonings in a bowl, stir in the oil and gradually add the vinegar, mixing well. Pour the dressing over the fruit mixture. Serve in individual dishes, garnished with a sprig of mint.

Serves 4

Grilled ginger grapefruit

METRIC/IMPERIAL/AMERICAN
2 grapefruit
2 tablespoons/2 tablespoons/3 tablespoons ginger wine
50 g/2 oz/$\frac{1}{4}$ cup demerara sugar
25 g/1 oz/1 oz stem or preserved ginger, chopped
mint sprigs to garnish

Cut the grapefruit in half and, using a serrated grapefruit knife, cut between the membrane of each segment. Cut round the grapefruit to release the segments from the pith. Carefully lift out the membrane leaving the segments in place. Sprinkle each half with a little of the ginger wine, sugar and chopped ginger.

Preheat a moderate grill. Remove the rack from the grill pan and place the fruit cut side uppermost in the pan. Cook until the sugar melts without burning the grapefruit. Garnish with the mint and serve.

Serves 4

Spicy prawn cocktail

METRIC/IMPERIAL/AMERICAN
1 small lettuce
6 tablespoons/6 tablespoons/½ cup mayonnaise
2 tablespoons/2 tablespoons/3 tablespoons tomato
  ketchup
1 teaspoon Worcestershire sauce
dash Tabasco sauce
2 teaspoons creamed horseradish sauce
225 g/8 oz/1⅓ cups peeled prawns

Wash and dry the lettuce leaves. Line 4 serving dishes with the
leaves.
  Mix the mayonnaise, tomato ketchup, Worcestershire sauce,
Tabasco and horseradish sauce together until blended. Stir in
the prawns and divide mixture between the dishes.

Serves 4

Chicken liver and egg pâté

METRIC/IMPERIAL/AMERICAN
50 g/2 oz/¼ cup butter or margarine
2 medium onions, finely chopped
1 clove garlic, crushed
225 g/8 oz/½ lb chicken livers, trimmed
4 hard-boiled eggs
2 tablespoons/2 tablespoons/3 tablespoons sherry or
  brandy
salt and pepper
GARNISH:
slices of cucumber
mustard and cress

Melt the butter or margarine in a large frying pan. Add the
onion and garlic and cook very gently for about 10 minutes
until soft. Add the chicken livers and cook for about
10 minutes, stirring occasionally. Place in a mixing bowl.
  Reserve one egg yolk for the garnish and put the remaining
shelled hard-boiled eggs through a mincer. Place in the bowl,
add the sherry or brandy and seasoning, and mix. Transfer to
individual dishes. Cover and chill in the refrigerator for several
hours before serving. Garnish with sliced cucumber, a
sprinkling of the reserved chopped egg yolk and mustard and
cress.

Serves 6–8

Fish dishes

When time is at a premium, fish makes an ideal choice for a meal as it does not require lengthy cooking. Use fresh fish on the same day it is purchased; if you do not have a reliable wet fishmonger in your area it is better to choose frozen fish which is processed within hours of being caught. For a speedy meal, make use of canned fish such as tuna and salmon which lend themselves to many tasty dishes.

Halibut with savoury butter

METRIC/IMPERIAL/AMERICAN
salt and pepper
3 halibut steaks
50 g/2 oz/¼ cup butter
**2 tablespoons/2 tablespoons/3 tablespoons chopped fresh
    herbs (parsley, chives, thyme or summer savory)**
1 tablespoon lemon juice
slices of lemon to garnish

Preheat a moderate grill. Lightly season the fish and place the butter on top. Put the fish in the grill pan (rack removed) and grill gently, turning once, for about 15 minutes depending on thickness. Remove the fish to a heated serving dish.

Pour the grill pan juices into a saucepan and add the herbs and lemon juice. Heat through, stirring, and spoon over the cooked fish. Serve immediately with French fried potatoes and garnished with lemon slices.

Serves 3

Crispy curried plaice

METRIC/IMPERIAL/AMERICAN
2 large plaice, filleted
salt and pepper
75 g/3 oz/$\frac{3}{4}$ cup flour
egg and breadcrumbs to coat
175–225 g/6–8 oz/1 cup long-grain rice
25 g/1 oz/2 tablespoons butter or margarine
1 clove garlic, crushed
50 g/2 oz/$\frac{1}{2}$ cup onion, chopped
2 teaspoons curry powder
$\frac{1}{2}$ teaspoon turmeric
600 ml/1 pint/2$\frac{1}{2}$ cups stock
$\frac{1}{2}$ teaspoon finely grated lemon rind
1 teaspoon marmalade
parsley sprig to garnish

Cut the plaice diagonally into strips. Season 25 g/1 oz/$\frac{1}{4}$ cup flour and use to coat the fish. Dip the fish in beaten egg, then toss in fresh or golden breadcrumbs.

Cook the rice in a pan of boiling salted water. Melt the butter or margarine, add the garlic and onion and cook until soft. Add the curry powder and turmeric. Stir in the remaining flour and blend in stock. Bring to the boil, stirring, simmer for 10 minutes. Stir in lemon rind, marmalade and seasoning.

Meanwhile, heat oil for deep frying and fry the plaice until crisp and golden; drain. Arrange the rice on a serving dish. Pile the fish on top and garnish. Serve the sauce separately with accompaniments illustrated.

Serves 4–6

Haddie omelette

METRIC/IMPERIAL/AMERICAN
225 g/8 oz/$\frac{1}{2}$ lb smoked haddock
25 g/1 oz/2 tablespoons butter
25 g/1 oz/$\frac{1}{4}$ cup flour
150 ml/$\frac{1}{4}$ pint/$\frac{2}{3}$ cup milk
1 (92-g/3$\frac{1}{4}$-oz/3$\frac{1}{4}$-oz) can peeled prawns, drained (optional)
1 tablespoon chopped parsley
1 teaspoon lemon juice
4 eggs
3 tablespoons/3 tablespoons/$\frac{1}{4}$ cup water
salt and pepper

Cover the fish with water and poach gently for 10 minutes. Drain, reserving 150 ml/$\frac{1}{4}$ pint/$\frac{2}{3}$ cup of the fish liquor. Remove the skin and bones from the fish and flake the flesh.

Melt the butter in a pan. Add the flour, stirring, and cook for 1 minute. Stir in the milk and reserved fish liquor, cook for 2 minutes. Stir in the flaked fish, prawns, parsley and lemon juice.

Separate yolks from whites of the eggs and place in separate bowls. Add the water and seasoning to yolks, beat thoroughly. Whisk the whites stiffly and fold into the yolk mixture.

Heat a little oil in an omelette pan and pour in half the egg mixture. Cook gently until the mixture sets. Place the pan under the grill and cook until the surface is golden. Turn out on to a hot plate, spoon half the sauce filling on top. Cook a second omelette, fill and serve.

Serves 2

Anchovy fish pie

METRIC/IMPERIAL/AMERICAN
4 frozen cod steaks, thawed
1 (64-g/2¼-oz/2¼-oz) packet instant potato
40 g/1½ oz/3 tablespoons butter
40 g/1½ oz/6 tablespoons plain flour
150 ml/¼ pint/⅔ cup milk
4 teaspoons anchovy essence
salt and pepper
2 large eggs, hard-boiled
50 g/2 oz/½ cup cheese, grated
melted butter
7 anchovy fillets
parsley sprigs to garnish

Cover the cod steaks with water and poach for 10–15 minutes. Drain, reserving 150 ml/¼ pint/⅔ cup of the fish stock.

Make up instant potato according to packet directions.

Melt the butter in a pan. Stir in the flour, cook for 1 minute and gradually add the reserved stock and milk. Bring to the boil, stirring, and simmer for 2 minutes. Stir in the anchovy essence, flaked fish and seasoning.

Pipe the potato around the edge of a large ovenproof dish. Halve the eggs and place in the bottom of the dish. Cover these with the fish sauce, sprinkle with the grated cheese. Brush the potato with melted butter. Cut the anchovy fillets in half lengthways and arrange in a lattice over the fish. Place under the grill and heat through for about 15 minutes. Garnish.

Serves 4

Trout with almonds

METRIC/IMPERIAL/AMERICAN
4 medium trout, gutted
4 tablespoons/4 tablespoons/¼ cup flour
salt and pepper
75 g/3 oz/6 tablespoons butter
2 tablespoons/2 tablespoons/3 tablespoons corn oil
75 g/3 oz/¾ cup blanched slivered almonds
1 tablespoon lemon juice
1 tablespoon chopped parsley
GARNISH:
twists of lemon
parsley sprigs

Wash the trout and wipe on kitchen paper. Remove the eyeballs and any fins. Put the flour on a plate and season with the salt and pepper. Coat the fish well in the seasoned flour and fry gently in 50 g/2 oz/¼ cup of the butter and the oil for about 5 minutes each side, depending on thickness of the fish. Remove the fish from the pan and keep hot.

Add the remaining butter to the pan, stir in the almonds and fry until lightly browned. Add the lemon juice and parsley, heat through for a few seconds.

Spoon the almond mixture over the trout. Serve immediately garnished with lemon twists and parsley sprigs.

Serves 4

Stuffed herrings with mustard sauce

METRIC/IMPERIAL/AMERICAN
1 (99-g/3½-oz/3½-oz) packet country stuffing mix
15 g/½ oz/1 tablespoon butter, melted
1 small apple, diced
4 medium herrings, cleaned and boned
SAUCE:
15 g/½ oz/1 tablespoon butter or margarine
1 small onion, chopped
1 teaspoon mustard powder
15 g/½ oz/2 tablespoons plain flour
300 ml/½ pint/1¼ cups milk
salt and pepper
watercress and lemon butterflies to garnish

Make up the stuffing according to the directions on the packet and stir in the butter and apple. Divide the mixture between the 4 fish, spreading the filling along the length of each. Fold the herrings over and place them in a buttered ovenproof dish. Cover with foil and bake in the centre of a moderately hot oven (190°C, 375°F, Gas Mark 5) for about 25–30 minutes.

Place butter or margarine in a saucepan, add the onion and sauté gently without browning for about 5 minutes. Stir in the mustard powder and cook gently for a further 5 minutes. Add the flour and gradually stir in the milk. Bring to the boil and simmer for 2 minutes. Season to taste and spoon over the fish or serve separately. Garnish with watercress and lemon butterflies.

Serves 4

Tuna and macaroni bake

METRIC/IMPERIAL/AMERICAN
175 g/6 oz/1½ cups macaroni or pasta shells
2 eggs, hard-boiled
1 (198-g/7-oz/8-oz) can tuna
3 tomatoes
CHEESE SAUCE:
40 g/1½ oz/3 tablespoons butter or margarine
40 g/1½ oz/6 tablespoons plain flour
600 ml/1 pint/2½ cups milk
75 g/3 oz/¾ cup cheese, grated
salt and pepper
GARNISH:
slices of tomato
parsley sprig

Cook the pasta in plenty of boiling salted water for about 12 minutes until tender. Drain well. Shell and chop the eggs. Drain the tuna. Slice the tomatoes.

Melt the butter or margarine in a saucepan, add the flour and gradually beat in the milk. Bring to the boil stirring and cook for 3 minutes. Stir in 50 g/2 oz/½ cup of the cheese and the pasta. Taste and adjust the seasoning.

Arrange all the ingredients in layers in a deep casserole dish finishing with a layer of sauce. Sprinkle the remaining cheese over the top. Bake in the centre of a moderate oven (180°C, 350°F, Gas Mark 4) for 30 minutes. Garnish with sliced tomato and parsley.

Serves 4–6

Tuna kedgeree

METRIC/IMPERIAL/AMERICAN
225 g/8 oz/generous cup long-grain rice
1 (198-g/7-oz/8-oz) can tuna
4 eggs, hard-boiled
75 g/3 oz/6 tablespoons butter or margarine
1 medium onion, chopped
7.5-cm/3-inch/3-inch length cucumber, peeled and diced
2 teaspoons lemon juice
1 tablespoon chopped parsley
salt and pepper
quartered cucumber slices to garnish

Cook the rice in a large saucepan of boiling salted water for 10–15 minutes until tender. Drain well.

Drain the liquid from the tuna and flake the fish. Remove the yolks from 2 of the eggs and sieve on to a plate. Chop the remaining eggs and whites.

Place the butter or margarine in a frying pan, add the onion and sauté for about 5 minutes until soft without browning. Stir in the cucumber and lemon juice and cook for a further 2 minutes. Stir in the rice, tuna, chopped egg and parsley. Season to taste. Heat through for about 5 minutes. Place in a heated serving dish, garnish with the sieved egg yolk sprinkled in the middle and quartered cucumber slices.

Serves 4

Scalloped kippers

METRIC/IMPERIAL/AMERICAN
2 medium kippers
50 g/2 oz/¼ cup butter or margarine
25 g/1 oz/¼ cup flour
300 ml/½ pint/1¼ cups milk
salt and pepper
1 teaspoon lemon juice
4 stuffed olives, sliced
2 eggs, hard-boiled
1 tablespoon chopped parsley (optional)
1 (148-g/5¼-oz/5¼-oz) packet instant potato
twists of lemon and parsley sprigs to garnish

Cover kippers with water and poach for 10 minutes.

Make a sauce by melting 25 g/1 oz/2 tablespoons of the butter or margarine in a pan. Stir in the flour, cook for 1 minute and gradually add the milk. Bring to the boil and cook for 2 minutes, stirring.

Remove the flesh from the bones of the kippers; flake, and add to the sauce. Add seasoning to taste, lemon juice, sliced olives, coarsely chopped eggs and parsley, if used.

Divide the mixture between 4 scallop shells or individual flameproof dishes. Make up the instant potato according to the packet directions using the remaining 25 g/1 oz/2 tablespoons butter or margarine. Place in a piping bag and pipe potato around the edge of each dish. Place under a hot grill to heat through and brown. Garnish.

Serves 4

Creamed scallops

METRIC/IMPERIAL/AMERICAN
8 scallops, washed and quartered
150 ml/¼ pint/⅔ cup water
40 g/1½ oz/3 tablespoons butter
40 g/1½ oz/6 tablespoons plain flour
150 ml/¼ pint/⅔ cup milk
50 g/2 oz/½ cup button mushrooms, sliced
1 teaspoon chopped fresh fennel
1 teaspoon lemon juice
salt and pepper
1 (64-g/2¼-oz/2¼-oz) packet instant potato
parsley sprigs to garnish

Poach the scallops in the water for about 5 minutes until they become opaque. Remove with a slotted spoon and reserve the liquor.

To make the sauce, melt the butter in a saucepan, stir in the flour and cook for a few minutes. Gradually add the milk and reserved fish stock. Bring to the boil, stirring, and cook for 2 minutes. Stir in the mushrooms, fennel, lemon juice, scallops and seasoning.

Divide the mixture between 4 ovenproof dishes or scallop shells. Preheat a moderate grill.

Make up the instant potato according to the directions on the packet and pipe a border round the edge of each dish. Place under the grill to lightly brown the potato. Serve immediately garnished with the parsley.

Serves 4

Prawns creole

METRIC/IMPERIAL/AMERICAN
100 g/4 oz/generous ½ cup long-grain rice
1 medium onion, chopped
1 clove garlic, crushed
1 tablespoon oil
1 (227-g/8-oz/8-oz) can peeled tomatoes
½ small green pepper, deseeded and chopped
8 pimento-stuffed olives, halved
salt and pepper
350 g/12 oz/2 cups peeled prawns

Cook the rice in boiling salted water for about 10–15 minutes until just tender. Drain and keep hot.

Place the onion, garlic and oil in a saucepan, cook gently to soften without browning, about 5 minutes. Add the tomatoes, pepper, olives and seasoning to taste. Simmer for about 10 minutes to reduce the liquor. Stir in the prawns and heat through for 5 minutes.

Arrange the rice round the edge of a heated serving dish, pour the prawns creole in the centre.

Serves 3

Meat, offal and poultry dishes

There are many ways to prepare quick main meals. Choose cuts of meat which cook quickly and need little preparation such as frying steak, chops, cutlets and veal escalopes; also make use of canned meats such as corned beef. Minced beef is marvellous for quick meals as it can be transformed into a host of exciting meals.

Paprika beef

METRIC/IMPERIAL/AMERICAN
1 large onion, sliced
2 tablespoons/2 tablespoons/3 tablespoons oil
0.75 kg/1½ lb/1½ lb frying steak
1 green pepper
150 ml/¼ pint/⅔ cup beef stock
½–1 teaspoon paprika
pinch sugar
salt and pepper
2 canned red peppers
2 tablespoons/2 tablespoons/3 tablespoons plain flour

Place the onion in a large frying pan with the oil. Saute gently, without browning, for 5 minutes. Cut the frying steak into 4 pieces and fry quickly until lightly browned.

Remove the meat from the pan and arrange in an ovenproof casserole with the onion rings placed over the top. Slice the pepper, add to the pan and fry for 3 minutes. Remove and add to the casserole.

Stir the stock into the pan, add paprika, sugar and seasoning. Blend and add to the meat.

Drain and slice the canned red peppers and arrange over the meat. Cover the dish and cook in the centre of a moderate oven (180°C, 350°F, Gas Mark 4) for ½–1 hour until the meat is tender. When cooked, remove to a heated serving dish.

Pour the liquid into a small saucepan, blend the flour with a little water, add to the pan and bring to the boil, stirring. Cook for 3 minutes then pour over the meat. Serve with broccoli.

Serves 4

Betty's quick country steaks

METRIC/IMPERIAL/AMERICAN
40 g/1½ oz/3 tablespoons butter
1 medium onion, chopped
2 cloves garlic, crushed
100 g/4 oz/1 cup mushrooms, sliced
2 quick-frying steaks
2 teaspoons French mustard
salt and pepper
1 teaspoon Worcestershire sauce
1 teaspoon tomato purée
2 tablespoons/2 tablespoons/3 tablespoons chopped
   parsley

Melt the butter in a frying pan. Add the onion and garlic and cook slowly to brown and soften the onion. Add the mushrooms and cook for a few seconds.

Meanwhile, spread the steaks on both sides with the French mustard, season liberally.

Push the onion mixture to one side and place the steaks in the pan. Cook quickly at first then reduce the heat and cook slowly for about 10 minutes. Remove the steaks on to a serving dish. Add the Worcestershire sauce and tomato purée to the pan, heat and add the chopped parsley. Spoon this mixture over the meat. Serve with a tossed salad.

Serves 2

Boeuf stroganoff

METRIC/IMPERIAL/AMERICAN
0.5 kg/1¼ lb/1¼ lb fillet of beef
50 g/2 oz/¼ cup unsalted butter
100 g/4 oz/1 cup onion, finely chopped
100 g/4 oz/1 cup mushrooms, sliced
150 ml/¼ pint/⅔ cup soured cream
1 tablespoon French mustard
salt and freshly ground pepper
chopped parsley to garnish

Trim the meat and cut into narrow strips. Heat half the butter in a large frying pan, add the onion and cook slowly until just beginning to colour – about 5 minutes. Stir in the mushrooms and cook for about 2 minutes. Remove these on to a plate and keep hot.

Add the remaining butter and half the beef, cook quickly to seal in the juices. Remove to the plate with the mushrooms and onion, keep warm. Add the remaining meat to the pan and cook quickly as before. Return the beef, mushrooms and onion to the pan, stir in most of the soured cream and the French mustard. Season to taste. Reheat and serve immediately with rice or potatoes and a salad or vegetables. Garnish the stroganoff with the remaining soured cream poured down the centre and parsley.

Serves 4

Corned cabbage sweet and sour

METRIC/IMPERIAL/AMERICAN
25 g/1 oz/2 tablespoons butter or margarine
1 large onion, sliced
0.5 kg/1 lb/1 lb white cabbage
salt and pepper
1 tablespoon water
1 (340-g/12-oz/12-oz) can corned beef
2 tablespoons/2 tablespoons/3 tablespoons vinegar
2 teaspoons demerara sugar
2 tablespoons/2 tablespoons/3 tablespoons mixed pickle
1 teaspoon poppy seeds
parsley sprig to garnish

Melt the butter or margarine in a frying pan, add the onion and fry gently without browning until soft.

Prepare and shred the cabbage, add to the onion with the seasoning and water. Cover the pan and simmer gently, stirring occasionally, for about 10–15 minutes. Place the cabbage in an ovenproof casserole leaving a space in the centre.

Cut the corned beef into slices and arrange in the centre of the casserole. Place the vinegar, sugar and pickle in a small saucepan, heat gently until the sugar dissolves. Pour the sauce over the corned beef, cover with foil and heat in the centre of a moderate oven (180°C, 350°F, Gas Mark 4) for about 20 minutes. Remove the foil. Sprinkle the cabbage with poppy seeds and garnish with a sprig of parsley.

Serves 3–4

Veal with capers

METRIC/IMPERIAL/AMERICAN
4 veal escalopes
seasoned flour
50 g/2 oz/¼ cup butter
juice of ½ lemon
2 tablespoons/2 tablespoons/3 tablespoons capers
GARNISH:
anchovy fillets
chopped parsley
lemon butterflies

If the veal has not been flattened by the butcher, place between 2 pieces of greaseproof paper and flatten with a rolling pin. Coat each piece of veal with the seasoned flour.

Melt the butter in a frying pan and cook the veal very slowly on both sides for about 10 minutes. Remove and keep hot. Add the lemon juice and capers to the pan, heat through and spoon over the veal. Garnish with curled anchovy fillets, capers, chopped parsley and lemon butterflies.

Serves 4

Quick curry

METRIC/IMPERIAL/AMERICAN

1 tablespoon oil
1 small onion, chopped
1 (440-g/15½-oz/16-oz) can mulligatawny soup
2 teaspoons concentrated curry sauce
1 tablespoon tomato ketchup
1 tablespoon cornflour
2 tablespoons/2 tablespoons/3 tablespoons water
25 g/1 oz/3 tablespoons sultanas
350 g/12 oz/12 oz cold cooked meat (beef, lamb, luncheon
    meat or 4 chicken joints)
chopped parsley to garnish

Place the oil in a saucepan, add the onion and sauté gently until soft. Stir in the soup, curry sauce and tomato ketchup. Blend the cornflour with the water and add to the pan. Bring to the boil, stirring, and simmer for about 3 minutes until the cornflour has thickened. Stir in the sultanas.

If not using chicken joints, cut the meat into cubes. Add the chicken joints or cubed meat to the saucepan. Heat through gently for 10–15 minutes. Garnish with chopped parsley.

Serve with chopped green pepper, croûtons of bread and small savoury biscuits. An accompanying tomato salad may be served separately.

Serves 4

Sweet and sour lamb kebabs

METRIC/IMPERIAL/AMERICAN

0.75 kg/1½ lb/1½ lb piece of top leg of lamb, boned
8 rashers streaky bacon
2 lambs' kidneys
1 small green pepper
100 g/4 oz/1 cup button mushrooms
12 bay leaves
2 tomatoes, quartered
oil for brushing
225 g/8 oz/generous cup long-grain rice
1 teaspoon turmeric
SWEET AND SOUR SAUCE:
1 tablespoon thick honey
1 tablespoon vinegar
1 (227-g/8-oz/8-oz) jar redcurrant jelly

Cut the meat into 2.5-cm/1-inch cubes. Derind the bacon, cut each rasher in half and roll up. Skin the kidneys, cut in half and remove the core. Cut the pepper into bite-size pieces. Thread the lamb, bacon, kidneys, pepper and mushrooms alternately on to 4 large skewers with the bay leaves and tomatoes. Brush the kebabs with a little oil and cook under the grill for 15 minutes.

Meanwhile, cook the rice in boiling salted water with the turmeric for 12–15 minutes. Place the honey, vinegar and redcurrant jelly in a small saucepan. Bring to the boil and reduce. Drain the rice and arrange on a serving dish. Place the kebabs on top. Serve the sauce separately with a tossed salad.

Serves 4

Baked spiced chops

METRIC/IMPERIAL/AMERICAN
6 tablespoons/6 tablespoons/$\frac{1}{2}$ cup mango chutney sauce
2 tablespoons/2 tablespoons/3 tablespoons clear honey
1 teaspoon dried mixed herbs
1 tablespoon made mustard
$\frac{1}{4}$ teaspoon curry powder
salt and freshly ground black pepper
8 best end of neck lamb chops
parsley sprigs to garnish

Mix the chutney sauce, honey, herbs, mustard, curry powder and seasonings together.

Place the chops in a shallow roasting tin, spoon over half the sauce and cook in the centre of a moderately hot oven (200°C, 400°F, Gas Mark 6) for about 15 minutes. Turn the chops over, spoon over the remaining sauce and cook for a further 10 minutes. When cooked, drain on kitchen paper to remove excess fat. Serve hot with baked potatoes and tomatoes or cold. Garnish with parsley. These chops are ideal to take on a picnic.

Serves 4 as a main course, or 8 if taken on a picnic

Lamb chops with apple and mint sauce

METRIC/IMPERIAL/AMERICAN
4 loin of lamb chops
40 g/1$\frac{1}{2}$ oz/3 tablespoons butter or margarine
100 g/4 oz/1 cup onion, chopped
50 g/2 oz/$\frac{1}{2}$ cup cooking apple, peeled and diced
25 g/1 oz/$\frac{1}{4}$ cup plain flour
300 ml/$\frac{1}{2}$ pint/1$\frac{1}{4}$ cups milk
1 tablespoon chopped mint
1 teaspoon white wine vinegar
salt and pepper

Thread the lamb chops on to skewers to keep their shape and place under a moderate grill. Cook slowly for about 20 minutes, turning once.

Meanwhile, make the sauce by placing the butter or margarine in a saucepan, add the onion and cook gently without browning for about 10 minutes until soft. Add the apple and cook for a further 5 minutes. Stir in the flour and gradually add the milk, beating well after each addition. Bring to the boil, stirring, reduce the heat and cook for 2 minutes. Stir in the mint, vinegar and seasoning to taste. Serve separately with the chops.

Serves 4

Danish pilaff

METRIC/IMPERIAL/AMERICAN
25 g/1 oz/2 tablespoons butter or margarine
1 tablespoon oil
1 medium onion, chopped
2 sticks celery, sliced
175–225 g/6–8 oz/$\frac{1}{2}$ lb forehock bacon steak
225 g/8 oz/generous cup long-grain rice
450–600 ml/$\frac{3}{4}$–1 pint/2–2$\frac{1}{2}$ cups chicken stock
50 g/2 oz/$\frac{1}{3}$ cup sultanas
1 medium green pepper
toasted flaked almonds to garnish

Place the butter and oil in a frying pan, add the onion and celery and cook slowly until soft – about 10 minutes.

Remove the rind from the bacon and cut into small strips. Add to the pan and cook slowly, stirring, for about 5 minutes. Stir in the rice and cook for 2 minutes until the rice is opaque. Add 450 ml/$\frac{3}{4}$ pint/2 cups of the chicken stock, cook gently, stirring occasionally, for 20 minutes; add the extra stock if the rice becomes too dry.

Stir in the sultanas, cut the pepper into strips, removing seeds and pith, and add to the rice. Cook for a further 10 minutes. Spoon the pilaff on to a serving dish and sprinkle with the toasted almonds.

Serves 4

Sausage stew

METRIC/IMPERIAL/AMERICAN
0.5 kg/1 lb/1 lb cocktail sausages or chipolatas, twisted in half
25 g/1 oz/2 tablespoons lard
1 large onion, sliced
50 g/2 oz/$\frac{1}{4}$ cup streaky bacon, chopped
25 g/1 oz/$\frac{1}{4}$ cup plain flour
300 ml/$\frac{1}{2}$ pint/1$\frac{1}{4}$ cups beef stock
100 g/4 oz/1 cup button mushrooms, sliced
1 tablespoon tomato purée
salt and pepper
1 (220-g/7$\frac{3}{4}$-oz/8-oz) can baked beans
chopped parsley to garnish

Place the sausages and lard in a saucepan and fry the sausages very slowly until lightly browned, turning frequently, for about 10 minutes. Remove and keep warm.

Add the onion to the fat, sauté gently until lightly browned. Add the streaky bacon and cook for 2–3 minutes. Stir in the flour, add the stock, mushrooms, tomato purée and seasoning. Blend thoroughly.

Return the sausages to the pan, stir in the baked beans, cover and cook slowly for 10–15 minutes. Remove to a serving dish and garnish with parsley. Serve with mashed potato and carrots.

Serves 4

Peasant pork

METRIC/IMPERIAL/AMERICAN
0.5 kg/1¼ lb/1¼ lb pork fillet
25 g/1 oz/2 tablespoons butter
1 tablespoon corn oil
3 medium onions, sliced
2 cloves garlic, crushed (optional)
350 g/12 oz/¾ lb tomatoes, skinned and quartered
225 g/8 oz/2 cups mushrooms
salt and pepper
1 tablespoon tomato purée
1 teaspoon dried basil
150 ml/¼ pint/⅔ cup soured cream
chopped parsley to garnish

Trim the pork fillet and cut into 2.5-cm/1-inch cubes.
    Melt the butter and oil in a large saucepan and fry the pork quickly to lightly brown and seal in the juices. Add the onions, garlic, tomatoes, mushrooms, seasoning, tomato purée and basil. Blend thoroughly. Cover and cook slowly for 30 minutes or until the meat is tender. Stir in the soured cream, garnish with parsley and serve with cooked rice or noodles.

Serves 4

Grilled gammon with marmalade sauce

METRIC/IMPERIAL/AMERICAN
4 medium gammon steaks
corn oil
1 small onion, chopped
4 tablespoons/4 tablespoons/⅓ cup marmalade
2 teaspoons white wine vinegar
2 teaspoons demerara sugar
watercress to garnish

Preheat a moderate grill. Remove the rind from gammon and snip the fat at intervals with a pair of scissors. Place the steaks in a large bowl, cover with boiling water and leave for about 5 minutes. Drain and brush with oil. Place the gammon steaks on the grill rack and cook gently for 10–15 minutes, turning once.
    Place the onion in a small saucepan with 1 teaspoon oil, cook without browning for 5 minutes. Stir in the marmalade, vinegar and sugar, heat gently to dissolve. Bring to the boil and reduce to a syrupy sauce.
    Place the gammon on a serving dish and pour over the sauce. Garnish with watercress.

Serves 4

Spicy sausagemeat patties

METRIC/IMPERIAL/AMERICAN
0.5 kg/1 lb/2 cups pork or beef sausagemeat
1 teaspoon dried mixed herbs
1 tablespoon tomato ketchup
½ teaspoon powdered cumin
25 g/1 oz/½ cup fresh breadcrumbs
seasoned flour
oil for frying

Place the sausagemeat in a bowl with the herbs, ketchup, cumin and breadcrumbs, mix evenly. Divide the mixture into 6 portions, using a little of the seasoned flour to shape the mixture into rounds about 1.5 cm/¾ inch thick. Heat a little oil in the frying pan and cook the patties gently for about 6 minutes each side.

Serve either hot or cold in baps, with baked beans and tomato quarters secured on cocktail sticks.

Makes 6

Liver and bacon kebabs

METRIC/IMPERIAL/AMERICAN
350 g/12 oz/¾ lb lamb's liver, in one piece
6 rashers streaky bacon
2 medium onions, quartered
oil for brushing
salt and pepper

Trim the liver and cut into 1-cm/½-inch cubes. Remove the rind from the bacon and 'stretch' each rasher with the back of a knife. Cut each rasher in half and roll up. Thread the liver, bacon and onion alternately on to 4 skewers (as shown in photograph).

Preheat a moderate grill, place the skewers in the grill pan, brush with the oil and season liberally. Place under the grill and cook for 10 minutes, turning frequently and basting with the pan juices when necessary.

Serves 4

Piquant liver with noodles

METRIC/IMPERIAL/AMERICAN
350 g/12 oz/¾ lb lamb's liver
225 g/8 oz/2 cups onion, chopped
1 clove garlic, crushed
75 g/3 oz/6 tablespoons butter or margarine
1 tablespoon dry sherry
salt and pepper
12 pimento-stuffed olives, sliced
1 tablespoon chopped parsley
225 g/8 oz/2 cups noodles
chopped parsley to garnish

Cut the liver into small slices, place in a bowl and cover with boiling water. Leave for about 3 minutes then drain. Place the onion and garlic in a frying pan with 50 g/2 oz/¼ cup of the butter or margarine. Sauté, without browning, until soft. Add the liver and cook for about 5 minutes. Stir in the sherry and seasoning, simmer for a further 5 minutes. Add half of the olives and the parsley.

Meanwhile, cook the noodles in boiling salted water until just tender – about 12 minutes. When tender, drain well and add the remaining butter.

Arrange the noodles in a heated serving dish and pile the liver on top. Garnish with chopped parsley and remaining sliced olives.

Serves 4–5

Veal and chicken liver gratin

METRIC/IMPERIAL/AMERICAN
1 tablespoon oil
40 g/1½ oz/3 tablespoons butter
1 large onion, chopped
0.5 kg/1 lb/1 lb minced veal
225 g/8 oz/½ lb chicken livers, trimmed and chopped
1 tablespoon tomato purée
½ teaspoon dried thyme
salt and pepper
1 tablespoon cornflour
1 kg/2 lb/2 lb potatoes
slices of tomato and parsley sprig to garnish

Place the oil and 15 g/½ oz/1 tablespoon butter in a large saucepan, add the onion and cook for about 10 minutes to soften. Stir in the veal and cook for about 5 minutes, add the chicken livers, tomato puree, thyme and seasoning. Blend the cornflour with 1 tablespoon water, stir into the mixture and cook for about 10 minutes to thicken.

Meanwhile, cut the potatoes in half and cook in boiling salted water until just tender. Cut into slices.

Place layers of the mince and sliced potato in a deep flameproof dish, finishing with a layer of potato. Melt the remaining butter and use to brush over the potato. Place under a preheated grill and cook until the potato is golden. Garnish. Serve with a tossed green salad.

Serves 5

Kidneys in sherry cream sauce

METRIC/IMPERIAL/AMERICAN
175 g/6 oz/1½ cups onion, chopped
25 g/1 oz/2 tablespoons butter or margarine
12 lambs' kidneys
3 tablespoons/3 tablespoons/¼ cup seasoned flour
100 g/4 oz/1 cup mushrooms, quartered
300 ml/½ pint/1¼ cups stock
2 tablespoons/2 tablespoons/3 tablespoons sherry
salt and pepper
150 ml/¼ pint/⅔ cup double cream
chopped parsley to garnish

Sauté the onion gently in a frying pan with the butter or margarine for about 10 minutes.

Meanwhile, remove skin from kidneys, cut in half and remove the core with a pair of scissors. Toss lightly in the seasoned flour. Remove the onion from the pan then add the kidneys. Cook, turning occasionally, for about 5 minutes. Add the onion, mushrooms, stock, sherry and seasoning, simmer for about 15–20 minutes. Spoon into a serving dish and pour over the cream. Garnish with chopped parsley and serve with noodles tossed in butter.

Serves 4

Devilled kidneys

METRIC/IMPERIAL/AMERICAN
25 g/1 oz/2 tablespoons butter or margarine
100 g/4 oz/1 cup onion, chopped
9 lambs' kidneys
1 tablespoon plain flour
150 ml/¼ pint/⅔ cup chicken stock
1 teaspoon brown fruit sauce
¼ teaspoon French mustard
1 tablespoon tomato purée
salt and pepper

Place the butter or margarine and onion in a frying pan and cook gently until lightly browned. Meanwhile, prepare the kidneys by cutting each in half, removing the outer skin and cutting out the core with a pair of scissors. Toss lightly in the flour. Add the kidneys to the pan and fry briskly for about 3 minutes to seal in the juices. Stir in the remaining ingredients. Gradually bring to the boil, stirring gently, and cook for about 10 minutes, stirring occasionally. Place in a serving dish and serve with plain boiled rice or noodles.

Serves 3

Lemon and honey chicken

METRIC/IMPERIAL/AMERICAN
50 g/2 oz/$\frac{1}{4}$ cup butter
4 chicken joints
2 sprigs lemon thyme (if available)
2 tablespoons/2 tablespoons/3 tablespoons chopped
   parsley
4 tablespoons/4 tablespoons/$\frac{1}{3}$ cup clear honey
juice of 1 lemon
freshly ground black pepper
GARNISH:
lemon slices
parsley sprig

Melt the butter in a frying pan with a lid. Place the chicken
joints in the pan and cook until lightly browned all over. Cover
and cook gently for about 25 minutes, turning once. Wash and
chop the lemon thyme, if used. Add to the chicken with the
parsley, honey, lemon juice and pepper. Turn up the heat and
baste the chicken with this mixture, cooking for a further
2 minutes.
   Place the chicken on a serving dish and keep hot. Reduce the
sauce a little over a high heat then spoon over the chicken.
Garnish with lemon slices and parsley.

Serves 4

Asparagus chicken suprême

METRIC/IMPERIAL/AMERICAN
4 chicken breasts
1 small carrot, quartered
1 onion, quartered
bouquet garni
salt and pepper
40 g/1$\frac{1}{2}$ oz/3 tablespoons butter or margarine
25 g/1 oz/$\frac{1}{4}$ cup plain flour
1 tablespoon dry Vermouth (optional)
1 (283-g/10-oz/10-oz) can asparagus spears
lemon butterflies and slices of stuffed olives to garnish

Carefully remove skin and bone from the chicken breasts,
keeping a neat shape. Place in a large shallow pan with a lid.
Add the carrot and onion with the bouquet garni and a little
seasoning. Pour over enough water to cover. Bring slowly to
simmering point, cover and cook slowly for 25–30 minutes
until chicken is tender. When the chicken is cooked, remove to
a serving dish, cover and keep hot. Reserve 300 ml/$\frac{1}{2}$ pint/1$\frac{1}{4}$
cups cooking liquor.
   Make the sauce by melting the butter or margarine in a small
saucepan, add the flour and cook for 1 minute, stir in the dry
Vermouth (if used). Gradually stir in the reserved chicken
stock, bring to the boil and cook for about 3 minutes, stirring.
Season to taste. Pour the sauce over the chicken breasts to coat.
Garnish. Heat the asparagus spears and serve with the chicken.

Serves 4

Barbecued chicken

METRIC/IMPERIAL/AMERICAN
50 g/2 oz/¼ cup butter or margarine
1 medium onion, chopped
1 clove garlic, crushed (optional)
1 (396-g/14-oz/14-oz) can tomatoes
1 tablespoon Worcestershire sauce
salt and pepper
1 tablespoon demerara sugar
4 chicken quarters
oil for brushing
watercress sprigs to garnish

Place the butter or margarine in a small saucepan. Add the onion and garlic and cook until soft, without browning, for about 10 minutes. Stir in the tomatoes, Worcestershire sauce, seasoning and sugar. Stir well, bring to the boil, reduce the heat and simmer for 20 minutes until reduced and thick.

Preheat a moderate grill and place the chicken quarters in a grill pan. Brush the chicken with oil and cook slowly, turning once, for 10 minutes. Remove the chicken from the grill, spoon the sauce over the quarters and continue cooking slowly for a further 15 minutes, turning once. Baste with the remaining sauce during the cooking. Serve hot, garnished with watercress.

Serves 4

Chicken and mushroom casserole

METRIC/IMPERIAL/AMERICAN
4 chicken joints
1 teaspoon paprika pepper
1 teaspoon mustard powder
25 g/1 oz/2 tablespoons butter or margarine
2 teaspoons corn oil
100 g/4 oz/1 cup onion, chopped
225 g/8 oz/2 cups button mushrooms, sliced
1 (396-g/14-oz/14-oz) can tomatoes
2 teaspoons chicken stock powder
salt and pepper

Coat the chicken joints with the paprika pepper and mustard. Melt the butter and oil in a frying pan and cook the chicken gently to seal and lightly brown it — about 5–10 minutes. Remove from the pan. Add the onion and cook for about 5 minutes. Add the mushrooms, tomatoes and chicken stock powder. Season to taste. Bring to the boil and return the chicken to the pan. Cover and simmer gently for 25 minutes until the chicken is tender.

Serves 4

Vegetable dishes and salads

These dishes can either be served on their own as a lunch or supper snack or may be the accompanying vegetable to a main meal. The salad ideas are particularly inspired without taking hours of preparation.

Courgette and tomato grill

METRIC/IMPERIAL/AMERICAN
1 medium onion
0.5 kg/1 lb/1 lb courgettes
50 g/2 oz/$\frac{1}{4}$ cup butter or margarine
1 (396-g/14-oz/14-oz) can tomatoes or use fresh tomatoes
1 teaspoon dried marjoram
salt and pepper
50 g/2 oz/$\frac{1}{2}$ cup Cheddar cheese, grated
2 tablespoons/2 tablespoons/3 tablespoons browned
    breadcrumbs
chopped parsley to garnish

Slice the onion. Wash the courgettes, trim off the ends and cut into 0.5-cm/$\frac{1}{4}$-inch slices.

Melt the butter or margarine in a large pan, add the onion, courgettes, tomatoes, marjoram and seasoning. Cover and simmer gently for 30 minutes, stirring frequently.

Preheat a medium grill. Turn the vegetables into a flameproof dish, mix the cheese and breadcrumbs together and sprinkle over the top. Place under the grill for about 5 minutes until the cheese is melted and lightly browned. Garnish with chopped parsley.

Serves 4

Vegetable pancakes

METRIC/IMPERIAL/AMERICAN
50 g/2 oz/¼ cup butter or margarine
225 g/8 oz/½ lb onions, finely sliced
175 g/6 oz/1½ cups mushrooms, chopped
350 g/12 oz/¾ lb tomatoes, skinned and chopped
50 g/2 oz/1 cup fresh brown breadcrumbs
½ teaspoon garlic salt
½ teaspoon paprika pepper
50 g/2 oz/½ cup shelled Brazil nuts, sliced
PANCAKE BATTER:
125 g/4 oz/1 cup plain flour
salt
1 large egg
1 tablespoon oil
300 ml/½ pint/1¼ cups milk

Melt the butter or margarine in a frying pan, add the onion and cook for about 10 minutes until soft. Stir in the mushrooms, tomatoes, breadcrumbs, salt, paprika and nuts. Keep warm.

Sift the flour and salt into a bowl, make a well in the centre. Break in the egg and oil, then gradually add the milk. Grease a 20–23-cm/8–9-inch frying pan and pour in just enough batter to cover the pan. Cook 8 pancakes lightly on both sides.

Fold the pancakes into four and fill each with the stuffing. Place on a serving dish and garnish with watercress. Mix 150 ml/¼ pint/⅔ cup soured cream, 1 tablespoon tomato puree and ½ teaspoon dried herbs. Serve this sauce separately.

Serves 4

Vegetable risotto

METRIC/IMPERIAL/AMERICAN
2 tablespoons/2 tablespoons/3 tablespoons corn oil
100 g/4 oz/1 cup onion, sliced
2 carrots, diced
15 g/½ oz/1 tablespoon dried peppers
1 tablespoon vegetable extract
1 litre/1¾ pints/4¼ cups boiling water
175 g/6 oz/scant cup long-grain rice
2 tablespoons/2 tablespoons/3 tablespoons tomato purée
25 g/1 oz/3 tablespoons sultanas
1 (113-g/4-oz/¼-lb) packet frozen peas
grated cheese to garnish

Place the oil in a frying pan, add the onion and saute gently for about 5 minutes. Add the carrots and cook for a further 5 minutes. Stir in the dried peppers, vegetable extract and boiling water. Add the rice, tomato puree and sultanas. Cook for about 20 minutes, stirring occasionally. Add a little more water if necessary. Stir in the peas and cook for about 10 minutes.

Serve immediately sprinkled with grated cheese.

Serves 4

Piquant spaghetti

METRIC/IMPERIAL/AMERICAN

225 g/8 oz/½ lb spaghetti
25 g/1 oz/2 tablespoons butter or margarine
175 g/6 oz/1½ cups onion, chopped
25 g/1 oz/¼ cup plain flour
1 teaspoon dry mustard
1 (396-g/14-oz/14-oz) can tomatoes
150 ml/¼ pint/⅔ cup chicken stock
1 tablespoon tomato purée
1 tablespoon vinegar
1 tablespoon Worcestershire sauce
pinch sugar
salt and pepper
1 tablespoon chopped parsley
1 teaspoon dried oregano
grated Parmesan cheese
chopped parsley

Cook the spaghetti in boiling salted water until tender. Drain.
   Meanwhile, melt the butter or margarine in a saucepan, add the onion and sauté until soft. Stir in the flour and mustard and cook for 1 minute. Add the tomatoes, chicken stock, tomato purée, vinegar, Worcestershire sauce, sugar, seasoning, parsley and oregano. Bring to the boil, simmer for 10 minutes. Place the spaghetti on a serving plate or plates. Pour the sauce in the centre and serve sprinkled with Parmesan and parsley.

Serves 4

Stuffed marrow rings

METRIC/IMPERIAL/AMERICAN

1 medium marrow, peeled, deseeded and cut into 3.5-
   cm/1½-inch rings
2 tablespoons/2 tablespoons/3 tablespoons corn oil
225 g/8 oz/2 cups onion, chopped
2 cloves garlic, crushed
0.5 kg/1 lb/1 lb tomatoes, skinned and chopped
75 g/3 oz/1½ cups fresh breadcrumbs
2 tablespoons/2 tablespoons/3 tablespoons chopped
   parsley
1 teaspoon dried mixed herbs
100 g/4 oz/¼ lb aubergine, chopped
salt and pepper
25 g/1 oz/¼ cup Parmesan cheese, grated
watercress sprig to garnish

Cook the marrow in boiling salted water until just tender – about 5–10 minutes. Drain well and arrange these rings in a large ovenproof dish.
   Place the oil, onion and garlic in a frying pan and sauté for about 10 minutes until soft. Add the tomatoes, breadcrumbs, parsley, mixed herbs, aubergine and seasoning, blend thoroughly and cook for about 5 minutes.
   Divide the mixture between the marrow rings, sprinkle each with a little cheese. Place under a moderate grill to lightly brown the cheese and heat through. Garnish with the watercress.

Serves 3–4

Malayan curried salad

METRIC/IMPERIAL/AMERICAN
100 g/4 oz/generous ½ cup long-grain rice
150 ml/¼ pint/⅔ cup mayonnaise
1–2 teaspoons concentrated curry sauce
1 (226-g/8-oz/8-oz) can pineapple slices
1 small green pepper, diced
225 g/8 oz/1 cup cooked chicken, diced
25 g/1 oz/3 tablespoons seedless raisins
chopped green pepper to garnish

Cook the rice in boiling salted water for 12–15 minutes until tender. Drain well and spread on kitchen paper to cool.

Place the mayonnaise in a bowl and stir in the curry sauce. Drain the pineapple, dry on kitchen paper and cut into small pieces. Add the green pepper, pineapple, chicken and raisins to the mayonnaise and stir to coat evenly.

Place the rice on a serving dish and top with the curried chicken mixture. Garnish with chopped green pepper.

Serves 3–4

Crunchy bacon salad

METRIC/IMPERIAL/AMERICAN
4 slices white bread, cut 1 cm/½ inch thick
50 g/2 oz/¼ cup butter or margarine
5 tablespoons/5 tablespoons/6 tablespoons oil
8 rashers streaky bacon
225 g/8 oz/2 cups button mushrooms, thickly sliced
½ small onion
salt and pepper
pinch dry mustard
1 tablespoon vinegar
50 g/2 oz/⅓ cup pimento-stuffed olives, sliced
2 tablespoons/2 tablespoons/3 tablespoons chopped
  parsley

Remove the crusts and cut the bread into large cubes. Melt the butter or margarine in a frying pan with 2 tablespoons/ 2 tablespoons/3 tablespoons of the oil. Heat gently and fry the bread cubes, turning frequently, until crisp and golden. Remove and drain on kitchen paper.

Remove the rind from the bacon and cut into large pieces. Fry until slightly crisp. Remove from the pan and drain well. Add the mushrooms to the pan and fry slowly until just soft. Remove, drain and place in a salad bowl.

Grate the onion and add to the mushrooms with the seasoning and mustard. Blend the remaining oil and vinegar into mushroom mixture. Cool and add remaining ingredients.

Serves 4

Mixed vegetable pasta

METRIC/IMPERIAL/AMERICAN
225 g/8 oz/½ lb macaroni
225 g/8 oz/½ lb frozen mixed vegetables, thawed
3 large tomatoes, skinned and chopped
1 (298-g/10½-oz/10½-oz) can condensed mushroom soup
1 tablespoon vegetable extract (optional)
croûtons of toast to garnish

Cook the macaroni in boiling salted water for about 8 minutes, then add the thawed mixed vegetables and cook for about 5 minutes. Drain well. Add the chopped tomatoes.

Heat the soup in a saucepan, stir in the pasta, vegetables, vegetable extract, if used, and heat for about 5 minutes.

Place in a heated serving dish and serve with croutons of toast.

Serves 4

Parsnip fritters

METRIC/IMPERIAL/AMERICAN
0.5 kg/1 lb/1 lb parsnips
50 g/2 oz/½ cup plain flour
salt
2 teaspoons cornflour
1 tablespoon oil
4 tablespoons/4 tablespoons/⅓ cup tepid water
1 egg white
oil for frying
grated cheese to garnish (optional)

Prepare the parsnips and cut into quarters lengthways. Cook in boiling salted water until tender.

To make the batter, sift the flour, salt and cornflour into a bowl. Make a well in the centre and add the oil and water gradually, beating well to give a smooth consistency. Allow the batter to stand while cooking the parsnips.

Drain the parsnips well on kitchen paper. Whisk the egg white until stiff and dry, and fold into the batter mixture until thoroughly incorporated. Heat a pan of oil until a piece of bread turns golden in about 20 seconds.

Dip some of the parsnip pieces into the batter. Drain off any excess batter and fry carefully in the oil for about 4 minutes. Drain on kitchen paper. Repeat in batches until all the parsnips have been fried.

Serve sprinkled with grated cheese, if liked.

Serves 2–3

Sweets

To complete the meal most people like to have a sweet dish and a look through the recipes in this section will convince you that speedy desserts are possible. Make use of store cupboard ingredients such as canned fruit and present them as shown in these mouthwatering pictures.

Pineapple and ginger creams

METRIC/IMPERIAL/AMERICAN
1 (226-g/8-oz/8-oz) can pineapple slices
100 g/4 oz/¼ lb gingernut biscuits
2 tablespoons/2 tablespoons/3 tablespoons dry sherry
300 ml/½ pint/1¼ cups double cream
grated chocolate to decorate

Drain the pineapple well and chop into small pieces. Crush the gingernut biscuits with a rolling pin and mix in the sherry.

Whisk the double cream until lightly whipped and gently fold in the crushed biscuits and pineapple. Spoon into individual glasses and sprinkle with the grated chocolate.

Serves 4–6

Mixed berry salad

METRIC/IMPERIAL/AMERICAN
225 g/8 oz/2 cups blackcurrants
150 ml/¼ pint/⅔ cup sweet white wine
150 ml/¼ pint/⅔ cup water
100 g/4 oz/1 cup icing sugar
3 teaspoons arrowroot
225 g/8 oz/1½ cups strawberries
225 g/8 oz/1½ cups raspberries

Place the blackcurrants in a pan with the wine, water and the icing sugar. Heat gently to dissolve the sugar and soften the fruit – about 10 minutes. Sieve the cooked fruit and allow to cool. Blend the arrowroot with a little water and some of the fruit purée and place in a saucepan with the remaining purée. Bring to the boil, stirring, and cook for about 3 minutes until the mixture thickens and clears. Allow to cool.

Place the remaining prepared fruit in a serving dish, pour over the cooled, thickened sauce. Serve with crisp biscuits or wafers.

Note: This would also be delicious served with ice cream or meringues.

Serves 4–6

Apricot soufflé omelette

METRIC/IMPERIAL/AMERICAN
25 g/1 oz/2 tablespoons butter
1 heaped tablespoon apricot jam
225 g/8 oz/½ lb fresh apricots or use dried
25 g/1 oz/2 tablespoons castor sugar
OMELETTE:
2 eggs
25 g/1 oz/2 tablespoons castor sugar
1 teaspoon cornflour
½ teaspoon vanilla essence

Place the butter and jam in a small saucepan. Heat until just melted. Meanwhile, wash and halve the apricots removing the stones, add to the melted butter and jam. (Soak dried apricots.) Cover and cook very gently for about 5–10 minutes until soft, shaking the saucepan occasionally. Stir in the sugar.

To make the omelette, separate the yolks from the whites and place in separate bowls. Stir the sugar, cornflour and vanilla essence into the yolks. Cream together until thick and pale. Whisk the egg whites until stiff. Fold the whites into the yolk mixture using a metal spoon.

Butter a 25-cm/10-inch frying pan, heat gently. Pour the egg mixture into the pan and cook slowly until the sides are beginning to set. Place the pan under a moderate grill to lightly brown the surface. Spoon the apricot filling on to the centre of the omelette and fold over. Sprinkle with sugar.

Serves 2

Orange and lychee compote

METRIC/IMPERIAL/AMERICAN
2 medium oranges
1 (312-g/11-oz/11-oz) can lychees
2 teaspoons arrowroot
15 g/½ oz/1 tablespoon seedless raisins

Finely grate the rind from one of the oranges and reserve.

Using a sharp knife, cut off the rind and pith from the oranges. Cut out the orange segments from in between the membranes.

Drain the juice from the lychees into a small saucepan. Squeeze any remaining juice from the orange membrane and add to the pan with the grated orange rind.

Blend a little of the juice with the arrowroot, add to the pan and bring to the boil, stirring. Cook for a few seconds until the mixture thickens and clears. Stir in the raisins, lychees and orange segments. Allow to chill before serving.
Note: This compote would make a delicious sauce to serve with ice cream.

Serves 4

Baked bananas and oranges

METRIC/IMPERIAL/AMERICAN
2 large oranges
50 g/2 oz/¼ cup demerara sugar
6 bananas
juice of ½ lemon
25 g/1 oz/2 tablespoons butter
brandy, rum or Grand Marnier (optional)

Grate the rind from one orange and mix with 40 g/1½ oz/3 tablespoons of the sugar. Grate the rind from the other orange and reserve for decoration. Using a sharp knife, remove the pith from the oranges and cut out the segments from in between the membranes. Peel the bananas and cut diagonally into slices. Arrange in alternate layers in an ovenproof dish sprinkling the sugar mixture between each layer. Pour over the lemon juice. Sprinkle the top layer with the remaining sugar and dot with the butter.

Bake for 20 minutes on the centre shelf of a moderately hot oven (190°C, 375°F, Gas Mark 5). Sprinkle with either brandy, rum or Grand Marnier, if liked. Decorate with the grated orange rind and serve with almond twirls.

Serves 4

Chocolate brandy whip

METRIC/IMPERIAL/AMERICAN
75 g/3 oz/3 oz plain chocolate
3 eggs
few drops vanilla essence
1 teaspoon hot water
1 tablespoon brandy
15 g/½ oz/1 tablespoon butter
GARNISH:
whipped cream
grated chocolate (optional)

Melt the chocolate in a bowl over a pan of hot water. Separate the yolks from the whites of the eggs. Beat each egg yolk separately and add one by one to the chocolate, beating well between each addition. Beat in the vanilla essence, water, brandy and gradually add the butter in small pieces, blending thoroughly. Remove the bowl from the heat and allow the chocolate mixture to cool.

When cooled, whisk the egg whites until stiff and carefully fold into the chocolate mixture.

Divide between 4 individual dishes and leave to chill in the refrigerator. Top each with a swirl of cream and a little extra grated chocolate, if liked.

Note: Substitute 1 tablespoon rum for the brandy, if preferred.

Serves 4

Quick chocolate trifle

METRIC/IMPERIAL/AMERICAN
1 jam Swiss roll
1 (212-g/7½-oz/8-oz) can sliced pears, diced
375 ml/13 fl oz/1⅔ cups milk
4 teaspoons custard powder
1 tablespoon cocoa powder
2 teaspoons castor sugar
150 ml/¼ pint/⅔ cup double cream
DECORATION:
glacé cherries
angelica

Cut the Swiss roll into slices and use to line the sides and base of a glass serving dish. Pour over the juice from the canned pears and cover with the diced fruit.

Place most of the milk in a saucepan and bring almost to the boil; blend the remaining milk with the custard and cocoa powder. Stir the hot milk on to the mixture, blend thoroughly and return to the saucepan. Bring to the boil, stirring, and cook for 2–3 minutes until thickened. Stir in the sugar. Allow to cool slightly. Pour the custard over the fruit. Cool.

Pour a little cream over the surface of the trifle then whip the remainder and pipe around the edge. Decorate with glacé cherries and angelica.

Serves 4–5

Lemon tutti-frutti

METRIC/IMPERIAL/AMERICAN

1 (255-g/9-oz/9-oz) packet frozen lemon mousse,
  thawed
150 ml/¼ pint/⅔ cup double cream
2 tablespoons/2 tablespoons/3 tablespoons lemon curd
25 g/1 oz/3 tablespoons sultanas, chopped
25 g/1 oz/3 tablespoons dried mixed peel
1 tablespoon Grand Marnier or Curaçao

Place the thawed mousse in a bowl, beat gently with a fork to
make smooth. Whisk the cream until it stands in soft peaks and
stir into the mousse with the remaining ingredients. Spoon into
individual glasses and serve slightly chilled with russe biscuits.

Serves 4

Mandarin crunch

METRIC/IMPERIAL/AMERICAN
BASE:
1 (312-g/11-oz/11-oz) can mandarin oranges
100 g/4 oz/½ cup cottage cheese
grated rind of 1 orange
TOPPING:
50 g/2 oz/¼ cup butter
50 g/2 oz/¼ cup demerara sugar
75 g/3 oz/1 cup porridge oats

Drain the juice from the mandarins. Place the cottage cheese in a
bowl and stir in the mandarins and orange rind. Divide between
4 individual flameproof dishes or use one large dish.
  Melt the butter and sugar together, stir in the porridge oats
and mix well. Divide between the dishes or dish and smooth the
surface. Place under a hot grill to brown the surface. Serve
immediately.

Serves 4

Egg and cheese dishes

When a quick meal is called for everyone thinks of eggs and cheese which do make nutritious, quick meals. By looking through these recipes you will see that the scope is wider than omelettes and egg on toast – both eggs and cheese go well with all kinds of pasta. For freezer owners, quick meals are no problem as pastry cases for delicious savoury flans can be partly baked and frozen in advance, and when required a tasty filling added.

Spaghetti eggs

METRIC/IMPERIAL/AMERICAN
175 g/6 oz/6 oz spaghetti
40 g/1½ oz/3 tablespoons butter
40 g/1½ oz/6 tablespoons plain flour
300 ml/½ pint/1¼ cups milk
175 g/6 oz/1½ cups Cheddar cheese, grated
2 teaspoons grated onion
4 large eggs, hard-boiled
2 tablespoons/2 tablespoons/3 tablespoons dried
   breadcrumbs
2 large tomatoes

Bring a large pan of salted water to the boil. Break the spaghetti into convenient lengths for serving, add to the water and cook for about 8 minutes. When cooked, drain, reserving 150 ml/¼ pint/⅔ cup of the liquor.

Melt the butter in a pan, add the flour and cook for 1 minute. Gradually stir in the milk and reserved cooking liquor. Bring to the boil, stirring, and simmer for 2 minutes. Add most of the cheese, the onion and salt and pepper to taste.

Preheat a moderately hot grill. Place half the spaghetti in a shallow flameproof casserole. Halve the eggs and arrange on the spaghetti. Cover with half the cheese sauce, top with the remaining spaghetti and cover this with the remainder of the cheese sauce. Mix the rest of the cheese and the breadcrumbs together and sprinkle over the top. Slice the tomatoes and arrange around the edge of the dish. Grill for 10 minutes.

Serves 4

Egg and onion casserole

METRIC/IMPERIAL/AMERICAN
75 g/3 oz/6 tablespoons butter
225 g/8 oz/$\frac{1}{2}$ lb onions, sliced
175 g/6 oz/$1\frac{1}{2}$ cups mushrooms, washed and sliced
salt and pepper
$\frac{1}{2}$–1 teaspoon dried thyme
100 g/4 oz/2 cups fresh brown breadcrumbs
25 g/1 oz/$\frac{1}{4}$ cup Parmesan cheese, grated
6 eggs, hard-boiled
SAUCE:
40 g/$1\frac{1}{2}$ oz/3 tablespoons butter
40 g/$1\frac{1}{2}$ oz/6 tablespoons plain flour
450 ml/$\frac{3}{4}$ pint/2 cups milk
1 teaspoon made mustard
slices of tomato and parsley sprig to garnish

Melt 25 g/1 oz/2 tablespoons butter in a saucepan, add the onion and sauté for about 10 minutes until soft. Stir in the mushrooms and cook for 2 minutes. Add seasoning and half the thyme. Melt remaining butter in a pan and fry breadcrumbs until crisp and golden, allow to cool before adding the Parmesan. Place half the crumbs in a well-greased casserole.

Melt the butter, stir in the flour and cook for 1 minute. Add the milk. Bring to the boil, stirring. Add thyme, seasoning and mustard. Mix with onion and mushrooms.

Slice the eggs and arrange over breadcrumbs in the casserole. Pour the sauce over and top with remaining crumbs. Bake in the oven (180°C, 350°F, Gas Mark 4) for 20 minutes. Garnish.

Serves 4

Cheese and pineapple flan

METRIC/IMPERIAL/AMERICAN
1 (18–20-cm/7–8-inch/7–8-inch) baked pastry flan case
100 g/4 oz/$\frac{1}{2}$ cup cooked bacon, diced finely
1 (200-g/7-oz/8-oz) can pineapple cubes
2 eggs, beaten
100 g/4 oz/$\frac{1}{2}$ cup cottage cheese
100 g/4 oz/1 cup Cheddar cheese, grated
pepper
1 teaspoon dried mustard
chopped parsley to garnish

Place the flan case on a baking sheet. Mix the bacon, drained pineapple, eggs, cheeses, pepper and mustard together, blending thoroughly. Pour the filling into the pastry case and bake on centre shelf of a moderate oven (180°C, 350°F, Gas Mark 4) for about 20–25 minutes until the filling is set. Sprinkle with chopped parsley and serve hot or cold.

Serves 4

Cheese and mushroom noodles

METRIC/IMPERIAL/AMERICAN
40 g/1½ oz/3 tablespoons butter or margarine
1 medium onion, chopped
100 g/4 oz/1 cup mushrooms, washed and halved
1 (106-g/3¾-oz/4-oz) packet cheese slices
175 g/6 oz/6 oz ribbon noodles
salt and pepper
1 teaspoon lemon juice
chopped parsley to garnish

Melt the butter or margarine in a frying pan, add the onion and cook gently for about 10 minutes until soft. Add the mushrooms and cook for a further 2 minutes. Cut the cheese into matchstick lengths.

Meanwhile, cook the noodles in boiling salted water for about 8 minutes until just tender. Drain well and return the noodles to the pan. Stir in the cooked onion and mushroom mixture, the cheese, seasoning and lemon juice. Blend thoroughly and serve immediately, garnished with parsley.

Serves 3

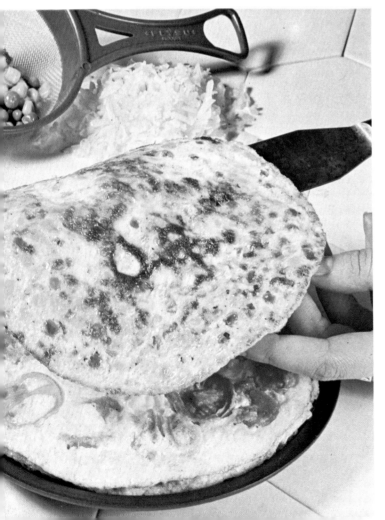

Omelette layer cake

METRIC/IMPERIAL/AMERICAN
1 (198-g/7-oz/8-oz) can sweetcorn with peppers
1 (113-g/4-oz/4-oz) packet frozen peas, thawed
6 large eggs
6 tablespoons/6 tablespoons/½ cup milk
salt and pepper
3 teaspoons corn oil
2 large tomatoes, skinned and sliced
40 g/1½ oz/⅓ cup Cheddar cheese, grated

Place the sweetcorn and peas in a pan of boiling salted water. Heat gently for about 5 minutes, drain well and cool.

Break 2 eggs into each of 3 basins and add one third milk to each basin with seasoning. Heat a teaspoon oil in an omelette pan. Place a third of the vegetables into two of the basins. Pour the contents of one basin into the omelette pan, cook gently for about 5 minutes until the base is set. Place the pan under the grill to brown. Lift out on to an ovenproof plate and keep warm in the oven.

Place another teaspoon of oil in the pan, pour in the egg mixture without vegetables. Arrange tomatoes on top and cook gently to lightly brown the base, brown the top under the grill. Remove from the pan and place on the first omelette.

Make the third omelette as the first. Place on top of the other 2 omelettes. Place remaining vegetables on top, sprinkle over the cheese and heat under the grill to melt cheese.

Serves 3–4

Eggs mulligatawny

METRIC/IMPERIAL/AMERICAN
175 g/6 oz/1 cup long-grain rice
750 ml/1¼ pints/3 cups chicken stock (or water and stock cube)
6 large eggs, hard-boiled
SAUCE:
1 (440-g/15½-oz/16-oz) can mulligatawny soup
1 tablespoon cornflour
1 tablespoon tomato purée
2 tablespoons/2 tablespoons/3 tablespoons sweet chutney
40 g/1½ oz/4 tablespoons sultanas
watercress sprigs to garnish

Cook the rice in the boiling stock until just tender – about 12–15 minutes.

Place the soup in a saucepan, blend the cornflour with a little water, add to the soup with the remaining ingredients. Bring slowly to the boil, stirring, and cook for about 5 minutes until the cornflour thickens and clears.

Drain the rice and arrange on a heated dish, cut the eggs into halves lengthways and arrange on the rice. Spoon the sauce over the eggs and garnish with watercress. Serve with redcurrant jelly and salted peanuts, if liked.

Serves 4

Fried egg ratatouille

METRIC/IMPERIAL/AMERICAN
50 g/2 oz/¼ cup butter or margarine
2 medium onions, sliced
1 medium green pepper, deseeded and diced
1 small aubergine, sliced
350 g/12 oz/¾ lb tomatoes, peeled and chopped
1 small clove garlic, crushed (optional)
salt and pepper
4 large eggs
1 tablespoon corn oil
8 anchovy fillets to garnish

Melt the butter or margarine in a frying pan, add the onion and cook gently until soft without browning – about 10 minutes. Add the green pepper and aubergine and cook very slowly, covered, for about 10 minutes without browning. Add the tomatoes, garlic if used and seasoning.

Fry the eggs in the oil. Arrange the vegetable mixture on a flat heated serving dish or individual dishes. Place the eggs on top. Garnish each egg with 2 anchovy fillets. Serve with warmed French bread.

Serves 4

Snacks

Snack meals may be required at any time during the day, particularly during the school holidays. These recipes have been created to inspire you to prepare tasty snacks from store cupboard ingredients and convenience foods with the minimum of effort.

Pizza discs

METRIC/IMPERIAL/AMERICAN
1 medium onion, chopped
1 clove garlic (optional)
25 g/1 oz/2 tablespoons butter or margarine
1 (396-g/14-oz/14-oz) can tomatoes
1 teaspoon dried mixed herbs
salt and pepper
1 tablespoon cornflour
2 tablespoons/2 tablespoons/3 tablespoons water
10 rusks or toast rounds
100 g/4 oz/1 cup Gruyère cheese, grated
1 (56-g/2-oz/2-oz) can anchovies, drained
watercress sprigs to garnish

Place the onion, garlic and butter in a medium saucepan and cook gently for 5 minutes until soft. Drain the tomatoes and add to the pan with the dried herbs and seasoning. Stir well and simmer for 10–15 minutes until thickened. Blend the cornflour with the water, stir into the tomatoes and cook, stirring, until the cornflour has thickened and cleared.

Place the rusks on a baking sheet and divide the sauce between the biscuits spreading the mixture evenly. Top each with grated cheese. Cut the anchovy fillets in half lengthways and arrange these in a criss-cross pattern on top of each biscuit.

Place in a moderately hot oven (200°C, 400°F, Gas Mark 6) for 8–10 minutes to heat through and melt the cheese. Garnish with watercress.

Makes 10

T.V. toppers

METRIC/IMPERIAL/AMERICAN
4 rashers streaky bacon, halved
8 large flat mushrooms, washed and trimmed
4 large eggs
3 tablespoons/3 tablespoons/¼ cup milk
salt and pepper
15 g/½ oz/1 tablespoon butter or margarine
4 round crusty bread rolls, warmed
parsley sprigs to garnish

Remove the rind from the bacon rashers and roll up. Secure
with a skewer and grill until slightly crisp. Put on one side and
keep warm. Place the mushrooms in the pan and cook on each
side for a few minutes, remove and keep warm.

Whisk together the eggs, milk and seasoning. Melt the butter
or margarine in a small pan, add the eggs and heat gently,
stirring until lightly scrambled.

Cut the warmed rolls in half, butter if liked and place a
mushroom on each half. Divide the scrambled egg between the
rolls and top each with a bacon roll. Garnish with the parsley.

Makes 8

Fried savoury scone

METRIC/IMPERIAL/AMERICAN
4 tablespoons/4 tablespoons/⅓ cup oil
50 g/2 oz/½ cup onion, chopped
1 (396-g/14-oz/14-oz) can tomatoes
½–1 teaspoon dried mixed herbs or marjoram
salt and pepper
175 g/6 oz/1½ cups self-raising flour
¼ teaspoon baking powder
25 g/1 oz/2 tablespoons margarine
5 tablespoons/5 tablespoons/6 tablespoons milk
100 g/4 oz/¼ lb pork and ham slices, in strips
2 slices processed cheese, cut into strips
3 pimento-stuffed olives, sliced, to garnish

Place 1 tablespoon of the oil in a saucepan, sauté the onion for
5 minutes. Drain the tomatoes and add to the onion with the
herbs and seasoning. Cook for about 5 minutes.

Sieve the flour, baking powder and salt into a mixing bowl,
rub in the margarine. Add the milk and mix until the mixture
forms a fairly soft dough. Knead gently on a floured surface and
roll out to a 26-cm/10-inch circle.

Heat the remaining oil in a 26-cm/10-inch frying pan. Add
the dough and cook to lightly brown the base – about 3–5
minutes. Turn the pizza over and cook for the same time.
Spread the tomato mixture over the dough, cover with strips of
meat and cheese. Garnish and place under the grill to melt the
cheese.

Serves 4

Creamed kippers

METRIC/IMPERIAL/AMERICAN
1 pair kippers
40 g/1½ oz/3 tablespoons butter or margarine
40 g/1½ oz/6 tablespoons plain flour
300 ml/½ pint/1¼ cups milk
1 egg
1 teaspoon lemon juice
4 slices toast
parsley sprigs to garnish

Poach the kippers by placing in a shallow pan of cold water. Bring to just below the boil, remove from the heat and leave for about 5 minutes. Remove the kippers and drain well. Remove the bones carefully and flake the fish.

Make the sauce by melting the butter or margarine, stir in the flour and gradually beat in the milk. Bring to the boil, stirring, and cook for about 2 minutes. Stir in the flaked kipper.

Separate the yolk from the white of the egg. Add the yolk to the fish, blending thoroughly. Whisk the egg white until stiff and fold into the mixture with the lemon juice.

Place the pieces of toast on a baking sheet, divide the mixture between them and place on the centre shelf of a moderate oven (180°C, 350°F, Gas Mark 4) for about 10–15 minutes. Serve immediately, garnished with parsley.

Serves 4

Baked bean hash

METRIC/IMPERIAL/AMERICAN
1 large onion, sliced
0.5 kg/1 lb/1 lb potatoes, peeled and diced
50 g/2 oz/¼ cup butter or margarine
1 (340-g/12-oz/12-oz) can corned beef
1 (220-g/7¾-oz/8-oz) can baked beans
1 tablespoon tomato ketchup
2 teaspoons dried mixed herbs
salt and pepper

Place the onion, potato, butter or margarine in a frying pan and sauté gently for about 20 minutes, stirring frequently.

Cut the corned beef into dice and add to the pan with the baked beans, ketchup, herbs and seasoning. Heat through gently for about 5 minutes, shaking the pan occasionally. Serve immediately.

Serves 3–4

Mixer and Blender Cookery

The mixer and blender are two very versatile pieces of kitchen equipment, but it's important to get the best possible use out of them, and in this chapter you will find a wide range of recipes enabling you to use your appliances to the maximum. So choose a machine of a capacity to suit your needs. Do not buy a small hand mixer if you will be using it for batch baking or bread making, and avoid small blenders if you need to process large quantities of food. Blenders which are attached to a hand mixer or the less powerful free-standing ones can only handle a small amount of food at a time, and in order to achieve the best results it is advisable never to overfill any mixer or blender.

The recipes here put these appliances to their best use for whisking, liquidising, mixing, making crumbs, beating and making purées. Many of the dishes are suitable for freezing, so prepare extra quantities with no extra effort and make all your catering easier.

The mixer and blender will make it simple to prepare otherwise time-consuming dishes effortlessly in minutes with the best results, enabling you to spend less time in the kitchen.

Appetisers, soups and spreads

Most of the appetisers and spreads in this chapter have been devised to serve as starters or for informal entertaining with drinks. They are very quick to make and may be made in advance and stored in the refrigerator for 3–4 days, if you prefer.

Pâtés are an absolute must with a liquidiser and home-made soups are really worth making. No more messy sieving; all the nutrients remain in the soup making it full of goodness and tasty too.

Avocado pâté

METRIC/IMPERIAL/AMERICAN
3 avocado pears
225 g/8 oz/1 cup cream cheese
1 teaspoon lemon juice
1 tablespoon grated onion
pinch salt
freshly ground black pepper
100 g/4 oz/½ cup butter, melted

Halve, stone and peel the avocado pears. Slice one of the pears into six, toss in a little lemon juice and reserve for the garnish. Place the remaining avocados, the cheese, lemon juice, grated onion and seasoning in the liquidiser, and blend until smooth. Turn into individual dishes, pour a little melted butter over each and place a slice of avocado on top. Serve immediately with croûtons.

Serves 6

Cheese pears

METRIC/IMPERIAL/AMERICAN
2 ripe pears
lemon juice
100 g/4 oz/½ cup cream cheese
1–2 tablespoons/1–2 tablespoons/1–3 tablespoons cream
salt and pepper
shredded lettuce
slices of radish to garnish

Peel the pears and slice in half lengthwise.

Remove the cores with a teaspoon and rub a little lemon juice over surface of the pears to prevent them discolouring. Place the cream cheese and cream in the mixer with the seasoning and switch on to a slow speed for 1–2 minutes. Pipe the mixture into the centre of each pear. Place some shredded lettuce on individual serving dishes with a pear half on top. Garnish with slices of radish.

Serves 4

Curried shrimp cocktails

METRIC/IMPERIAL/AMERICAN
150 ml/¼ pint/⅔ cup mayonnaise (see page 208)
1 teaspoon curry powder
225 g/8 oz/1 cup peeled shrimps
2 sticks celery, chopped
2 tomatoes, peeled and chopped
few lettuce leaves, shredded

Make the mayonnaise (see page 56) and stir in the curry powder, shrimps, celery and chopped tomatoes.

Place the shredded lettuce in the bottom of four individual serving glasses or dishes. Just before serving spoon the shrimp mixture on top.

Serves 4

Sardine cheese dip

METRIC/IMPERIAL/AMERICAN
2 (125-g/4¼-oz/4¼-oz) cans sardines
2 hard-boiled eggs
150 g/5 oz/generous 1 cup cream cheese
salt
freshly ground black pepper
few drops of lemon juice

Place all the ingredients in the liquidiser and blend until smooth. Chill.

Serve with sticks of raw celery, carrot or florets of cauliflower, spring onions, slices of apple and savoury biscuits.

Serves 6

Curd cheese creams

METRIC/IMPERIAL/AMERICAN
1 (290-g/10½-oz/10½-oz) can condensed consommé soup
15 g/½ oz/2 envelopes gelatine
175 g/6 oz/¾ cup curd cheese
pinch curry powder
1 tablespoon chopped chives
GARNISH:
slices of lemon
parsley sprigs

Place half the can of soup and gelatine in a saucepan and dissolve over a gentle heat. Cool and place in the liquidiser with the cheese and curry powder. Blend until smooth. Stir in the chives and pour into four individual ramekin dishes. Allow to chill for a few hours in the refrigerator.

Gently heat the remaining soup until liquid enough to pour on top of the chilled mixture. Allow to chill. Garnish each ramekin dish with a slice of lemon and a sprig of parsley. Serve with melba toast.

Note: These are even better if left to set in the refrigerator overnight.

Serves 4

Chilled mulligatawny soup

METRIC/IMPERIAL/AMERICAN

75 g/3 oz/6 tablespoons butter
1 onion, finely chopped
1 carrot, finely chopped
75 g/3 oz/¾ cup flour
25 g/1 oz/¼ cup curry powder
scant 1.5 litres/2½ pints/6¼ cups beef stock
salt
freshly ground black pepper
florets of cauliflower to garnish

Melt the butter and sauté the vegetables until soft, but not browned.

Stir in the flour, curry powder and stock. Whisking all the time, bring to the boil. Cover and simmer for 30 minutes.

Allow to cool slightly, then pour into the liquidiser. Blend until smooth. Season to taste.

Chill and skim off any fat. Serve chilled garnished with florets of cauliflower.

Serves 6

Cream of lettuce soup

METRIC/IMPERIAL/AMERICAN

25 g/1 oz/2 tablespoons butter
2 lettuces, washed and shredded
1 onion, finely chopped
20 g/¾ oz/3 tablespoons flour
900 ml/1½ pints/3¾ cups milk
salt
freshly ground black pepper
2 egg yolks
4 tablespoons/4 tablespoons/⅓ cup cream

Melt the butter in a saucepan and add lettuce and onion. Cover and cook gently for 5 minutes. Add the flour and milk and, whisking all the time, bring to the boil. Reduce the heat and simmer for 15–20 minutes.

Allow to cool, then pour the soup into the liquidiser. Blend until smooth. Return to the saucepan and add the seasoning.

Mix the egg yolks and cream together and pour into the soup. Heat gently until thickened. Serve hot or cold with fried garlic croûtons.

Serves 4

Main dishes

The *mixer and liquidiser can be used to help speed up the
preparation of many main course dishes.*

*Several recipes necessitate the use of breadcrumbs
whether for coatings or for stuffings. These can be made in
a matter of seconds in the liquidiser. Pastry can be made
very successfully in the mixer, eliminating all the messy
rubbing-in.*

*Batters are excellent made in the liquidiser and a mixer
takes the hard work out of preparing soufflés.*

Crispy fried fish balls

METRIC/IMPERIAL/AMERICAN
50 g/2 oz/¼ cup butter
50 g/2 oz/½ cup flour
150 ml/¼ pint/⅔ cup milk
350 g/12 oz/¾ lb smoked haddock, cooked
grated rind of ½ lemon
salt and pepper
1 tablespoon chopped parsley
2 hard-boiled eggs, chopped
COATING:
beaten egg
fresh white breadcrumbs

oil for deep frying

Place the butter, flour and milk in the liquidiser and switch on
to maximum speed for 30 seconds. Pour into a saucepan and,
whisking all the time, bring to the boil. Simmer gently for
1 minute. Stir in the remaining ingredients and then spread over
a plate and mark into 12 portions. Chill until firm enough to
handle.

Roll into balls, using a little flour if necessary. Dip in the
beaten egg and then toss in the breadcrumbs.

Heat the oil to 180°C/360°F and fry the fish balls until
golden. Drain well on absorbent paper. Serve with tomato
sauce (see page 206).
Note: These fish balls may be cooked fondue style at the table.

Serves 4

Stuffed plaice mimosa

METRIC/IMPERIAL/AMERICAN
4 slices white bread, crusts removed
2 hard-boiled eggs
few parsley sprigs
50 g/2 oz/½ cup cheese, grated
50 g/2 oz/¼ cup butter, melted
salt
freshly ground black pepper
2 plaice, filleted and skinned
broccoli spears to garnish

Place the bread in the liquidiser and make into breadcrumbs. Roughly chop the eggs and add to the breadcrumbs with the parsley. Blend for a few seconds only. Turn into a bowl and stir in the cheese, melted butter and seasoning. Mix well together.

Spread the filling over the skinned side of each fillet and roll up, starting at the tail end. Secure with a wooden cocktail stick and place in a greased ovenproof dish. Cook in a moderate oven (180°C, 350°F, Gas Mark 4) for 15–20 minutes. Remove the cocktail sticks, garnish with broccoli spears and serve with parsley sauce (see page 205).

Serves 4

Puff top fish pie

METRIC/IMPERIAL/AMERICAN
2 sticks celery, chopped
1 onion, chopped
75 g/3 oz/6 tablespoons butter
675 g/1½ lb/1½ lb smoked cod or haddock, cubed
450 ml/¾ pint/2 cups milk
25 g/1 oz/¼ cup flour
salt and pepper
1 egg yolk
1 tablespoon cream
3 tablespoons/3 tablespoons/¼ cup chopped parsley
75 g/3 oz/¾ cup cheese, grated
1 (212-g/7½-oz/7½-oz) packet frozen puff pastry
twist of lemon and watercress sprigs to garnish

Sauté the vegetables in 50 g/2 oz/¼ cup of the butter until softened. Stir in the fish and simmer for 5 minutes. Add the milk, bring to the boil and simmer for 10 minutes. Drain and reserve liquor. Place the remaining butter, the flour and strained fish liquor in the liquidiser. Blend until smooth then pour into a saucepan. Bring to the boil, whisking all the time. Stir in the vegetables, fish, seasoning, egg yolk, cream, parsley and cheese. Pour into an ovenproof dish; cool. Roll out the pastry and cut out 5-cm/2-inch circles. Overlap them around the edge of the dish. Brush with milk and bake in a hot oven (230°C, 450°F, Gas Mark 8) for 15–25 minutes.

Serves 4–6

Beef and walnut cobbler

METRIC/IMPERIAL/AMERICAN
675 g/1½ lb/1½ lb chuck steak, cubed
25 g/1 oz/¼ cup seasoned flour
100 g/4 oz/½ cup margarine
2 onions, sliced
1 clove garlic, crushed
1 green pepper, sliced
450 ml/¾ pint/2 cups beef stock
1½ tablespoons tomato purée
225 g/8 oz/2 cups plain flour
½ teaspoon bicarbonate of soda
1 teaspoon cream of tartar
1 egg, beaten
5 tablespoons/5 tablespoons/6 tablespoons milk
25 g/1 oz/¼ cup walnuts, chopped

Toss the meat in seasoned flour. Melt half the margarine and sauté the vegetables for 5 minutes. Remove. Brown the meat, then replace the vegetables; add seasoning, stock and the tomato purée. Cover and cook in a moderately hot oven (190°C, 375°F, Gas Mark 5) for 1½ hours. Place the remaining margarine, flour, pinch salt, bicarbonate, cream of tartar, egg and milk in the mixer bowl and switch on to a slow speed to form a soft dough. Knead lightly and roll out and cut into 5-cm/2-inch circles. Place overlapping on top of the meat, glaze and sprinkle with the walnuts. Return to a hot oven (220°C, 425°F, Gas Mark 7) for 20–25 minutes. Garnish with parsley.

Serves 4–6

Guard of honour with apricot stuffing

METRIC/IMPERIAL/AMERICAN
2 joints best end neck of lamb, chined
4 slices white bread, crusts removed
few sprigs parsley and mint
40 g/1½ oz/3 tablespoons margarine
1 small onion, chopped
75 g/3 oz/½ cup dried apricots, chopped
salt and pepper
beaten egg to bind
broccoli spears to garnish

Choose joints of lamb with six or seven chops on each. Trim the bones to within 2.5 cm/1 inch of the top. Place the joints together allowing the bones to cross alternately with the bases together. Secure with string.

Place the bread in the liquidiser with the parsley and mint. Switch on to a medium speed for 6–8 seconds. Turn into a bowl. Melt the margarine and sauté the onion. Stir into the breadcrumb mixture with the remaining ingredients, adding egg to bind.

Fill the cavity between the two joints of meat with the stuffing. Cover the end of each bone with foil to prevent burning. Place the meat in a roasting tin and roast in a moderately hot oven (190°C, 375°F, Gas Mark 5) for 1¼–1½ hours. Remove the foil and replace with cutlet frills.

Serves 6

Savoury meat loaf

METRIC/IMPERIAL/AMERICAN

25 g/1 oz/2 tablespoons butter or margarine
175 g/6 oz/$\frac{3}{4}$ cup onions, diced
75 g/3 oz/$\frac{3}{4}$ cup mushrooms, chopped
25 g/1 oz/$\frac{1}{4}$ cup plain flour
175 ml/6 fl oz/$\frac{3}{4}$ cup milk
2 eggs
1 teaspoon Worcestershire sauce
salt and pepper
1 teaspoon mixed herbs
3 tablespoons/3 tablespoons/$\frac{1}{4}$ cup tomato purée
1 tablespoon chopped parsley
450 g/1 lb/2 cups minced beef
175 g/6 oz/$\frac{3}{4}$ cup minced pork
75 g/3 oz/$1\frac{1}{2}$ cups fresh white breadcrumbs
slices of tomato and cucumber, radish roses, lettuce, cress
    to garnish

Melt the butter or margarine and sauté the onions until soft but
not browned. Stir in the mushrooms and flour and cook for 1
minute. Add the milk gradually, stirring all the time and bring
to the boil. Allow to cool slightly.

Add the remaining ingredients to the cooked mixture and
mix well together. Place in a 1-kg/2-lb greased loaf tin and cook
in a moderate oven (180°C, 350°F, Gas Mark 4) for 1–1$\frac{1}{4}$ hours.
Allow to cool slightly in the tin before turning out. When cold
wrap in foil and chill. Garnish before serving.

Serves 4–6

Beef olives

METRIC/IMPERIAL/AMERICAN

1 onion, chopped roughly
1 slice bread, crusts removed
few parsley sprigs
1 teaspoon mixed herbs
175 g/6 oz/1 cup pork, minced
1 apple, peeled, cored and finely chopped
1 egg, beaten
8 thin slices beef topside
2 tablespoons/2 tablespoons/3 tablespoons oil
2 onions, chopped
4 tomatoes, peeled and chopped
300 ml/$\frac{1}{2}$ pint/1$\frac{1}{4}$ cups red wine or stock
slices of tomato and cress to garnish

Place the onion, bread and parsley in the liquidiser and blend for
30 seconds. Add the herbs, pork, apple, seasoning and beaten
egg. Divide the stuffing between the slices of meat, and spread
evenly. Roll up and secure with string. Heat the oil and sauté
the beef olives until brown. Remove, add the vegetables and
sauté for 5 minutes. Place vegetables and beef olives in a
casserole. Pour over wine, cover and cook in a moderate oven
(180°C, 350°F, Gas Mark 4) for 1–1$\frac{1}{2}$ hours.

Remove olives and keep hot. Pour the sauce and vegetables
into the liquidiser and blend until smooth. Reheat and pour
over the beef olives. Pipe a border of potato around edge of the
beef olives and serve garnished.

Serves 4–8

Chicken gougère

METRIC/IMPERIAL/AMERICAN
150 ml/¼ pint/⅔ cup water
50 g/2 oz/¼ cup butter
65 g/2½ oz/generous ½ cup plain flour
2 eggs, beaten
1 onion, chopped
15 g/½ oz/2 tablespoons butter
25 g/1 oz/¼ cup flour
300 ml/½ pint/1¼ cups milk
450 g/1 lb/2 cups cooked chicken, chopped
2 hard-boiled eggs, chopped
1½ tablespoons chopped parsley
grated rind of ½ lemon
1 tablespoon each breadcrumbs and grated cheese
25 g/1 oz/¼ cup flaked almonds

Heat the water and butter. Bring to the boil, remove and beat in the flour and seasoning until the mixture leaves the sides of the pan. Cool then place in the mixer bowl. Add eggs with the mixer on slow speed. Place in a piping bag with a 1-cm/½-inch plain nozzle and pipe two rows around edges of four 13-cm/5-inch ovenproof dishes. Cook in a hot oven (220°C, 425°F, Gas Mark 7) for 20 minutes. Sauté the onion in the butter until soft. Stir in the flour and cook for 1 minute. Gradually stir in the milk and bring to the boil. Add the chicken, eggs, parsley and lemon rind. Spoon into the dishes. Mix the breadcrumbs, cheese and almonds and sprinkle over. Bake for 5–10 minutes.

Serves 4

Cheese and herb soufflé

METRIC/IMPERIAL/AMERICAN
50 g/2 oz/¼ cup butter or margarine
50 g/2 oz/½ cup flour
300 ml/½ pint/1¼ cups milk
salt and pepper
1 tablespoon chopped parsley
½ teaspoon basil
pinch dry mustard
3 eggs, separated
100 g/4 oz/1 cup Cheddar cheese, grated
parsley sprig to garnish

Place the butter or margarine, flour and milk in the liquidiser and switch on to maximum speed for 30 seconds. Pour into a saucepan and whisking all the time bring to the boil. Simmer gently for 1 minute, still stirring. Stir in the seasoning, parsley, basil and mustard. Allow to cool slightly.

Pour the sauce into the mixer bowl and whisk in the egg yolks. Fold in the grated cheese. Whisk the egg whites until stiff, then fold into the mixture. Pour into 4 greased individual ramekin dishes and cook in a moderately hot oven (190°C, 375°F, Gas Mark 5) for 20–25 minutes. Serve immediately garnished with parsley.

Serves 4

Stuffed lamb chops

METRIC/IMPERIAL/AMERICAN
4 loin lamb chops
STUFFING:
2 slices white bread, crusts removed
few mint sprigs
few rosemary sprigs
½ small onion, roughly chopped
grated rind of ½ lemon
beaten egg to bind
GARNISH:
watercress sprigs
quarters of tomato

Slit the chops horizontally through to the bone, to form a
pocket.

Place the bread in the liquidiser with the remaining
ingredients and switch on to a medium speed. Blend until a
fairly moist stuffing is formed. Divide into four and fill the
cavity in each of the chops. Wrap each one in foil. Cook in a
moderately hot oven (190°C, 375°F, Gas Mark 5) for 20–25
minutes. Unwrap and garnish with watercress sprigs and
quarters of tomato. Serve with sautéed mushrooms.

Serves 4

Minted lamb and apricot kebabs

METRIC/IMPERIAL/AMERICAN
MARINADE:
175 ml/6 fl oz/¾ cup oil
4 tablespoons/4 tablespoons/⅓ cup wine vinegar
1 clove garlic, crushed
few fresh mint leaves
salt and pepper
few parsley sprigs
KEBABS:
675 g/1½ lb/1½ lb lean leg of lamb, cubed
8 bay leaves
4 courgettes, sliced thickly
12 dried apricots, soaked overnight in cold water and
**   drained**

Place all the marinade ingredients in the liquidiser and blend
until smooth. Place the lamb in a shallow dish, pour over the
marinade and set aside in the refrigerator for 1–2 hours.

Thread the lamb and the remaining ingredients on to four
long skewers. Brush with the marinade and cook under a hot
grill, turning and basting the kebabs frequently.

Serve with barbecue sauce (see page 206).

Serves 4

Hot and
cold
puddings

Puddings can be a real joy to make with the aid of a mixer or liquidiser. You can make soufflés and meringues at the flick of a switch.

Fruit purées and biscuit crumb crusts can be made in a matter of seconds. Nuts can be chopped finely or coarsely as required, and almonds can be made into ground almonds.

Pineapple fritters

METRIC/IMPERIAL/AMERICAN
FRITTER BATTER:
50 g/2 oz/½ cup plain flour
1 egg, separated
5 tablespoons/5 tablespoons/6 tablespoons milk
1 tablespoon water

oil for deep frying
1 (439-g/15½-oz/15½-oz) can pineapple rings, drained
castor sugar to sprinkle

Place the flour, egg yolk, milk and water in the liquidiser and blend until smooth. Pour into a bowl.

Heat the oil in a deep fat pan to 180°C/360°F, or when a cube of day-old bread turns golden brown.

Whisk the egg white and fold into the batter. Dip the pineapple rings in the batter and coat evenly. Fry in the oil until golden brown. Drain on absorbent paper and sprinkle with castor sugar.

Serves 4

Apple-berry charlotte

METRIC/IMPERIAL/AMERICAN
1 kg/2 lb/2 lb cooking apples
lemon juice
225 g/8 oz/½ lb blackberries
50 g/2 oz/¼ cup sugar
3 cloves
75 g/3 oz/2 slices white bread, crusts removed
50 g/2 oz/¼ cup butter
25 g/1 oz/2 tablespoons demerara sugar

Peel and core the apples. Reserve three slices for decoration and sprinkle with a little lemon juice to prevent discoloration. Quarter the remaining apples.

Reserve a few blackberries for decoration and mix remainder with the quartered apples. Place in an ovenproof dish with the sugar and cloves.

Place the bread in the liquidiser and blend into fine breadcrumbs. Melt the butter in a frying pan and stir in the breadcrumbs; fry until golden. Mix with the demerara sugar and sprinkle over the fruit.

Bake in a moderately hot oven (190°C, 375°F, Gas Mark 5) for 35–45 minutes. Decorate with reserved slices of apple filled with the blackberries.

Serves 4–6

Pineapple meringue pie

METRIC/IMPERIAL/AMERICAN
Shortcrust pastry (see page 230)
FILLING:
25 g/1 oz/2 tablespoons butter or margarine
25 g/1 oz/¼ cup cornflour
1 (376-g/13¼-oz/13¼-oz) can pineapple pieces
50 g/2 oz/¼ cup sugar
2 egg yolks
MERINGUE:
2 egg whites
75 g/3 oz/scant ½ cup castor sugar
glacé cherries and angelica to decorate

Make the pastry and use to line a 20-cm/8-inch flan ring, placed on a baking sheet. Bake blind in a moderately hot oven (200°C, 400°F, Gas Mark 6) for 15 minutes. Reduce the oven temperature to moderate (180°C, 350°F, Gas Mark 4) and bake the flan for a further 10–15 minutes. Place the butter or margarine, cornflour, juice made up to 300 ml/½ pint/1¼ cups, and the sugar in a saucepan. Whisking all the time, bring to the boil and cook for 2–3 minutes. Cool slightly. Beat in the egg yolks and fold in the drained pineapple pieces. Pour into the partly-cooked flan case. Place the egg whites in the mixer bowl and whisk until stiff. Add the sugar and whisk again until stiff. Pile on top of the pineapple mixture. Bake in a moderately hot oven (200°C, 400°F, Gas Mark 6) for 10–15 minutes. Decorate.

Serves 4–6

Brandied mincemeat soufflé

METRIC/IMPERIAL/AMERICAN
25 g/1 oz/2 tablespoons butter or margarine
50 g/2 oz/½ cup plain flour
150 ml/¼ pint/⅔ cup milk
25 g/1 oz/2 tablespoons castor sugar
3 egg yolks
1 tablespoon mincemeat
1 tablespoon brandy
3 egg whites
icing sugar to decorate

Place the butter, flour, milk and sugar in the liquidiser and switch on to maximum speed for 30 seconds. Pour into a saucepan and whisking all the time bring to the boil. Simmer gently for 1 minute, still stirring. Cool slightly.

Whisk the egg yolks into the cooled sauce. Fold in the mincemeat and brandy. Place the egg whites in the mixer bowl and whisk until stiff. Fold the whisked egg whites into the mincemeat mixture.

Pour into 4 individual greased soufflé dishes and cook in a moderately hot oven (190°C, 375°F, Gas Mark 5) for 40–45 minutes. Sprinkle with icing sugar and serve immediately with cream.

Serves 4

Fruity bakewell tart

METRIC/IMPERIAL/AMERICAN
ORANGE PASTRY:
100 g/4 oz/½ cup margarine
175 g/6 oz/1½ cups plain flour
grated rind of 1 orange
FILLING:
50 g/2 oz/¼ cup margarine
50 g/2 oz/½ cup ground almonds
100 g/4 oz/½ cup castor sugar
2 eggs
4–5 tablespoons/4–5 tablespoons/⅓ cup–6 tablespoons redcurrant jelly
2 bananas, sliced
angelica leaves to decorate

Place the margarine, 1 tablespoon water and one-third of the flour in the mixer bowl. Using a slow speed combine until just mixed. Add the remaining flour and the orange rind and mix again until a dough is formed. Knead lightly on a floured board. Roll out and line a 20-cm/8-inch flan ring placed on a baking sheet.

Place the margarine, ground almonds, sugar and eggs in the mixer bowl. Mix together on a slow speed until well mixed. Spread the redcurrant jelly over the base of the flan case. Arrange the bananas (reserving a few for decoration) on top and then cover with the almond mixture. Bake in a moderate oven (160°C, 325°F, Gas Mark 3) for 45–60 minutes. Decorate.

Serves 6

Mocha fudge pudding

METRIC/IMPERIAL/AMERICAN
75 g/3 oz/6 tablespoons soft margarine
50 g/2 oz/½ cup self-raising flour
25 g/1 oz/¼ cup cocoa powder
15 g/½ oz/2 tablespoons instant coffee granules
75 g/3 oz/6 tablespoons castor sugar
1 egg
50 g/2 oz/4 tablespoons brown sugar
40 g/1½ oz/scant ½ cup walnuts, chopped
SAUCE:
300 ml/½ pint/1¼ cups hot black coffee
50 g/2 oz/¼ cup castor sugar
DECORATION:
icing sugar
halved walnuts

Place the margarine, flour, half the cocoa powder, the coffee, sugar and egg in the mixer bowl and whisk on a slow speed until well mixed. Place in a 1-litre/2-pint ovenproof dish.

Sprinkle with the brown sugar, remaining cocoa powder and the walnuts. Mix the black coffee and sugar together and pour over. Bake in a moderate oven (160°C, 325°F, Gas Mark 3) for 50–60 minutes. Dredge with icing sugar, decorate with halved walnuts and serve with cream.

Serves 4–6

Gooseberry creams

METRIC/IMPERIAL/AMERICAN
1 kg/2 lb/2 lb gooseberries, topped and tailed
100 g/4 oz/½ cup castor sugar
green food colouring (optional)
½ teaspoon gelatine
1 tablespoon hot water
150 ml/¼ pint/⅔ cup double cream

Place the gooseberries and sugar in a saucepan and heat very gently until the sugar has dissolved. Pour into the liquidiser and blend into a purée. Add a few drops green colouring if liked.

Dissolve the gelatine in the water. Cool slightly, then stir into the gooseberry purée. Lightly whisk the cream and gently swirl into the gooseberry mixture. Chill and serve in individual glasses, with sponge finger biscuits.

Serves 6

Strawberry cream sorbet

METRIC/IMPERIAL/AMERICAN
350 g/12 oz/1¼ cups strawberries, hulled
50 g/2 oz/¼ cup castor sugar
1 (142-g/5-oz/5-oz) carton strawberry yogurt
few drops of lemon juice
150 ml/¼ pint/⅔ cup double cream
2 egg whites, whisked
DECORATION:
strawberries
mint leaves

Place the strawberries, sugar and yogurt in the liquidiser and blend until smooth. Add the lemon juice to taste.

Pour into a rigid polythene container and freeze for 1 hour. Turn out into a bowl and break up with a fork. Whisk the cream lightly and fold into the strawberry mixture with the whisked egg whites. Return to the freezer until firm. Spoon into glasses and decorate with strawberries and mint leaves.

Note: Raspberries may be substituted for strawberries.

Serves 4

Citrus cornflake freeze

METRIC/IMPERIAL/AMERICAN
75 g/3 oz/3 cups crushed cornflakes
25 g/1 oz/2 tablespoons castor sugar
25 g/1 oz/2 tablespoons butter, melted
2 eggs, separated
grated rind of 1 lemon
1 small can condensed milk
4 tablespoons/4 tablespoons/⅓ cup lemon juice
100 g/4 oz/½ cup castor sugar
slices of lemon to decorate

Mix together the crushed cornflakes, sugar and melted butter. Press half into the base of a 1-kg/2-lb loaf tin and chill.

Whisk the egg yolks until thick and creamy. Add the lemon rind, condensed milk and lemon juice and whisk until thickened.

Whisk the egg whites until stiff and fold in the sugar. Fold into the lemon mixture and pour on to the chilled cornflake base. Sprinkle the top with the remaining cornflakes. Freeze until firm. Carefully remove from the loaf tin and cut into slices. Decorate with slices of lemon.

Serves 4–6

Orange syllabub

METRIC/IMPERIAL/AMERICAN

300 ml/½ pint/1¼ cups double cream
2 tablespoons/2 tablespoons/3 tablespoons clear honey
2 tablespoons/2 tablespoons/3 tablespoons white wine
2 tablespoons/2 tablespoons/3 tablespoons fresh orange
   juice
finely grated rind of 1 orange
15 g/½ oz/1 tablespoon castor sugar

Place the cream, honey, wine, orange juice and half of the
orange rind in the mixer bowl and whisk until stiff. Spoon into
individual glasses and chill.

   Just before serving mix the remaining orange rind with the
sugar and sprinkle on top of the syllabub.

Serves 4

Blackberry meringue

METRIC/IMPERIAL/AMERICAN

4 egg whites
225 g/8 oz/1 cup castor sugar
CRÈME PATISSIÈRE:
25 g/1 oz/2 tablespoons butter
20 g/¾ oz/3 tablespoons plain flour
6 tablespoons/6 tablespoons/½ cup milk
25 g/1 oz/2 tablespoons castor sugar
1 egg yolk
1 tablespoon cream

225 g/8 oz/2 cups blackberries
150 ml/¼ pint/⅔ cup double cream, whipped

Place the egg whites in the mixer bowl and whisk until stiff.
Gradually add the sugar whisking all the time until stiff again.
Place the mixture in a piping bag fitted with a large star tube.
Line two baking sheets with silicone paper and pipe two circles,
20 cm/8 inches in diameter. Smooth evenly. Pipe the remaining
meringue into small rosettes. Bake in a cool oven (110°C, 225°F,
Gas Mark ¼) for 4–5 hours. Cool, then remove the paper.

   Place the butter, flour and milk in a saucepan and whisking all
the time over a moderate heat, bring to the boil. Cool slightly,
before whisking in the remaining ingredients. Allow to cool
completely, then sandwich the meringue circles together with
the crème patissière. Top with blackberries, piped cream and
meringue rosettes.

Serves 4–6

Strawberry cheesecake

METRIC/IMPERIAL/AMERICAN
100 g/4 oz/$\frac{1}{4}$ lb digestive biscuits
50 g/2 oz/$\frac{1}{4}$ cup butter, melted
FILLING:
225 g/8 oz/1 cup cream cheese
150 g/5 oz/generous $\frac{1}{4}$ cup natural yogurt
$\frac{1}{2}$ packet lemon jelly
3 tablespoons/3 tablespoons/$\frac{1}{4}$ cup hot water
50 g/2 oz/$\frac{1}{4}$ cup castor sugar
grated rind and juice of 1 lemon
DECORATION:
150 ml/$\frac{1}{4}$ pint/$\frac{2}{3}$ cup double cream, whipped
few strawberries

Crush the digestive biscuits in the liquidiser. Place in a bowl and
stir in the melted butter. Press into the base of a 20-cm/8-inch
round loose-bottomed sandwich tin. Chill until firm.

Place the cheese and yogurt in the mixer bowl and whisk
slowly until smooth. Dissolve the jelly in the water with the
sugar and cool slightly. Pour into the cheese mixture together
with the lemon rind and juice. Whisk on a slow speed until
smooth. Pour over the biscuit base and chill until set. Carefully
remove from the cake tin and decorate with piped cream and
strawberries.

Serves 4–6

Coffee cream

METRIC/IMPERIAL/AMERICAN
3 teaspoons gelatine
3 tablespoons/3 tablespoons/$\frac{1}{4}$ cup water
450 ml/$\frac{3}{4}$ pint/2 cups double cream
150 ml/$\frac{1}{4}$ pint/$\frac{2}{3}$ cup single cream
75 g/3 oz/6 tablespoons castor sugar
1 tablespoon instant coffee powder
2 teaspoons hot water
DECORATION:
150 ml/$\frac{1}{4}$ pint/$\frac{2}{3}$ cup double cream, whipped
grated chocolate

Dissolve the gelatine in the water in a bowl placed over a
saucepan of hot water. Place the double and single creams in the
mixer bowl and whisk until the cream leaves a trail. Fold in the
sugar. Dissolve the coffee powder in the hot water and stir into
the dissolved gelatine and allow to cool slightly.

With the mixer at a medium speed pour in the dissolved
coffee and gelatine. Whisk until the cream is on the point of
setting. Pour into a rinsed out 1-litre/1$\frac{3}{4}$-pint mould and chill.
Turn out just before serving and decorate with whipped cream
and grated chocolate.

Serves 4–6

Orange zabaglione

METRIC/IMPERIAL/AMERICAN
2 eggs
2 egg yolks
40 g/1½ oz/3 tablespoons castor sugar
grated rind and juice of 1 orange
2 tablespoons/2 tablespoons/3 tablespoons brandy

Place the eggs and yolks in bowl and whisk until combined. Add the sugar and grated orange rind, place the bowl over a saucepan of hot water and whisk until thick and frothy. Lastly, whisk in the orange juice and brandy.

Pour into individual glasses and serve immediately.

Serves 6

Banana and blackcurrant fool

METRIC/IMPERIAL/AMERICAN
450 g/1 lb/4 cups blackcurrants, washed and hulled
2 tablespoons/2 tablespoons/3 tablespoons water
100 g/4 oz/½ cup castor sugar
2 bananas, sliced
300 ml/½ pint/1¼ cups double cream

Place the blackcurrants and water in a saucepan. Cover and simmer for 10–15 minutes. Stir in the sugar and sliced bananas. Place in the liquidiser and blend to a purée. Allow to cool.

Whip the cream and then fold in the fruit purée. Pour into a serving dish or individual dishes and chill well.

Serves 4–6

Soured apricot fool

METRIC/IMPERIAL/AMERICAN
1 kg/2 lb/2 lb ripe apricots
3 tablespoons/3 tablespoons/$\frac{1}{4}$ cup water
150 g/5 oz/$\frac{2}{3}$ cup castor sugar
grated rind of $\frac{1}{2}$ orange
2 tablespoons/2 tablespoons/3 tablespoons orange juice
300 ml/$\frac{1}{2}$ pint/$1\frac{1}{4}$ cups soured cream
DECORATION:
glacé cherries
angelica

Stone the apricots and place in a saucepan with the water and sugar. Bring to the boil and simmer gently until tender. Cool slightly, then place in the liquidiser and blend until smooth. Allow to cool.

Stir the orange rind and juice into the purée. Spoon into individual glasses with the soured cream. Swirl the purée and cream with a teaspoon. Chill well and decorate with a glacé cherry and angelica.

Serves 4–6

St Clements crunch flan

METRIC/IMPERIAL/AMERICAN
175 g/6 oz/$\frac{1}{3}$ lb chocolate digestive biscuits
50 g/2 oz/$\frac{1}{4}$ cup butter, melted
grated rind of 1 orange
FILLING:
150 ml/$\frac{1}{4}$ pint/$\frac{2}{3}$ cup double cream
1 small can condensed milk
3 tablespoons/3 tablespoons/$\frac{1}{4}$ cup lemon juice
2 tablespoons/2 tablespoons/3 tablespoons orange juice
grated rind of 1 lemon

slices of orange to decorate

Place the digestive biscuits in the liquidiser and blend until crumbled. Place crumbs in a bowl and pour in the melted butter and orange rind. Mix well and line the base and sides of six individual dishes or a 20-cm/8-inch flan dish, using the back of a metal spoon. Chill well.

Lightly whisk the cream and fold in the condensed milk, lemon juice, orange juice and lemon rind. Pour into the chilled biscuit shell. Chill until set.

Decorate with slices of orange.

Serves 6

Apricot sherbet

METRIC/IMPERIAL/AMERICAN
1 (411-g/14½-oz/14½-oz) can apricots, drained
2 eggs, separated
25 g/1 oz/2 tablespoons castor sugar
25 g/1 oz/¼ cup ground almonds
4 tablespoons/4 tablespoons/⅓ cup cream

Place apricots in the liquidiser and blend to a purée. Place the egg whites in the mixer bowl and whisk until stiff. Whisk in the sugar.

Combine the egg yolks, ground almonds and cream. Fold into the egg whites together with the apricot purée. Pour into a shallow rigid polythene container and freeze for 4 hours, or until hard. Scoop out with a spoon into serving dishes.

Serves 4

Blackberry flummery

METRIC/IMPERIAL/AMERICAN
450 g/1 lb/4 cups blackberries
600 ml/1 pint/2½ cups water
2 tablespoons cornflour
100 g/4 oz/½ cup castor sugar
1 tablespoon lemon juice
2 eggs
150 ml/¼ pint/⅔ cup double cream

Place the blackberries (reserving a few for decoration) and water in a saucepan. Bring to the boil, then simmer gently until tender. Allow to cool slightly then place in the liquidiser and blend to a purée.

Mix the cornflour with a little of the purée until smooth. Place the remaining purée in a saucepan, add the sugar and bring to the boil. Stir in the blended cornflour and lemon juice. Return to the heat and stir until thick. Cool.

Separate eggs and add the yolks to the cooled purée. Place the egg whites in mixer bowl and whisk until fairly stiff. Fold into the blackberry purée. Pour into individual dishes. Whip the cream lightly and swirl into the purée. Serve decorated with the reserved blackberries.

Serves 4–6

Gingered pear flan

METRIC/IMPERIAL/AMERICAN
225 g/8 oz/$\frac{1}{2}$ lb ginger biscuits
75 g/3 oz/6 tablespoons butter, melted
FILLING:
25 g/1 oz/2 tablespoons butter
25 g/1 oz/$\frac{1}{4}$ cup plain flour
100 ml/4 fl oz/$\frac{1}{2}$ cup milk
1 egg yolk
25 g/1 oz/2 tablespoons sugar
grated rind of 1 orange
1 tablespoon cream
1 tablespoon brandy
1 (411-g/14$\frac{1}{2}$-oz/14$\frac{1}{2}$-oz) can pear halves, drained
2 oranges, peeled and segmented
DECORATION:
whipped cream
angelica leaves

Roughly break up the ginger biscuits, then crush them in the liquidiser. Place in a bowl and mix with the melted butter. Press into the base and sides of a 20-cm/8-inch flan dish or shallow pie dish, using the back of a metal spoon. Chill.

Place the butter, flour and milk in a saucepan and whisking continuously bring to the boil. Cool slightly then whisk in the egg yolk, sugar, orange rind, cream and brandy. Pour into the biscuit shell. Arrange the pears and orange segments on top of the filling. Decorate with cream and angelica.

Serves 6

Normandy flan

METRIC/IMPERIAL/AMERICAN
Shortcrust pastry (see page 230)
450 g/1 lb/1 lb cooking apples, peeled, cored and sliced
1 tablespoon water
75 g/3 oz/6 tablespoons sugar
50 g/2 oz/$\frac{1}{4}$ cup butter
2 egg yolks
grated rind of 1 orange
2 red-skinned eating apples
sieved apricot jam to glaze
icing sugar to sprinkle

Make the pastry and use to line a 20-cm/8-inch flan dish. Bake blind in a moderately hot oven (200°C, 400°F, Gas Mark 6) for 15 minutes. Reduce the oven temperature to moderate (180°C, 350°F, Gas Mark 4) and continue to cook the flan for a further 10–15 minutes. Cool.

Cook the apples with the water and sugar until soft. Whisk into a purée. Remove from the heat and beat in the butter, egg yolks and orange rind. Pour into the flan case.

Slice the eating apples, leaving the skin on and arrange on top of the apple purée. Brush with apricot jam and return to a moderately hot oven (200°C, 400°F, Gas Mark 6) for 25 minutes. Dredge the surface of the flan with icing sugar and place under a hot grill to caramelise the apples. Serve cold with cream.

Serves 4–6

Citrus crunch pie

METRIC/IMPERIAL/AMERICAN
150 g/5 oz/5 oz semi-sweet biscuits
100 g/4 oz/½ cup butter, melted
100 g/4 oz/½ cup castor sugar
FILLING:
2 eggs, separated
100 g/4 oz/½ cup castor sugar
grated rind and juice of 1 small lemon
1 teaspoon gelatine
pinch cream of tartar
4 tablespoons/4 tablespoons/⅓ cup double cream
whipped cream and slices of lemon to decorate

Place the biscuits in the liquidiser and blend into fine crumbs.
Mix with the melted butter and sugar. Press the mixture over
the base and sides of a greased 20-cm/8-inch flan dish. Chill.

Place the egg yolks, half the sugar, the lemon rind and juice in
a bowl placed over a saucepan of hot water, and whisk until
thick and creamy. Dissolve the gelatine in 1 tablespoon hot
water then stir into the egg mixture; cool.

Place the egg whites in the mixer bowl and whisk with the
cream of tartar until foamy. Add the remaining sugar and whisk
until stiff. Whisk the cream until thick. When the egg mixture
begins to set, whisk lightly until smooth, then fold in the egg
whites and cream. Pour into the biscuit base and chill. Decorate.

Serves 4–6

Banana ice cream

METRIC/IMPERIAL/AMERICAN
100 g/4 oz/½ cup granulated sugar
300 ml/½ pint/1¼ cups water
300 ml/½ pint/1¼ cups banana purée (made in the
   liquidiser using 5 ripe bananas)
grated rind of ½ lemon
1 egg white
150 ml/¼ pint/⅔ cup double cream

Place the sugar and water in a saucepan and dissolve over a low
heat. Bring to the boil and cook quickly for 10 minutes. Allow
to become quite cold. Stir the banana purée into the syrup and
pour into a shallow rigid container and freeze until semi-solid.

Remove from the freezer and beat with an electric whisk until
smooth. Stir in the lemon rind. Place the egg white in the mixer
bowl and whisk until stiff. Fold into the banana mixture. Return
the mixture to the container and freeze again until semi-solid.
Beat again with the electric whisk. Whisk the cream lightly and
fold into the banana ice cream. Freeze again until firm.

Allow to soften slightly for 30 minutes in the refrigerator
before serving. Serve topped with slices of banana, dipped in
lemon juice.

Serves 4–6

Cakes, teabreads and cookies

In this chapter the mixer really comes into its own, taking all the hard work out of creaming and beating. Simply place all the ingredients in the mixer bowl and combine together – what could be quicker and easier!

Meringues and whisked sponges are effortless to make in the mixer.

Most cakes, teabreads and cookies freeze well, preferably un-iced. Batch baking becomes really speedy with the combination of a mixer and freezer.

Coffee almond gâteau

METRIC/IMPERIAL/AMERICAN
4 eggs
4 tablespoons/4 tablespoons/⅓ cup coffee essence
100 g/4 oz/½ cup castor sugar
75 g/3 oz/¾ cup plain flour
25 g/1 oz/¼ cup cornflour
225 g/8 oz/1 cup butter or margarine
275 g/10 oz/2¼ cups icing sugar
100 g/4 oz/1 cup flaked almonds, toasted
icing sugar

Place the eggs, half the coffee essence and the castor sugar in the mixer bowl (or if using a hand whisk, place in a bowl over a saucepan of hot water). Whisk until thick and creamy. If whisking over hot water, remove from the heat when thick and continue whisking for a few minutes. Sieve the flour and cornflour over the mixture and fold in. Pour into two 20-cm/8-inch greased and lined sandwich tins. Bake in a moderately hot oven (190°C, 375°F, Gas Mark 5) for 25–30 minutes. Cool on a wire tray.

Place the butter or margarine in the mixer bowl and gradually whisk in the sieved icing sugar with the remaining coffee essence. Sandwich the cakes together with a little of the icing. Spread the remainder over the sides and top. Press the toasted almonds all over the cake. Cut four 2.5-cm/1-inch wide strips of greaseproof paper and lay them across the top of the cake, leaving a gap between each. Dredge with icing sugar, then carefully lift off.

Tipsy coffee ring cake

METRIC/IMPERIAL/AMERICAN
100 g/4 oz/½ cup butter or margarine
100 g/4 oz/½ cup castor sugar
2 eggs
100 g/4 oz/1 cup self-raising flour
grated rind of 1 orange
1 tablespoon coffee essence
SYRUP:
100 g/4 oz/½ cup castor sugar
juice of 2 oranges, strained
1–2 teaspoons Tia Maria or sherry
150 ml/¼ pint/⅔ cup double cream to decorate

Place the butter or margarine and sugar in the mixer bowl and
beat until light and fluffy. Beat in the eggs one at a time, adding
a little flour with the second egg. Using a metal spoon fold in
the remaining flour. Divide the mixture in two. Add the orange
rind to one half and coffee essence to the other. Place alternate
spoonfuls of the mixtures in a greased fluted or plain ring
mould. Swirl with a skewer to give a marbled effect.

Bake in a moderate oven (180°C, 350°F, Gas Mark 4) for
40–50 minutes. Turn out and cool on a wire tray.

Dissolve the sugar and orange juice in a saucepan over a low
heat. Add the Tia Maria or sherry. Make holes in the base of the
cake with a skewer and pour over the syrup until it is all
absorbed.

Whisk the cream and pipe rosettes around the cake.

Rich fruit cake

METRIC/IMPERIAL/AMERICAN
150 g/5 oz/generous ½ cup butter or margarine
175 g/6 oz/¾ cup soft brown sugar
1 tablespoon black treacle
4 eggs
200 g/7 oz/1¾ cups plain flour
275 g/10 oz/2 cups currants
200 g/7 oz/generous 1 cup sultanas
65 g/2½ oz/generous ¼ cup glacé cherries, chopped
65 g/2½ oz/⅔ cup almonds, chopped
65 g/2½ oz/generous ¼ cup mixed peel
1 teaspoon mixed spice
½ teaspoon nutmeg
grated rind and juice of 1 orange
50 g/2 oz/½ cup ground almonds

Place the butter or margarine and sugar in the mixer bowl and
beat until well creamed. Beat in the treacle, then add the eggs
gradually, adding a little flour with each egg after the first. Fold
in the remaining ingredients. Place in a greased and lined 20-
cm/8-inch round or 18-cm/7-inch square cake tin. Smooth the
top. Bake in a cool oven (140°C, 275°F, Gas Mark 1). Test the
cake after the first 3 hours with a skewer. If it is not cooked
check at 30-minute intervals. The cake is cooked when the
skewer is no longer sticky. Leave to cool in the tin for 15
minutes before cooling on a wire tray.

Devil's food cake

METRIC/IMPERIAL/AMERICAN
CAKE:
100 g/4 oz/½ cup margarine
150 g/5 oz/⅔ cup castor sugar
3 eggs
150 g/5 oz/1¼ cups self-raising flour
1 teaspoon baking powder
3 tablespoons/3 tablespoons/¼ cup cocoa powder
2 teaspoons orange juice
100 g/4 oz/1 cup ground almonds
150 ml/¼ pint/⅔ cup natural yogurt
ICING:
75 g/3 oz/6 tablespoons margarine
225 g/8 oz/scant 2 cups icing sugar, sieved
1–2 tablespoons/1–2 tablespoons/1–3 tablespoons orange juice
circles of chocolate to decorate (see method)

Place all the cake ingredients in the mixer bowl and using a slow speed combine together. Place the mixture in three greased and lined 18-cm/7-inch sandwich cake tins. Bake in the centre of a very moderate oven (160°C, 325°F, Gas Mark 3) for 25–35 minutes. Cool on a wire tray.

Place icing ingredients in the mixer bowl and mix until smooth. Sandwich the cakes together with some icing. Spread some icing over the top and use the remainder to pipe a border. Decorate with circles of chocolate. To make these, spread melted chocolate over a sheet of waxed paper. Allow to set, then cut out circles using a small fluted cutter.

Strawberry gâteau

METRIC/IMPERIAL/AMERICAN
SPONGE BASE:
4 eggs
100 g/4 oz/½ cup castor sugar
100 g/4 oz/1 cup plain flour
¾ teaspoon baking powder
FILLING:
3 tablespoons/3 tablespoons/¼ cup strawberry jam
225 g/8 oz/2 cups strawberries
300 ml/½ pint/1¼ cups double cream, whipped
icing sugar to sprinkle

Place the eggs and sugar in the mixer bowl (or if using a hand whisk, place in a bowl over a saucepan of hot water). Whisk until thick and creamy and the mixture leaves a trail. If whisking over hot water, remove from the heat when thick and whisk for a few minutes to allow the mixture to cool. Sieve the flour and baking powder and carefully fold into the whisked mixture.

Line the bases of two 20-cm/8-inch sandwich tins, grease and dust with a little flour. Pour the mixture into the tins. Bake in a moderate oven (180°C, 350°F, Gas Mark 4) for 25–35 minutes. Turn out and cool on a wire tray. Cut one of the sponges into six wedges. Spread the jam over the uncut sponge with some sliced strawberries and a little whipped cream. Carefully arrange the wedges on the top to form a circle and sprinkle with sieved icing sugar. Pipe with cream and decorate with strawberries.

Mocha gâteau

METRIC/IMPERIAL/AMERICAN
CAKE:
175 g/6 oz/¾ cup butter or margarine
175 g/6 oz/¾ cup castor sugar
3 eggs
175 g/6 oz/1½ cups self-raising flour, sieved
1 tablespoon cocoa powder, sieved
ICING:
350 g/12 oz/2⅔ cups icing sugar, sieved
140 g/4½ oz/generous ½ cup butter or margarine
2 tablespoons/2 tablespoons/3 tablespoons milk
1 tablespoon coffee essence
browned flaked almonds to decorate

Place the butter or margarine and sugar in the mixer bowl and
cream together until light and fluffy. Beat in the eggs one at a
time adding a little of the flour with each egg after the first.
Using a metal spoon fold in the flour and cocoa powder. Place
the mixture in two greased and lined 18-cm/7-inch sandwich
tins. Bake in a moderate oven (160°C, 325°F, Gas Mark 3) for
25–35 minutes. Turn out and cool on a wire tray.

To make the icing, place all the ingredients in the mixer bowl
and using a slow speed combine until smooth.

Split each cake in half horizontally and sandwich the layers
together with a little of the icing. Spread some icing around the
sides and roll in the browned almonds. Use the remaining icing
to spread over the top of the cake and pipe rosettes around the
edge and on the top.

Fruit 'n' nut cake

METRIC/IMPERIAL/AMERICAN
100 g/4 oz/½ cup butter or margarine, softened
100 g/4 oz/½ cup castor sugar
2 eggs
grated rind of 1 orange
150 g/5 oz/1¼ cups plain flour
½ teaspoon nutmeg
100 g/4 oz/¾ cup raisins
25 g/1 oz/3 tablespoons chopped angelica
100 g/4 oz/1 cup glacé cherries, halved
50 g/2 oz/½ cup brazil nuts, chopped
50 g/2 oz/½ cup almonds, chopped
50 g/2 oz/½ cup walnuts, chopped
1–2 tablespoons/1–2 tablespoons/1–3 tablespoons orange
    juice
DECORATION:
glacé cherries
whole brazil nuts
pieces of angelica
apricot jam

Place all the ingredients in the mixer bowl and using a slow
speed gradually combine until well mixed. Place in a greased
and lined 15-cm/6-inch round cake tin. Smooth top with the
back of a spoon or palette knife. Arrange circles of cherries,
brazil nuts and angelica on top. Bake in a cool oven (140°C,
275°F, Gas Mark 1) for 2½–3 hours. Turn out on to a wire tray
and brush the topping with a little heated apricot jam to glaze.
Allow to cool before serving.

Coffee meringues

METRIC/IMPERIAL/AMERICAN
3 egg whites
150 g/6 oz/$\frac{3}{4}$ cup castor sugar
1 tablespoon coffee essence
300 ml/$\frac{1}{2}$ pint/1$\frac{1}{4}$ cups double cream
1–2 tablespoons/1–2 tablespoons/1–3 tablespoons brandy (optional)
DECORATION:
glacé cherries, chopped
angelica

Line two to three baking sheets with silicone paper. Place the egg whites in the mixing bowl and whisk until stiff. Add the sugar gradually, whisking all the time until stiff. Fold in the coffee essence.

Place the meringue in a piping bag fitted with a large star piping tube. Pipe stars on to the lined baking sheets. Bake in a very cool oven (110°C, 200°F, Gas Mark $\frac{1}{4}$) for 3–4 hours. Allow to cool on a wire tray.

Whisk the cream lightly, adding the brandy if used. Sandwich the meringues together in pairs with the cream and decorate with the cherries and angelica.

Wiltshire teabread

METRIC/IMPERIAL/AMERICAN
275 g/10 oz/2$\frac{1}{2}$ cups plain flour
1 teaspoon mixed spice
1 teaspoon bicarbonate of soda
100 g/4 oz/$\frac{1}{2}$ cup soft margarine
150 ml/$\frac{1}{4}$ pint/$\frac{2}{3}$ cup milk
1 tablespoon lemon juice
100 g/4 oz/$\frac{1}{2}$ cup soft brown sugar
100 g/4 oz/$\frac{2}{3}$ cup sultanas
100 g/4 oz/$\frac{2}{3}$ cup currants
grated rind of 1 lemon
1 egg

Place all the ingredients in the mixer bowl and using a slow speed mix until a dropping consistency is obtained. Cover and leave overnight.

Place the mixture in a 450-g/1-lb greased and lined loaf tin, smoothing the surface with a knife. Bake in a moderate oven (160°C, 325°F, Gas Mark 3) for 2 hours. Allow to cool in the tin before turning out.

Serve sliced and spread with butter.

Gingerbread loaf

METRIC/IMPERIAL/AMERICAN
175 g/6 oz/¾ cup butter
75 g/3 oz/6 tablespoons soft brown sugar
75 g/3 oz/¼ cup black treacle
3 eggs
225 g/8 oz/2 cups self-raising flour
1 tablespoon/1 tablespoon/1 tablespoon ground ginger
3 pieces stem ginger, finely chopped
25 g/1 oz/¼ cup flaked almonds

Place the butter, sugar and treacle in the mixer bowl and mix until light and fluffy. Add the eggs, beating well on a medium speed. Using a metal spoon fold in the flour, ground and stem ginger. Place in a greased and lined 1-kg/2-lb loaf tin. Sprinkle the flaked almonds over the surface, then bake in a moderate oven (180°C, 350°F, Gas Mark 4) for 1–1¼ hours. Turn out and cool on a wire tray.

Serve sliced and spread with butter.

Banana teabread

METRIC/IMPERIAL/AMERICAN
450 g/1 lb/1 lb ripe bananas
100 g/4 oz/½ cup butter or margarine
150 g/6 oz/¾ cup castor sugar
2 eggs
225 g/8 oz/2 cups self-raising flour
grated rind of 1 lemon
50 g/2 oz/¼ cup glacé cherries, chopped
100 g/4 oz/⅔ cup raisins

Mash the bananas, reserving a whole one for decoration. Place all the ingredients in the mixer bowl and beat slowly until well mixed. Place in a 1-kg/2-lb greased and lined loaf tin.

Bake in a moderate oven (160°C, 325°F, Gas Mark 3) for 1½–1¾ hours. Turn out and cool on a wire tray. Decorate with the reserved banana cut into slices and dipped in lemon juice. Slice and spread with butter.

Malted apricot and walnut teabread

METRIC/IMPERIAL/AMERICAN
75 g/3 oz/4½ tablespoons malt extract
50 g/2 oz/4 tablespoons soft brown sugar
25 g/1 oz/2 tablespoons margarine
225 g/8 oz/2 cups plain wholemeal flour
2 teaspoons baking powder
50 g/2 oz/½ cup walnuts, chopped
50 g/2 oz/6 tablespoons sultanas
25 g/1 oz/3 tablespoons dried apricots, chopped
grated rind of 1 orange
150 ml/¼ pint/⅔ cup milk
halved walnuts for topping

Melt the malt extract, sugar and margarine and allow to cool slightly. Place remaining dry ingredients in the mixer bowl and pour in the melted ingredients together with the milk. Mix on a slow speed until well combined. Place in a greased and lined 450-g/1-lb loaf tin. Lightly press halved walnuts over the top of the loaf. Bake in a moderate oven (160°C, 325°F, Gas Mark 3) for 1¼–1½ hours. Turn out and cool on a wire tray. Serve sliced and spread with butter.

Nutty cheese scone round

METRIC/IMPERIAL/AMERICAN
225 g/8 oz/2 cups self-raising flour
pinch dry mustard
salt and pepper
40 g/1½ oz/3 tablespoons butter or margarine
25 g/1 oz/¼ cup walnuts, finely chopped
75 g/3 oz/¾ cup cheese, finely grated
7 tablespoons/7 tablespoons/generous ½ cup milk
milk to glaze
few chopped or ground walnuts to decorate

Place all the ingredients, except the milk, in the mixer bowl. Using a slow speed gradually pour in the milk until the mixture forms a soft dough.

Turn out on to a lightly floured board and knead gently. Roll out into a 20-cm/8-inch round and score into eight sections using a sharp knife. Brush with milk and sprinkle with walnuts. Bake in a hot oven (220°C, 425°F, Gas Mark 7) for 15–20 minutes.

Serve hot or cold with butter.

Cheese and herb loaf

METRIC/IMPERIAL/AMERICAN
50 g/2 oz/¼ cup soft margarine
150 ml/¼ pint/⅔ cup milk
1 egg
75 g/3 oz/¾ cup Cheddar cheese, grated
225 g/8 oz/2 cups self-raising flour
1 teaspoon baking powder
pinch dry mustard
1 tablespoon chopped parsley
½ teaspoon chervil
parsley sprigs to garnish

Place all the ingredients in the mixer bowl and using a slow speed, beat until well mixed. Place the mixture in a greased and lined 450-g/1-lb loaf tin. Smooth the top. Bake in a moderate oven (180°C, 350°F, Gas Mark 4) for 1–1¼ hours. Turn out and serve either hot or cold. Garnish with parsley sprigs.
Note: Sliced and spread with butter, this loaf makes an ideal base for open sandwiches.

Grannie's cookies

METRIC/IMPERIAL/AMERICAN
100 g/4 oz/½ cup butter
350 g/12 oz/1½ cups castor sugar
1 large egg
250 g/9 oz/2¼ cups self-raising flour
1 teaspoon ground ginger
pinch ground nutmeg

Place the butter and sugar in the mixer bowl and beat until soft and well combined. Beat in the egg. Using a metal spoon stir in the flour, ginger and nutmeg. Place on a board and knead into a firm dough. Roll into balls the size of a walnut. Place on greased baking sheets, keeping well apart. Bake in a cool oven (150°C, 300°F, Gas Mark 2) for 30–40 minutes. Cool on a wire tray.

Makes approximately 30

Viennese biscuits

METRIC/IMPERIAL/AMERICAN
225 g/8 oz/1 cup margarine
75 g/3 oz/¾ cup icing sugar, sieved
grated rind of 1 lemon
200 g/7 oz/1¾ cups plain flour
50 g/2 oz/½ cup cornflour
ICING:
225 g/8 oz/2 cups icing sugar, sieved
75 g/3 oz/6 tablespoons margarine
2 teaspoons lemon juice
100 g/4 oz/4 squares chocolate, melted, to decorate

Place the margarine and icing sugar in the mixer bowl and beat together until light and creamy. Beat in the lemon rind, flour and cornflour and mix to a soft paste. Put the mixture in a piping bag fitted with a large star tube and pipe into fingers on a greased baking sheet, 2.5 cm/1 inch apart. Bake in a moderately hot oven (190°C, 375°F, Gas Mark 5) for 15–20 minutes. Cool on a wire tray.

To make the icing, place all the ingredients in the mixer bowl and using a slow speed gradually combine until the mixture is light and creamy.

Sandwich the biscuits together in pairs with the icing and dip the ends into the melted chocolate. Leave to set.

Makes 12–14 pairs

Butterscotch brownies

METRIC/IMPERIAL/AMERICAN
100 g/4 oz/½ cup butter or margarine
175 g/6 oz/¾ cup soft brown sugar
2 eggs
50 g/2 oz/½ cup walnuts, chopped
75 g/3 oz/¾ cup self-raising flour
¼ teaspoon baking powder
40 g/1½ oz/¾ cup cocoa powder
DECORATION:
icing sugar
walnut halves

Place all the ingredients in the mixer bowl and beat until well mixed. Place in a lined and greased 18-cm/7-inch square cake tin. Bake in a moderate oven (180°C, 350°F, Gas Mark 4) for 40–50 minutes. Turn out and cool on a wire tray.

Dredge with icing sugar and then cut into squares. Place a walnut half on each square.

Oatcakes

METRIC/IMPERIAL/AMERICAN
75 g/3 oz/6 tablespoons butter or margarine
100 g/4 oz/1 cup self-raising flour
pinch salt
100 g/4 oz/1 generous cup rolled oats
25 g/1 oz/2 tablespoons castor sugar
1 egg, beaten
1 teaspoon milk

Place the butter or margarine, flour, salt, oats and sugar in the mixer bowl. Using a slow speed mix the ingredients until just combined. Pour in the egg and milk and mix into a stiff dough. Turn on to a floured board and knead lightly.

Roll out thinly and cut out circles using a 6-cm/2½-inch plain cutter. Place on a greased baking sheet and prick lightly with a fork. Bake in a moderate oven (180°C, 350°F, Gas Mark 4) for 15–20 minutes. Cool on a wire tray and serve with cheese.

Macaroons

METRIC/IMPERIAL/AMERICAN
100 g/4 oz/½ cup castor sugar
100 g/4 oz/1 cup ground almonds
1 teaspoon ground rice
2 egg whites
few drops of almond essence
halved almonds

Place the sugar, ground almonds and ground rice in the mixer bowl and using a slow speed gradually beat in the egg whites and almond essence until the mixture is of a soft piping consistency. Place in a piping bag fitted with a 1-cm/½-inch plain tube. Pipe the mixture into 3.5–5-cm/1½–2-inch circles on rice paper placed on baking sheets. Press a halved almond into each macaroon. Bake in a moderate oven (160°C, 325°F, Gas Mark 3) for 15–20 minutes. Using a palette knife place the macaroons on a wire tray to cool.

Makes 20–24

Crispy peanut cookies

METRIC/IMPERIAL/AMERICAN
100 g/4 oz/½ cup soft margarine
100 g/4 oz/½ cup soft brown sugar
100 g/4 oz/1 cup salted peanuts
4 teaspoons coffee essence
150 g/5 oz/1¼ cups self-raising flour
¼ teaspoon cinnamon

Place all the ingredients in the mixer bowl and mix until a soft dough is formed. Roll into balls the size of a walnut. Place well apart on greased baking trays. Flatten each cookie with the back of a fork. Bake in a moderate oven (180°C, 350°F, Gas Mark 4) for 10–12 minutes. Cool on a wire tray.

If liked, sandwich the cookies in pairs with peanut butter.

Makes approximately 25–30

Orange shortbread

METRIC/IMPERIAL/AMERICAN
100 g/4 oz/½ cup butter
50 g/2 oz/¼ cup castor sugar
175 g/6 oz/1½ cups plain flour
grated rind of 1 orange
DECORATION:
castor sugar
orange segments

Place all the ingredients in the mixer bowl and using a slow speed combine them until sticky. Spoon into a 20-cm/8-inch round flan ring placed on a baking sheet. Press down using the back of a tablespoon to smooth the surface. Prick lightly with a fork and divide into portions marking halfway through the shortbread with a sharp knife. Bake in a cool oven (150°C, 300°F, Gas Mark 2) for 40–50 minutes. Remove the flan ring carefully and cool the shortbread on a wire tray.

Dredge the shortbread with castor sugar and decorate with orange segments.

Sauces and dressings

Sauces and dressings add the finishing touch to many dishes and are so easy to make with a liquidiser.

You can make a basic white sauce in seconds without the agony of wondering if it will turn out lumpy! A sauce usually has to be made at the last minute, but with your liquidiser you can combine all the ingredients in the goblet in advance and then leave in the saucepan until ready to heat and serve.

Mayonnaise and Hollandaise sauce are often thought to be difficult to make but, with the aid of your appliances, you can be sure of a perfect result every time.

White sauce

METRIC/IMPERIAL/AMERICAN
25 g/1 oz/2 tablespoons butter
25 g/1 oz/$\frac{1}{4}$ cup flour
300 ml/$\frac{1}{2}$ pint/1$\frac{1}{4}$ cups milk
salt and pepper

Place all the ingredients in the liquidiser and switch on to maximum speed for 30 seconds. Pour the mixture into a saucepan and whisking all the time bring to the boil. Simmer gently for 1 minute, still stirring. Serve as an accompaniment to vegetable dishes.

Variations
Béchamel sauce: Place the milk in a saucepan with 1 carrot, 1 onion, 1 bay leaf and pinch of nutmeg. Bring to the boil, remove from the heat and infuse for 30 minutes. Strain milk and use to make basic white sauce as above.
Cheese sauce: Stir 50 g/2 oz/$\frac{1}{2}$ cup grated cheese and a pinch of mustard into the cooked sauce. Do not allow to boil once the cheese has been added.
Mushroom sauce: Stir 50 g/2 oz/$\frac{1}{2}$ cup chopped sautéed mushrooms into the cooked sauce.
Parsley sauce: Stir 3 tablespoons/3 tablespoons/$\frac{1}{4}$ cup chopped parsley into the cooked sauce.
Anchovy sauce: Stir 2–3 teaspoons anchovy essence and a few drops of lemon juice into the cooked sauce.

Makes 300 ml/$\frac{1}{2}$ pint/1$\frac{1}{4}$ cups

Tomato sauce

METRIC/IMPERIAL/AMERICAN
50 g/2 oz/¼ cup butter or margarine
1 rasher bacon, derinded and chopped
2 onions, chopped
450 g/1 lb/1 lb tomatoes, roughly chopped
1 clove garlic, crushed
bouquet garni
pinch sugar
salt and pepper
few parsley sprigs
few drops of Worcestershire sauce

Melt the butter or margarine and sauté the bacon, onions and tomatoes for 10 minutes in a covered pan, shaking occasionally.

Add the remaining ingredients and simmer gently for 30 minutes. Remove the bouquet garni. Pour into the liquidiser and blend until smooth. Sieve and return to a clean saucepan and reheat. Serve with spaghetti or other pasta.

Serves 4–6

Barbecue sauce

METRIC/IMPERIAL/AMERICAN
1 onion, chopped
2 sticks celery, chopped
1 clove garlic, crushed
150 ml/¼ pint/⅔ cup water
300 ml/½ pint/1¼ cups red wine
1 tablespoon wine vinegar
1 tablespoon brown sugar
few drops of Tabasco sauce
1 tablespoon Worcestershire sauce
2 tablespoons/2 tablespoons/3 tablespoons redcurrant
    jelly
salt
freshly ground black pepper
1 tablespoon cornflour blended in a little water

Place all the ingredients except the blended cornflour in a saucepan and bring to the boil. Simmer for 10 minutes and then allow to cool slightly.

Pour into the liquidiser and blend until smooth. Return to the saucepan, stir in the blended cornflour and heat until thickened.

Serve as an accompaniment to kebabs, ham, pork or lamb dishes.

Serves 4

Hollandaise sauce

METRIC/IMPERIAL/AMERICAN
225 g/8 oz/1 cup butter
1 tablespoon water
4 egg yolks
2 tablespoons/2 tablespoons/3 tablespoons lemon juice
freshly ground black pepper
pinch cayenne pepper
salt to taste

Melt the butter in the water in a saucepan, but do not allow to brown. Place the egg yolks, lemon juice, black pepper and cayenne pepper in the liquidiser. Turn on to the slowest speed and pour in the melted butter mixture in a steady stream, until the sauce has emulsified. Add salt to taste.

Serve cold with fish and vegetable dishes.

Serves 4

Cranberry sauce

METRIC/IMPERIAL/AMERICAN
225 g/8 oz/2 cups cranberries
100 g/4 oz/$\frac{1}{2}$ cup sugar
3 tablespoons/3 tablespoons/$\frac{1}{4}$ cup water
grated rind of $\frac{1}{2}$ lemon

Place the cranberries, sugar, water and lemon rind in a saucepan and bring to the boil. Simmer for 10–15 minutes. Allow to cool slightly.

Pour into the liquidiser and blend until smooth.

Chill before serving as an accompaniment to poultry and game dishes.

Serves 4

Mixer mayonnaise

METRIC/IMPERIAL/AMERICAN
2 egg yolks
pinch dry mustard
salt and pepper
pinch castor sugar
300 ml/½ pint/1¼ cups oil
1–2 tablespoons/1–2 tablespoons/1–3 tablespoons wine
    vinegar or lemon juice

Place the egg yolks, mustard, seasoning and sugar in the mixer bowl and whisk gently until combined. Continue whisking and gradually pour the oil in drop by drop. When thick and smooth add the wine vinegar or lemon juice to thin the mayonnaise to the required consistency.

Note: If making mayonnaise in the liquidiser use 1 whole egg in place of the 2 egg yolks. Place the whole egg, seasonings and half the vinegar or lemon juice in the liquidiser and switch on at a slow speed. Pour the oil in a thin stream until the mixture begins to thicken, add the remaining vinegar or lemon juice. Then add any remaining oil, increasing the speed.

When making mayonnaise, have all the ingredients at room temperature.

Garlic mayonnaise: Add 1 crushed clove of garlic to the mayonnaise.
Herb mayonnaise: Add 2 tablespoons/2 tablespoons/3 tablespoons chopped parsley or chives.
Mayonnaise verte: Add ½ bunch finely chopped watercress just before serving.

French dressing

METRIC/IMPERIAL/AMERICAN
300 ml/½ pint/1¼ cups oil
3 tablespoons/3 tablespoons/¼ cup wine vinegar
pinch sugar
salt and pepper
pinch paprika pepper
pinch mixed herbs

Place all the ingredients in the liquidiser and blend until an emulsion is formed. Store in an airtight bottle in a cool place and shake well before using.

Variations
Garlic dressing: Keep 1 peeled clove of garlic in dressing; this will impart a delicate flavour.
Orange dressing: Add the grated rind of ½ orange to the dressing.
Parsley dressing: Before blending add several sprigs of parsley to the dressing.

Blue cheese dressing

METRIC/IMPERIAL/AMERICAN
100 g/4 oz/½ cup blue cheese, crumbled
175 g/6 oz/¾ cup cream or curd cheese
150 ml/¼ pint/⅔ cup milk
1 teaspoon grated onion
salt
freshly ground black pepper
few parsley sprigs

Place all the ingredients in the liquidiser and blend until smooth.
    Serve with tomato or cucumber salad, or hamburgers.

Serves 4

Cucumber dressing

METRIC/IMPERIAL/AMERICAN
½ cucumber
few fresh mint leaves
few drops of lemon juice
salt
freshly ground black pepper
150 ml/¼ pint/⅔ cup soured cream

Cut the peeled cucumber into chunks and place in the liquidiser with the mint leaves and lemon juice. Blend until smooth. Mix in the seasoning and soured cream. Serve with salads, fish or chicken dishes.

Serves 4

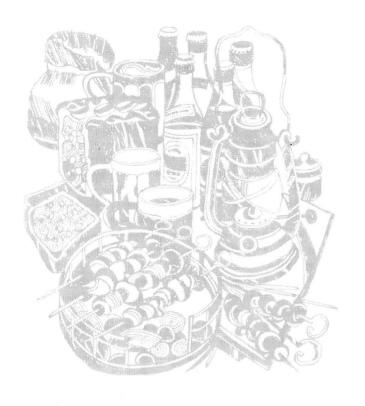

Drinks

A wide range of drinks can be made with the aid of your liquidiser.

Some of the larger liquidisers will crush ice in seconds. You can also colour sugar to decorate the rims of glasses by adding a couple of drops of food colouring to granulated sugar. Blend until the colour is distributed evenly. Dip the glass rims in a little lightly beaten egg white, then into the coloured sugar.

Lime soda

METRIC/IMPERIAL/AMERICAN
1 small banana
3 tablespoons/3 tablespoons/¼ cup lime cordial
1 family brick vanilla ice cream
250 ml/scant ½ pint/1 cup soda water
slices of lime or lemon to decorate

Place the banana, lime cordial and half of the ice cream in the liquidiser. Switch on to a medium speed and blend until smooth and frothy.

Pour into glasses and float the remaining ice cream on top. Top each glass up with soda water and serve with a lime or lemon slice on the rim of each glass.

Serves 4

Tipsy orange flip

METRIC/IMPERIAL/AMERICAN
juice of 2 oranges
2 teaspoons lemon juice
2 eggs, separated
2 tablespoons/2 tablespoons/3 tablespoons sherry
25 g/1 oz/2 tablespoons sugar
2 cinnamon sticks

Place the orange and lemon juices in the liquidiser with the egg yolks, sherry and sugar. Switch on to a high speed and blend until well mixed.

Place the egg whites in the mixer bowl and whisk until fairly stiff. Fold into the blended mixture and serve immediately with a cinnamon stick in each glass.

Serves 2

Yogurt fruit shake

METRIC/IMPERIAL/AMERICAN
150 ml/$\frac{1}{4}$ pint/$\frac{2}{3}$ cup fruit yogurt
$\frac{1}{2}$ banana
1 teaspoon honey
1 ice cube
2 tablespoons/2 tablespoons/3 tablespoons vanilla ice
  cream to decorate

Place all the ingredients in the liquidiser and blend until frothy. Pour into a glass and serve immediately with the ice cream floating on top.

Serves 1

Raspberry cooler

METRIC/IMPERIAL/AMERICAN
300 ml/½ pint/1¼ cups milk
150 ml/¼ pint/⅔ cup raspberry yogurt
100 g/4 oz/1 cup raspberries

Place the milk, raspberry yogurt and most of the raspberries, reserving some for decoration, in the liquidiser. Blend until mixture becomes frothy. Pour into glasses and float the reserved raspberries on top.

Serves 2

Brandy flip with clotted cream

METRIC/IMPERIAL/AMERICAN
2 eggs, separated
150 ml/¼ pint/⅔ cup brandy
2 tablespoons/2 tablespoons/3 tablespoons rum
150 ml/¼ pint/⅔ cup milk
sugar to taste
150 ml/¼ pint/⅔ cup clotted cream
nutmeg to decorate

Place the egg yolks in the liquidiser and mix for 2–3 seconds. Pour in the brandy, rum and milk. Blend until combined and pour into a bowl. Add sugar to taste. Chill.

Place the egg whites in the mixer bowl and whisk until fairly stiff. Fold into the brandy mixture. Pour into glasses. Top with clotted cream and sprinkle with nutmeg.

Serves 2

Minted chocolate

METRIC/IMPERIAL/AMERICAN
600 ml/1 pint/2½ cups milk
few drops of peppermint essence
1 family block vanilla ice cream
green food colouring
grated chocolate to decorate

Pour the milk into the liquidiser with the peppermint essence and mix for 3–4 seconds. Cut the ice cream into cubes and add to the liquidiser with a few drops of green colouring. Blend until well mixed and smooth. Pour into glasses and decorate with grated chocolate.

Serves 2–4

Hot mocha creams

METRIC/IMPERIAL/AMERICAN
600 ml/1 pint/2½ cups milk
1 tablespoon instant coffee
1 tablespoon cocoa powder
sugar to taste
2 tablespoons/2 tablespoons/3 tablespoons whipped
  cream

Heat the milk gently and stir in the coffee and cocoa. Pour into the liquidiser and blend until frothy. Add the sugar to taste. Pour into large mugs and top with a spoonful of whipped cream.

Serves 3–4

Orange frappé

METRIC/IMPERIAL/AMERICAN
**1 (178-ml/6¼-fl oz/6¼-fl oz) can concentrated frozen
    orange juice
24 ice cubes, lightly crushed
4 tablespoons/4 tablespoons/⅓ cup gin or vodka**

Place all the ingredients in the liquidiser and blend until the
mixture resembles crushed ice. Spoon into frosted glasses and
serve immediately.

Variation: Substitute concentrated grapefruit juice for the
orange juice.
To frost glasses, dip the rims of glasses in a little beaten egg white
and then in castor sugar. Allow to harden before spooning in
the frappé.

Serves 4

Honeyed lemonade

METRIC/IMPERIAL/AMERICAN
**2 thin-skinned lemons
50 g/2 oz/¼ cup sugar
2 tablespoons/2 tablespoons/3 tablespoons clear honey
600 ml/1 pint/2½ cups water
slices of lemon to decorate**

Roughly chop the lemons and place in the liquidiser with the
sugar, honey and water. Blend until mixed, then strain into a
jug. Serve chilled with a lemon slice on the rim of each glass.

Serves 2

Freezer Cookery

A freezer can be an enormous advantage to a household if it is used sensibly; home grown or glut produce can be packed and stored for the winter months, shopping can be made cheaper by bulk buying and storing in a freezer. Just as useful in saving time and trouble are ready prepared dishes or parts of dishes, frozen when you have time to cook, ready to reheat and serve when you are busy.

Here you will find recipes for basic freezer dishes, a good supply of which will ensure you are never at a loss for a good meal at short notice. These recipes can be used for a large variety of sweet and savoury dishes which will make your everyday cooking easier.

Freezer dishes need not necessarily be ready cooked – it might be helpful to prepare and freeze dishes such as

chicken Kiev or lasagne in advance, then cook them when the occasion arises.

Frozen desserts are not only an excellent standby, but ices and sorbets can capture the flavour of summer for a special occasion when soft fruits are out of season.

All manner of soups, pâtés, main dishes, desserts and bakes can be prepared and stored – the recipes here give the best ways to freeze and thaw each dish, to give you the very best results from your freezer.

All about freezing

When you are thinking of buying a freezer the first things to decide are where you will put it and which type you would prefer. Any well-ventilated, dry place with a strong floor is suitable, as long as there is an electric socket nearby. Floor area is usually the main consideration when choosing between a chest and an upright but there are several other factors to be borne in mind. A chest freezer offers more storage space for less money, is more economical to run because less cold air escapes when the lid is opened, and only needs to be defrosted once a year. An upright is more convenient, easier to load and unload and more likely to fit into the average kitchen, but it will need to be defrosted twice a year unless you buy a model which defrosts automatically.

Packaging materials

Once you have purchased and installed your freezer, and are faced with the exciting task of stocking it, one of the most important rules to remember is that all food stored in the freezer must be packed properly in moisture/vapour-proof material, and tightly sealed. This is absolutely essential to prevent it losing moisture and becoming dry. Careless packing can result in freezer burn appearing particularly on meat, fish and poultry. This causes toughness and loss of flavour and produces greyish-white marks on the surface. Good packaging also stops cross-flavouring between strongly flavoured foods.

There are many different packaging materials to choose from:

Foil Heavy-duty freezer foil is the best, but ordinary foil can be used double. It is easy to handle and makes an effective wrapping material for unevenly shaped foods like meat, poultry and fish. Be sure to mould it closely to exclude all air, and seal the edges with freezer tape.

Foil can also be used for lining casseroles so that the contents can be removed when frozen and the dish used again. Line the dish carefully with foil, leaving a large 'frill' of extra foil around the top. Pour in the food. This can then be cooked in the lined dish or it may be more convenient to cook a large quantity in one big casserole and then divide it between several smaller foil-lined dishes for freezing in meal-size portions. Cool and freeze until solid. Lift the foil-wrapped block out of the dish, fold the foil 'frill' over the top and seal with freezer tape. Overwrap with a polythene bag before returning to the freezer. To serve, strip off the foil and place the food in the casserole again for thawing and reheating.

Alternatively, cooked food can be frozen in the dish in which it was cooked. When the food is solid, dip the dish quickly into hot water, turn out the frozen block and wrap it in foil.

Freezerproof china Ovenproof china which can withstand long-term storage in the freezer is now available. This means that, after cooling, covering with foil, sealing and labelling, food can be transferred to the freezer in the dish in which it was cooked.

Freezer tape Special adhesive tape which does not peel off at low temperatures. Particularly useful for sealing foil packages and polythene bags. The type which looks like masking tape has the advantage that it can be written on but the clear variety can be used to protect paper labels.

Foil bags Particularly suitable for storing liquid and semi-liquid foods like soups or stews.

Foil dishes These are very useful for freezing cooked food as it can be reheated in the same dish. They are available in many different shapes and sizes, some of which have lids. The dishes can be re-used after careful washing and drying. If the lids are not re-usable the tops can be covered with double-thickness foil and then sealed.

Polythene bags Heavy-duty extra thick polythene bags should be used for freezing – the coloured ones are particularly useful for easy identification. Polythene bags are very popular for packing solids such as vegetables, pastries, cakes, meat, fish and poultry, and as added protection around foil-wrapped parcels. As much air as possible should be extracted and the bag sealed with a twist tie or freezer tape. They can be washed and used again but are best as overbags after the first time.

If they are to be used for liquids, it is a good idea to form them into a square shape to save storage space. Line a square polythene container with a polythene bag. Pour in the food to be frozen and seal, leaving a headspace. Freeze until hard, then remove the wrapped frozen food from the container.

Rigid polythene containers These can be re-used indefinitely but do make sure that they are guaranteed to withstand the low temperatures without warping or cracking. They come in a variety of shapes and sizes but the square ones take up the least freezer space. They are ideal for storing casseroles, soups or other liquid foods, but be sure to leave a space to allow for expansion. Delicate items like decorated cakes are well protected in the larger polythene containers.

Boil-in-bags These are made of specially thick polythene in which food can be frozen and then cooked or reheated in boiling water. They must be heat-sealed with a heat sealer or iron.

Cling film Freezer cling film is much thicker and stronger than the ordinary film, and is very good for moulding around difficult shapes. Ordinary cling film is useful for separating individual items like chops or steaks before they are over-wrapped.

Twist ties These are made of wire covered with either paper or plastic and are used for sealing the tops of polythene bags or opened bags of commercially frozen foods.

Labels Some are adhesive and come in various sizes and colours. Be sure to stick them on to polythene bags before filling. Labels attached to twist ties are useful for shapes on which it is difficult to write or stick labels.

Heat sealers These are useful if you freeze a lot of produce in heavy-gauge polythene bags. They seal the two pieces of polythene together, providing an airtight seal.

Freezing tips

Labelling and recording You may think that you will remember what you have put in the freezer, and what you have already used, but you will soon find that this is extremely difficult. It is much better to label everything clearly with the name of the food, the date it was frozen, the quantity or the number it is to serve. A log is also a very helpful guide as to when restocking is necessary.

Fast freezing It is very important to freeze down food as quickly as possible because slow freezing damages the cell structure which may result in a loss of nutrients, flavour and texture when the food is thawed or cooked. The fast freeze switch by-passes the thermostat, causing continuous running to bring the temperature below the normal storage temperature of $-18°C/0°F$. It should be switched on at least 2 hours before packing fresh food into the freezer, and left on for a further 24 hours.

It is not worth using the fast freeze switch if you are only freezing down a very small weight of food, say 1 kg/2 lb or less. When loading fresh food for freezing, ensure that it is not placed in contact with any already frozen food and that, as far as possible, it is put on refrigerated shelves in an upright freezer or against the walls of a chest freezer.

Only freeze within 24 hours the weight of food recommended by the freezer manufacturer and if the maximum weight is to be frozen, operate the fast freeze switch according to the manufacturer's recommendations. If weights are not given, do not exceed 10 per cent of the loading capacity. It is generally accepted that an upright freezer holds 7.5 kg/15 lb per 28.3 litres/1 cubic foot and a chest holds 10 kg/20 lb per 28.3 litres/1 cubic foot so this figure should be multiplied by the net capacity of the freezer to find out the weight of the food which can be frozen down at one time.

Open freezing Commercially frozen fruit and vegetables are 'blast' frozen to keep them separate and free flowing. To keep them separate at home, they have to be spread out on trays and frozen until hard before being packed. It is also a good idea to open freeze very delicate items like decorated cakes and soufflés before packing in rigid polythene containers. Fragile foods should not be packed in bags as they can easily be damaged even when frozen.

Dividers Another way of preventing food from freezing together is to place a sheet of foil, cling film, waxed paper or greaseproof paper between such items as chops, steaks, sausages, pastry rounds or pancakes before packing them in polythene bags. This way the required number can be removed easily when needed.

Freezing cooked dishes One of the greatest joys of owning a freezer is the way that it enables you to cook in bulk when it is convenient and you have the time, or to prepare for a dinner party in advance and save all that last-minute panic.

Instructions on freezing and thawing have been given with the individual recipes in this book but it must also always be remembered that all cooked food must be completely cooled as quickly as possible and then frozen.

Food which has already been frozen can be used with complete safety in dishes which are to be frozen as long as it is thoroughly cooked in between and not left lying around in a warm kitchen.

Rigid polythene or foil containers are the most popular packaging materials for freezing cooked dishes but sheet foil can also be used, as already explained.

Excluding air All air must be expelled from packs containing solid food. Foil and cling film should be moulded closely and air must be withdrawn from bags with the aid of a pump or by dipping the bag into water to expel the air – dry before freezing. Fill spaces above solids packed in rigid containers with a piece of crumpled foil.

Headspace Remember that liquids expand on freezing so always leave a headspace of 1–2.5 cm/$\frac{1}{2}$–1 inch above casseroles, soups, sauces or any other liquids.

Defrosting This operation is made easier if it is undertaken when freezer stocks are low, but it is not essential to run the food down deliberately.

Disconnect the freezer and remove all the food. Small items and those which thaw quickly (e.g. ice cream) can be kept in a refrigerator. The remainder will keep perfectly well for the duration of the defrosting if they are packed closely together and covered with plenty of newspaper and a thick blanket.

Place a bowl of hot water in the bottom of the freezer to loosen the ice, then remove the ice from the sides and shelves with a plastic scraper. Do not use metal implements because they damage the interior surface. The ice can either be collected up in a thick towel placed in the bottom of the freezer, or with a dustpan and brush.

Wipe out with a solution of 1 tablespoon bicarbonate of soda to each generous litre/2 pints/2$\frac{1}{2}$ pints water, rinse, and dry with a clean absorbent cloth. Reconnect and replace the food. The whole defrosting process should not take more than 2 hours.

To keep the outside of the cabinet in good condition and to prevent it from rusting it is a good idea to give it an occasional coat of wax polish.

Emergencies and power cuts If you tape over the switch and plug and make sure that the freezer is never switched off, emergencies are extremely unlikely. Most freezers are very reliable and as a full load of food will remain in perfect condition in the cabinet for over 12 hours after the power has been turned off (provided the lid or door is not opened), there is little need to worry about power cuts. However, it is wise to take out a freezer insurance and to have a good maintenance engineer on call.

When moving house it is sensible to reduce the stocks and to make sure that the freezer is the last thing to go into the removal van and the first to come out at your destination. If the journey is to take more than 12 hours the freezer should be emptied completely if the removal firm cannot arrange for it to be connected to an electrical supply overnight.

Basic freezing recipes

It is an excellent idea to keep in the freezer a supply of basics such as a meat sauce which can be thawed out and added to other ingredients to make a variety of quick, interesting dishes. It is also always handy to have in stock a basic sandwich cake to serve with tea or coffee and a few savouries to accompany drinks.

Meat sauce

METRIC/IMPERIAL/AMERICAN
1 large onion, chopped
1 tablespoon corn oil
0.5 kg/1 lb/2 cups minced beef
40 g/1½ oz/6 tablespoons plain flour
100 g/4 oz/1 cup mushrooms, chopped
1–2 cloves garlic, crushed
1 (227-g/8-oz/8-oz) can peeled tomatoes
2 tablespoons/2 tablespoons/3 tablespoons tomato purée
1 bay leaf
150 ml/¼ pint/⅔ cup beef stock

Place the onion and oil in a saucepan and cook gently for about 10 minutes. Add the mince and cook until no longer red. Blend in the flour and the remaining ingredients.

Cover and simmer very gently for 40 minutes.

To serve at once: Use half the above quantity of sauce to make the meat and vegetable pasties (see page 28) or pancake layer pie (see page 27). Use the full quantity for the individual shepherd's pies (see page 29).

To freeze: Put into rigid polythene containers. Seal, label and freeze.

To thaw: Leave at room temperature for 3–4 hours, in the refrigerator overnight, or slowly heat through from frozen in a saucepan.

Serves 4 as a sauce for spaghetti
Makes 4 pasties, or 1 meat and pancake pie to serve 6

Curry sauce

METRIC/IMPERIAL/AMERICAN
2 large onions, finely chopped
25 g/1 oz/2 tablespoons butter
2 tablespoons/2 tablespoons/3 tablespoons corn oil
2 tablespoons/2 tablespoons/3 tablespoons curry powder
1½ tablespoons/1½ tablespoons/2 tablespoons flour
½ teaspoon ground ginger
2 tablespoons/2 tablespoons/3 tablespoons tomato purée
2 tablespoons/2 tablespoons/3 tablespoons mango
  chutney
1 tablespoon redcurrant jelly or clear jam
2 teaspoons lemon juice
½ teaspoon salt
450 ml/¾ pint/2 cups stock

Sauté the onions (and 1 crushed clove garlic, if liked) for 10 minutes in the butter and oil. Stir in the remaining ingredients.
  Cover and simmer for about 1 hour, stirring occasionally.
To serve at once: Strain, if liked, and mix with any left-over meat or hard-boiled eggs. Serve with rice.
To freeze: When cold, heat seal in a freezer boil-in-the-bag or thick polythene bag. Seal, label and freeze.
To thaw: If using a boil-in-the-bag, put the frozen bag into a pan of cold water and bring to the boil slowly. Simmer for 30 minutes. If using an ordinary freezer polythene bag or other disposable container thaw overnight in the refrigerator and then heat through in a saucepan, or gently heat from frozen.

Serves 4

Chicken and mushroom filling for vol-au-vents

METRIC/IMPERIAL/AMERICAN
50 g/2 oz/¼ cup butter or margarine
50 g/2 oz/½ cup plain flour
300 ml/½ pint/1¼ cups milk
100 g/4 oz/⅔ cup cooked chicken meat, chopped
100 g/4 oz/1 cup mushrooms, chopped
vol-au-vent cases to finish

Melt the butter or margarine in a saucepan, add the flour and cook for 1 minute. Gradually beat in the milk, stirring continuously. Bring to the boil and cook for 2 minutes. Stir in the chicken and mushrooms and heat through.
To serve at once: Warm approximately thirty-six 2.5-cm/1-inch cocktail vol-au-vent cases or ten 5-cm/2-inch main-course cases in a cool oven (150°C, 300°F, Gas Mark 2), then fill with the sauce. Allow 2 main-course vol-au-vents per person.
To freeze: Put the cooled sauce in a rigid polythene container and seal, or heat seal the sauce in a freezer boil-in-the-bag. Label and freeze.
To thaw: If frozen in a rigid polythene container, thaw at room temperature for about 2 hours then heat through in a saucepan. If frozen in a boil-in-the-bag, place the frozen bag in a saucepan of cold water, bring to the boil and simmer for 30 minutes. Spoon into warmed vol-au-vent cases.

Fills 36 vol-au-vents as a cocktail, 10 as a main course

Tomato and onion relish

METRIC/IMPERIAL/AMERICAN
0.5 kg/1 lb/4 cups onions, chopped
1 tablespoon/1 tablespoon/2 tablespoons corn oil
1 kg/2 lb/4 cups tomatoes, peeled and chopped
3–4 tablespoons/3–4 tablespoons/¼–⅓ cup tomato purée
salt and pepper
1 teaspoon sugar

Place the onions and oil in a saucepan and heat gently for about 10 minutes to soften the onions without browning. Add the chopped tomatoes, cover the pan and cook gently for 2 hours. Remove the lid and cook for a further 30 minutes to evaporate the excess moisture. (If the tomatoes are particularly wet, it may be necessary to cook for longer without a lid.) The mixture should be thick. Stir in the tomato purée to taste and for colour as some tomatoes can be very pale. Add salt and pepper to taste and 1 teaspoon sugar to take away any acidity.
To serve at once: Use in selected recipes (see page 226).
To freeze: Allow to become cold. Divide between suitable rigid polythene containers or freezerproof ramekins. Seal, label and freeze.
To thaw: Thaw overnight in the refrigerator or for a few hours at room temperature. The exact time will depend on the size of the container. Use for the chosen recipe.

Makes 0.75 kg/1¾ lb/1¾ lb relish

Duchesse potatoes

METRIC/IMPERIAL/AMERICAN
1.25 kg/2½ lb/2½ lb potatoes, peeled and sliced
salt
75 g/3 oz/6 tablespoons butter or margarine
pepper
pinch grated nutmeg
1 large egg, lightly beaten
beaten egg for brushing

Cook the potatoes in boiling salted water until tender – about 10–15 minutes. Drain and mash well.
   Beat in the butter or margarine, pepper, nutmeg and egg. Mix well, allow to cool and place in a large nylon piping bag with a star vegetable nozzle. Pipe rosettes on to a lightly greased or foil-lined baking sheet.
To serve at once: Brush the potato with beaten egg and cook for 15–20 minutes in the centre of a moderately hot oven (200°C, 400°F, Gas Mark 6).
To freeze: Do not brush with egg. Open freeze the piped rosettes on the baking sheets. When frozen, pack in rigid polythene containers. Seal, label and return to the freezer.
To thaw: Leave to thaw at room temperature for 1–2 hours. Brush with egg and place on lightly greased baking sheets. Cook in the centre of a moderately hot oven (200°C, 400°F, Gas Mark 6) for 15–20 minutes.

Makes about 20

Pancakes

METRIC/IMPERIAL/AMERICAN
100 g/4 oz/1 cup plain flour
salt
1 egg
300 ml/½ pint/1¼ cups milk
oil for frying

Place the flour and salt in a bowl. Break in the egg and gradually add the milk to make a smooth batter.

Heat a little oil in a 20–23-cm/8–9-inch frying pan and pour in a little of the batter to make a very thin coating. Cook until the underside is golden brown. Either toss or turn over with a palette knife and cook this side for only a few seconds.
To serve at once: Serve with your favourite topping.
To freeze: Turn the pancakes on to kitchen paper on a cake rack to cool. Make into piles of four with greaseproof paper or freezer layer tissue between each pancake.

Wrap each pile in foil and make a parcel, or place in a plastic bag. Seal, label and freeze.
To thaw: Leave in parcels at room temperature for 2 hours.

Makes 7–8 pancakes

Asparagus rolls

METRIC/IMPERIAL/AMERICAN
1 (340-g/12-oz/12-oz) can green asparagus spears
175 g/6 oz/¾ cup butter
1 large wholemeal loaf

Drain the asparagus and turn on to a plate. Cut off the crust from the bottom, top, both ends and one side of the loaf. Lay the loaf on a bread board with the remaining crust on one side. Holding the crusted side in one hand, lightly spread the opposite side with butter. Slice off the buttered side as thinly as possible, cutting along the length of the loaf. Continue buttering and slicing until the loaf is finished. Discard the remaining crust. Cut each slice in half and place an asparagus spear on each half with a little of the tip showing. Roll up carefully. Trim off any extra stalk. If the roll does not hold together spread a little extra butter along the edge.
To serve at once: Keep covered with cling film until ready to use.
To freeze: Pack carefully, interleaved with freezer layer tissue, in rigid polythene containers. Seal, label and freeze.
To thaw: Arrange on a plate, cover with foil and leave for about 1 hour before serving.

Makes approximately 16 rolls

Smoked salmon rolls

METRIC/IMPERIAL/AMERICAN
1 small wholemeal loaf
100 g/4 oz/½ cup butter
100 g/4 oz/¼ lb smoked salmon
freshly ground black pepper
lemon juice
chopped parsley to garnish

Cut the crusts from the top, bottom, both ends and one side of the loaf. Lay the loaf on a bread board with the remaining crust on one side. Holding the crusted side in one hand, lightly spread the opposite side with butter. Slice off the buttered side as thinly as possible, cutting along the length of the loaf. Continue in this way until the loaf is finished. Discard the crust. Place a piece of smoked salmon on each slice of bread, leaving a 1-cm/½-inch border along one short side and narrow borders around the other sides. Sprinkle with black pepper and lemon juice. Roll up neatly from the 1-cm/½-inch border, spreading the final edge with a little extra butter if it does not stick.
To serve at once: Trim the rolls and cut into 2 or 3 equal pieces. Garnish with parsley.
To freeze: Pack the whole rolls interleaved with freezer layer tissue, in rigid containers. Seal, label and freeze.
To thaw: Leave to thaw for 30 minutes then trim as before. Cover with foil and leave for a further hour. Cut each roll into 2 or 3 pieces and serve garnished with parsley.

Makes approximately 8 whole rolls

Pâté pinwheels

METRIC/IMPERIAL/AMERICAN
1 large uncut white sandwich loaf
225 g/8 oz/1 cup butter or margarine, softened
225 g/8 oz/1 cup soft Continental liver sausage or soft pâté
GARNISH:
parsley sprig
stuffed green olives

Cut the crusts from the top, bottom, both ends and one side of the loaf. Holding the remaining crusted side in one hand, spread the opposite side thinly with the butter or margarine and pâté. Slice thinly along the length of the bread. Roll up tightly from the short end along the length of the slice. Continue in this way until all the bread is used up.
To serve at once: Trim the ends and cut each roll into 5 equal slices like a Swiss roll. Serve garnished with parsley and green olives.
To freeze: Place the whole rolls, interleaved with freezer layer tissue, in rigid polythene containers, or make into foil parcels, being careful not to squash them. Seal, label and freeze.
To thaw: Remove the required number from the freezer. After 1 hour trim the ends and cut into 5 equal slices as before. Arrange on a plate and cover with cling film. Leave to thaw completely.

Makes approximately 50 pinwheels

Fruit purées

METRIC/IMPERIAL/AMERICAN
0.5 kg/1 lb/1 lb gooseberries or apricots
2–4 tablespoons/2–4 tablespoons/3–5 tablespoons water

Wash and top and tail the gooseberries or stone the apricots. Place in a saucepan with the water. Cover and cook very gently until pulpy, stirring occasionally to prevent the fruit sticking to the pan. Allow to cool, then sieve or liquidise.

Note: Soft fruits like raspberries and strawberries can be puréed by sieving without cooking and without the addition of any water.

To serve at once: Use as required in chosen recipe, adding sugar if necessary.

To freeze: Allow to cool completely, then pack in freezer boil-in-the-bags, foil bags, foil containers or rigid polythene containers. Seal, label and freeze.

To thaw: Thaw overnight in the refrigerator, for 6 hours at room temperature, or in hot water if frozen in a boil-in-the-bag.

Makes 300–450 ml/$\frac{1}{2}$–$\frac{3}{4}$ pint/$1\frac{1}{4}$–2 cups purée

Small choux buns

METRIC/IMPERIAL/AMERICAN
300 ml/$\frac{1}{2}$ pint/$1\frac{1}{4}$ cups water
50 g/2 oz/$\frac{1}{4}$ cup butter or margarine
150 g/5 oz/$1\frac{1}{4}$ cups plain flour
2 large eggs

Place the water and butter or margarine in a saucepan and heat gently to melt the butter. Bring to the boil, remove from the heat and sieve the flour into the pan. Return to a moderate heat and beat well until the mixture forms a ball in the centre of the pan. Allow the mixture to cool a little. Beat the eggs well and, off the heat, gradually add them to the mixture in the pan, beating until smooth and glossy.

Place in a large nylon piping bag fitted with a star vegetable nozzle. Pipe small rosettes on baking sheets. Cook in the centre of a moderately hot oven (200°C, 400°F, Gas Mark 6) for 20 minutes until risen and crisp. Pierce the sides immediately to release the steam, and place in the switched-off oven for 20 minutes to dry off a little. Allow to cool on a cake rack.

To serve at once: The choux buns can now be filled and served as profiteroles.

To freeze: Place the cooled buns on a baking sheet lined with greaseproof paper and open freeze. When solid, transfer to a polythene bag. Seal, label and return to the freezer.

To thaw: Unwrap and leave at room temperature for 1–2 hours. Serve as above.

Makes about 16

All-in-one sandwich cake

METRIC/IMPERIAL/AMERICAN
110 g/4 oz/$\frac{1}{2}$ cup soft margarine
110 g/4 oz/$\frac{1}{2}$ cup castor sugar
2 large eggs
110 g/4 oz/1 cup self-raising flour
1 teaspoon baking powder
TO FINISH:
4 tablespoons/4 tablespoons/$\frac{1}{3}$ cup freezer jam
100 ml/4 fl oz/$\frac{1}{2}$ cup double cream, whipped (optional)
icing sugar for dusting
walnuts, glacé cherries, angelica

Line the bases of two 18-cm/7-inch sandwich tins with greaseproof paper. Grease, and sprinkle with flour.

Using a wooden spoon, beat all the ingredients together for 2–3 minutes. Divide the mixture between the tins.

Bake in a moderate oven (160°C, 325°F, Gas Mark 3) for 25–35 minutes until firm. Allow to stand for a few minutes before turning out on to a cake rack. Leave to become cold.

To serve at once: Sandwich the cakes together with freezer jam and whipped double cream, if liked. Dust with icing sugar and decorate with walnuts, glacé cherries and angelica.

To freeze: Interleave the layers with freezer layer tissue and wrap in foil. Seal, label and freeze.

To thaw: Leave in the foil at room temperature for 2 hours, then finish as above.

Makes 1 (18-cm/7-inch) round cake

Freezer jam

METRIC/IMPERIAL/AMERICAN
0.75 kg/1$\frac{1}{2}$ lb/1$\frac{1}{2}$ lb raspberries, strawberries or
   loganberries
1 kg/2 lb/4 cups castor sugar
$\frac{1}{2}$ bottle Certo
2 tablespoons/2 tablespoons/3 tablespoons lemon juice

Mash the fruit lightly with the sugar. Stirring occasionally, leave to stand for about 2$\frac{1}{2}$ hours in a warm kitchen, or until the sugar has dissolved. Add the Certo and lemon juice and stir for about 2 minutes. Pour into rigid polythene containers, leaving a 1-cm/$\frac{1}{2}$-inch headspace.

To freeze: Allow to stand for 48 hours in a warm kitchen, until set. Seal, label and freeze.

To thaw: Leave at room temperature for about 30 minutes when the jam should be ready for spreading.

Makes 1.5 kg/3 lb

Soups and starters

Soups and pâtés are both very good candidates for the freezer and they are especially useful when planning a dinner party menu. They can be prepared well in advance and will require very little attention on the day. Frozen homemade stock can be used in the soups, making them even more delicious.

Tomato and cucumber soup

METRIC/IMPERIAL/AMERICAN
1 small onion, sliced
1 large cucumber, coarsely chopped
150 ml/$\frac{1}{4}$ pint/$\frac{2}{3}$ cup chicken stock
1 (794-g/1-lb 12-oz/28-oz) can peeled tomatoes
salt
$\frac{1}{2}$ teaspoon paprika
pinch sugar
TO SERVE:
150 ml/$\frac{1}{4}$ pint/$\frac{2}{3}$ cup natural yogurt
2 tablespoons/2 tablespoons/3 tablespoons single cream
    or creamy milk
chopped chives to garnish

Place the onion, cucumber and stock in a saucepan. Cover and simmer gently until the onion is soft. Sieve or liquidise with the tomatoes, salt, paprika and a pinch sugar. Chill well before serving.
To serve at once: Stir in the yogurt and single cream. Garnish each bowl with chopped chives.
To freeze: Do not add the yogurt or cream. Pour the tomato mixture into a rigid polythene container or foil bag. Allow to cool. Seal, label and freeze.
To thaw: Place in the refrigerator overnight as the soup should be served chilled. Finish as above.

Serves 6

Scampi with relish

METRIC/IMPERIAL/AMERICAN
0.5 kg/1 lb/2 cups tomato and onion relish, thawed (see
   page 220)
0.75 kg/1½ lb/1½ lb potatoes, peeled and sliced
salt and pepper
65 g/2½ oz/5 tablespoons butter
2 tablespoons/2 tablespoons/3 tablespoons milk
0.5 kg/1 lb/1 lb frozen scampi, thawed
150 ml/¼ pint/⅔ cup dry white wine
150 ml/¼ pint/⅔ cup water
1 small onion, sliced
bouquet garni
40 g/1½ oz/6 tablespoons plain flour
chopped parsley to garnish

Divide the relish between 6 individual flameproof dishes. Cook
the potatoes in boiling salted water, drain and mash with
25 g/1 oz/2 tablespoons butter, the milk and salt and pepper.
   Simmer the scampi with the wine, water, onion and bouquet
garni for 10–15 minutes. Drain well, reserving the stock.
Divide the scampi between the dishes. Melt the remaining
butter and stir in the flour. Gradually blend in the reserved
stock. Bring to the boil, stirring, and cook for 1 minute. Season
and pour over the scampi. Pipe potato around each dish. Place
under a moderate grill for 10 minutes. Sprinkle with parsley.
Note: This recipe uses frozen ingredients and is not for
refreezing.

Serves 4

Prawn and tomato cocktail

METRIC/IMPERIAL/AMERICAN
100 g/4 oz/½ cup tomato and onion relish, thawed (see
   page 220)
4 tablespoons/4 tablespoons/5 tablespoons mayonnaise
few drops Tabasco sauce
175 g/6 oz/1 cup frozen peeled prawns, thawed
1 small lettuce
paprika (optional)
4 fresh prawns or slices of lemon to garnish

Mix the tomato and onion relish with the mayonnaise and a few
drops Tabasco sauce. Drain the thawed prawns on kitchen
paper and then stir into the sauce.
   Shred the lettuce and use to line 4 ramekins or glasses suitable
for a prawn cocktail. Divide the prawn mixture between the
dishes and sprinkle with a little paprika if liked.
   Garnish each dish with a fresh prawn or a slice of lemon.
Serve with toast.
Note: This recipe uses frozen ingredients and is not for
refreezing.

Serves 4

Herbed chicken liver pâté

METRIC/IMPERIAL/AMERICAN
1 large onion, chopped
25 g/1 oz/2 tablespoons butter or margarine
1 tablespoon corn oil
0.5 kg/1 lb/1 lb chicken livers
$\frac{1}{4}$ teaspoon chopped fresh tarragon
$\frac{1}{4}$ teaspoon chopped fresh chives
pinch chopped fresh sage
1 teaspoon chopped fresh parsley
50 g/2 oz/$\frac{1}{4}$ cup cream cheese
4 tablespoons/4 tablespoons/$\frac{1}{3}$ cup natural yogurt
garlic salt
freshly ground pepper
1 bay leaf to garnish

Place the onion, butter and oil in a saucepan and cook without browning until soft – about 10 minutes. Add the livers to the onion together with the chopped herbs. Mix well and cook for about 10 minutes.

Remove from the heat and sieve or blend in a liquidiser. Add the cream cheese and stir in the yogurt, garlic salt and pepper.
To serve at once: Transfer to a serving dish and chill to allow flavours to develop. Garnish with a bay leaf.
To freeze: Divide into 2 rigid polythene or foil containers, each one to serve 4 people. When quite cold, seal, label and freeze.
To thaw: Overnight in the refrigerator. Serve as before.

Serves 8

Liver and mushroom pâté

METRIC/IMPERIAL/AMERICAN
100 g/4 oz/1 cup onion, chopped
1 clove garlic, crushed
350 g/12 oz/$\frac{3}{4}$ lb lambs' liver, sliced
100 g/4 oz/$\frac{1}{4}$ lb streaky bacon, derinded and chopped
100 g/4 oz/1 cup mushrooms, washed and chopped
50 g/2 oz/$\frac{1}{4}$ cup butter
40 g/1$\frac{1}{2}$ oz/6 tablespoons plain flour
300 ml/$\frac{1}{2}$ pint/1$\frac{1}{4}$ cups milk
$\frac{1}{2}$ teaspoon dried basil
salt and pepper
cucumber, tomato and mustard and cress to garnish

Sauté the onion, garlic, liver, bacon and mushrooms in 15 g/ $\frac{1}{2}$ oz/1 tablespoon butter for 10 minutes, then mince.

Melt the remaining butter, add the flour and gradually add the milk. Bring to the boil, stirring continuously, and cook for 2 minutes. Stir in the remaining ingredients and the minced mixture. Turn into a small terrine and cover. Place in a roasting tin half filled with water and cook in the centre of a moderate oven (160°C, 325°F, Gas Mark 3) for 1$\frac{1}{2}$ hours.
To serve at once: When cold, garnish and serve.
To freeze: When cold, remove the pâté from the dish, line the dish with foil, return the pâté and freeze. When frozen, lift the pâté out of the dish, wrap completely in foil and place in a polythene bag. Seal, label and return to the freezer.
To thaw: Overnight in the refrigerator.

Serves 6

Fish, meat and poultry

What could be better than to come home from a day at work or out with the family and have the dinner already prepared? Casseroles and stews are the usual favourites for freezing and this chapter provides some good ideas for these as well as giving you many other exciting recipes for freezing fish, meat and poultry.

Sole or plaice goujons

METRIC/IMPERIAL/AMERICAN
6–8 sole or plaice fillets
1 large egg
1 tablespoon water
salt and pepper
fresh breadcrumbs for coating
oil for deep frying

Wash the fillets and cut diagonally into strips about 1 cm/$\frac{1}{2}$ inch wide. Beat the egg with the water. Add salt and pepper. Spread the breadcrumbs on a sheet of greaseproof paper. Coat the fish strips in the egg and then toss in the breadcrumbs.

To serve at once: Place some of the goujons in a wire basket and fry for 1$\frac{1}{2}$ minutes in deep oil hot enough to brown a cube of bread in 30 seconds. Drain and keep hot while cooking a second batch. Serve with mixed salad and tartare sauce.

To freeze: Place the uncooked goujons on a baking sheet and open freeze. When frozen, place in a polythene bag. Seal, label and return to the freezer.

To thaw: Thaw for 30 minutes before frying. Heat deep fat until a cube of bread browns in 25 seconds. Place some of the goujons in the basket but do not overfill. Cook for about 1$\frac{1}{2}$ minutes, remove basket, allow fat to heat up again, then replace goujons for a further $\frac{1}{2}$–1 minute to cook through and become crisp. Serve as above.

Serves 4

Individual fish pies

METRIC/IMPERIAL/AMERICAN

1 (396-g/14-oz/14-oz) packet frozen cod steaks, thawed
150 ml/¼ pint/⅔ cup milk
150 ml/¼ pint/⅔ cup water
40 g/1½ oz/3 tablespoons butter
1 small onion, grated
25 g/1 oz/¼ cup flour
2 teaspoons anchovy essence
1 tablespoon chopped fresh parsley
pepper and salt
1 (64-g/2¼-oz/2¼-oz) packet instant potato
prawns, slices of lemon and parsley sprigs to garnish

Cut the cod into cubes and poach in the milk and water for 10 minutes. Drain, reserving the liquor. Divide the fish between 4 scallop shells.

Sauté the onion in 25 g/1 oz/2 tablespoons butter for 2 minutes. Stir in the flour and reserved stock. Add the anchovy essence, parsley, pepper and salt. Pour over the fish.

Make up the instant potato, adding the remaining butter. Season to taste and pipe around each shell.

To serve at once: Place under a moderate grill for 10 minutes. Garnish and serve with a green salad.

To freeze: Open freeze then wrap in foil. Seal, label and return to the freezer.

To thaw: Unwrap and place the frozen pies in a hot oven (220°C, 425°F, Gas Mark 7) for 25 minutes.

Serves 4

Russian fish pie

METRIC/IMPERIAL/AMERICAN

0.5 kg/1 lb/1 lb cod
150 ml/¼ pint/⅔ cup milk
25 g/1 oz/2 tablespoons butter, melted
25 g/1 oz/¼ cup plain flour
salt and pepper
1 tablespoon chopped fresh parsley
1 (368-g/13-oz/13-oz) packet frozen puff pastry, thawed
½ egg, beaten
lettuce and watercress to garnish

Simmer the fish gently in the milk for 10–12 minutes. Drain and leave to cool, reserving the liquor.

Whisk together the butter, flour and reserved milk. Bring to the boil and continue whisking for 2–3 minutes. Flake the fish and fold into the sauce with salt, pepper and parsley.

Roll out the pastry to a 30-cm/12-inch square. Trim the edges. Place on a baking sheet and spoon the fish and sauce into the centre. Dampen the pastry edges and bring the corners together to make a square envelope. Seal and flute. Decorate with pastry leaves. Brush with beaten egg and cook in a hot oven (220°C, 425°F, Gas Mark 7) for 30–40 minutes.

To serve at once: Garnish with lettuce and watercress.

To freeze: Open freeze when cold, then wrap in foil. Seal, label and return to the freezer.

To thaw: Unwrap and place, frozen, on a baking sheet in a moderate oven (160°C, 325°F, Gas Mark 3) for 40–50 minutes.

Serves 4–6

Meat and vegetable pasties

METRIC/IMPERIAL/AMERICAN
100 g/4 oz/1 cup potatoes, grated
50 g/2 oz/½ cup carrots, grated
25 g/1 oz/2 tablespoons butter
1 tablespoon plain flour
½ teaspoon dried mixed herbs
½ quantity meat sauce, thawed (see page 218)
SHORTCRUST PASTRY:
55 g/2 oz/¼ cup lard
55 g/2 oz/¼ cup butter
225 g/8 oz/2 cups plain flour, sifted
1 teaspoon salt
2 tablespoons/2 tablespoons/3 tablespoons cold water
beaten egg for brushing

Sauté the potatoes and carrots in the butter for 5 minutes. Stir in the flour, cook for 3 minutes. Add the herbs and meat sauce, cook for a further 5 minutes. Cool.

Rub the lard and butter into the flour and salt and add water to bind. Knead gently, then roll out as two 25-cm/10-inch circles. Divide the meat between the circles. Dampen the pastry edges and seal. Place on a baking sheet, brush with egg and bake in a hot oven (220°C, 425°F, Gas Mark 7) for 20–25 minutes. Serve with vegetables or cold with salad.
To freeze: Open freeze, wrap in foil and return to the freezer.
To thaw: To serve cold, thaw overnight in the refrigerator. To serve hot, unwrap and thaw overnight then place in a moderate oven (180°C, 350°F, Gas Mark 4) for 15–20 minutes.

Makes 2 pasties each serving 2

Sweet and sour meatballs

METRIC/IMPERIAL/AMERICAN
225 g/8 oz/1 cup minced beef
225 g/8 oz/1 cup beef sausagemeat
50 g/2 oz/½ cup onion, grated
½ teaspoon dried mixed herbs
2 teaspoons chopped parsley
salt and pepper
1 tablespoon seasoned flour
2 tablespoons/2 tablespoons/3 tablespoons oil
1 carrot, peeled and cut into small strips
450 ml/¾ pint/2 cups beef stock
4 tablespoons/4 tablespoons/⅓ cup malt vinegar
75 g/3 oz/6 tablespoons demerara sugar
1½ tablespoons/1½ tablespoons/2 tablespoons cornflour
1 teaspoon soy sauce

Mix together the mince, sausagemeat, onion, herbs and seasoning. Form into 18–20 balls and toss in the seasoned flour. Fry gently in the oil for 15–20 minutes, then drain well.

Place the carrot, stock, vinegar and sugar in a saucepan. Cover and cook slowly for 5 minutes. Blend the cornflour with the soy sauce and a little water. Stir in some of the hot liquid. Return to the pan and bring to the boil, stirring. Spoon the sauce over the meatballs and serve on noodles.
To freeze: Pack the cooled meatballs and sauce separately.
To thaw: Thaw the meatballs in the refrigerator overnight then place in a hot oven for 15 minutes. Heat the sauce in a pan.

Serves 4

Beef loaf

METRIC/IMPERIAL/AMERICAN
150 ml/¼ pint/⅔ cup beef stock
75 g/3 oz/1½ cups brown breadcrumbs
0.5 kg/1 lb/2 cups lean minced beef
50 g/2 oz/½ cup onion, finely chopped
¼ teaspoon dried thyme
50 g/2 oz/⅓ cup dried milk powder
1 egg, well beaten
2 teaspoons tomato purée
1 tablespoon chopped parsley
1 teaspoon Worcestershire sauce
tomato and mustard and cress to garnish

Mix together all the ingredients and place the mixture in the centre of a large piece of foil and form into a loaf shape. Seal the edges of the foil over the loaf.

Put the parcel in a tin half filled with water and cook in a moderately hot oven (200°C, 400°F, Gas Mark 6) for 1–1¼ hours.
To serve at once: Open the foil and drain off any liquid. If serving cold, wrap again in the foil so that the loaf keeps its shape while cooling. Garnish with mustard and cress and slices of tomato. Serve with potatoes sprinkled with parsley.
To freeze: Allow to cool completely, then wrap in fresh foil. Seal, label and freeze.
To thaw: Leave to thaw overnight in the refrigerator. To serve hot, unwrap and place in a moderate oven (180°C, 350°F, Gas Mark 4) for 20–30 minutes.

Serves 6–8

Individual shepherd's pies

METRIC/IMPERIAL/AMERICAN
1 quantity basic meat sauce (see page 218)
100 g/4 oz/1 cup carrot, grated
1 tablespoon flour
0.5 kg/1 lb/1 lb potatoes, peeled and boiled
salt and pepper
freshly ground nutmeg
parsley to garnish

Heat the meat sauce through to thaw, then stir in the grated carrot and flour. Cook for 10 minutes. Cool slightly, then divide between 6 ramekin dishes. For freezing, use freezerproof ramekins or line the dishes with foil.

Mash the potatoes with the salt, pepper and nutmeg. Pipe a whirl of potato on each ramekin.
To serve at once: Place in a moderately hot oven (190°C, 375°F, Gas Mark 5) for 25–30 minutes. Garnish with parsley and serve with grilled tomatoes.
To freeze: Open freeze before the final cooking. Pack freezerproof ramekins in polythene bags. If the ramekins have been lined with foil, lift out the solid pies and wrap in foil. Seal, label and return to the freezer.
To thaw: Unwrap freezerproof ramekins and thaw at room temperature for 30–50 minutes before placing in a moderately hot oven (200°C, 400°F, Gas Mark 6) for 30 minutes. Unwrap pies frozen in foil, replace in original ramekins and heat from frozen for 40 minutes in a moderately hot oven.

Serves 6

Lamb and olive stew

METRIC/IMPERIAL/AMERICAN
0.75 kg/1½ lb/1½ lb lamb fillet, cubed
175 g/6 oz/3 cups onion, chopped
1 stock cube, crumbled
1 large clove garlic, crushed
1 (396-g/14-oz/14-oz) can peeled tomatoes
10 pimento-stuffed olives
2 tablespoons/2 tablespoons/3 tablespoons tomato purée
1 teaspoon sugar
salt and pepper

Place the meat in a saucepan with the onion and heat gently to extract the fat from the meat. Cook for 10 minutes, then add the remaining ingredients. Mix well and pour into a casserole which should be lined with foil for freezing.

Cover and cook in the centre of a moderate oven (180°C, 350°F, Gas Mark 4) for 1 hour if the casserole is to be frozen or 1½ hours if not. Serve sprinkled with a little parsley.

To freeze: Cool thoroughly and then freeze until solid. Remove the foil parcel from the casserole, wrap completely in foil and place in a polythene bag. Seal, label and return to the freezer. The parsley can be frozen separately in a polythene bag.

To thaw: Unwrap and return to the casserole. Either thaw at room temperature for several hours and then place in a moderate oven (160°C, 325°F, Gas Mark 3) for about 1 hour, or heat through from frozen in the oven for 2 hours. The frozen parsley can be crumbled over the casserole.

Serves 4

Lamb curry

METRIC/IMPERIAL/AMERICAN
1 quantity curry sauce (see page 219)
0.5 kg/1¼ lb/1¼ lb lamb fillet
1 small eating apple, peeled, cored and chopped
GARNISH:
parsley sprigs
lemon wedges

Thaw the curry sauce, if frozen. Trim the lamb and cut into 2.5-cm/1-inch cubes. Place in a saucepan and cook slowly in its own fat to seal in the meat juices. Transfer the meat to a plate. Drain the fat from the pan and clean the pan round with kitchen paper.

Place the curry sauce in the pan, and add the apple and meat. Mix well.

Cover and cook very slowly for 1¼–1½ hours until the meat is tender.

To serve at once: Garnish with parsley sprigs and lemon wedges. Serve with plain boiled rice, salted peanuts, poppadums, redcurrant jelly, sliced banana and chopped tomatoes.

To freeze: When cold, transfer the curry to a rigid polythene container. Seal, label and freeze.

To thaw: Leave in the refrigerator overnight and then heat through in a saucepan, or heat through gently from frozen. Serve as above.

Serves 4

Kidney special

METRIC/IMPERIAL/AMERICAN
8–10 lambs' kidneys
4 rashers streaky bacon, derinded
1 medium onion, sliced
225 g/8 oz/1½ cups carrots, sliced
25 g/1 oz/2 tablespoons butter
1 tablespoon plain flour
1 (396-g/14-oz/14-oz) can peeled tomatoes
1 teaspoon sugar
2 bay leaves
salt and pepper
¼ teaspoon dried thyme

Halve, skin and core the kidneys. Stretch each rasher of bacon with the back of a knife, cut in half and roll up neatly.

Sauté the bacon rolls, onion and carrots in the butter until golden brown. Keep on one side of the pan and add the kidneys to the other side. Cook gently for 3 minutes. Stir in the flour and the juice from the can of tomatoes, then add the tomatoes and the remaining ingredients. Simmer gently for about 15–20 minutes.

To serve at once: Serve with mashed potato.
To freeze: Cool quickly and transfer to suitable freezer container. Seal, label and freeze.
To thaw: Thaw completely either overnight in the refrigerator or at room temperature for 3–4 hours. Heat through gently and serve with mashed potatoes as before.

Serves 4

Rabbit pie

METRIC/IMPERIAL/AMERICAN
1 (0.5-kg/1¼-lb/1¼-lb) rabbit, prepared
1 small onion, sliced
750 ml/1¼ pints/3 cups water
1 tablespoon cornflour blended with 3 tablespoons/
    3 tablespoons/¼ cup milk
50 g/2 oz/¼ cup streaky bacon, cooked and chopped
SHORTCRUST PASTRY:
65 g/2½ oz/5 tablespoons margarine
65 g/2½ oz/5 tablespoons lard
275 g/10 oz/2½ cups plain flour
¼ teaspoon salt
parsley sprig to garnish

Place the rabbit, onion and water in a casserole with seasoning. Cover and cook in a moderate oven (180°C, 350°F, Gas Mark 4) for 1¼ hours. Strip the meat from the bones. Strain the liquor into a saucepan and add the cornflour and bacon. Bring to the boil, stirring. Cool. Make the pastry in the usual way (see page 28) and roll out just under half to line a 25-cm/10-inch foil plate. Arrange the rabbit and sauce in the centre. Roll out the remaining pastry and use as a lid. Cook in a hot oven (220°C, 425°F, Gas Mark 7) for 15 minutes, then at 190°C, 375°F, Gas Mark 5 for 25–30 minutes. Garnish and serve with salad.
To freeze: Open freeze when cold, then wrap in foil.
To thaw: Unwrap and place, frozen, in a moderate oven (180°C, 350°F, Gas Mark 4) for 40–45 minutes.

Serves 4–6

Chicken Kiev

METRIC/IMPERIAL/AMERICAN
100 g/4 oz/½ cup butter
3 tablespoons/3 tablespoons/¼ cup chopped parsley
2 cloves garlic, crushed
salt and pepper
4 chicken breasts
2 tablespoons/2 tablespoons/3 tablespoons seasoned flour
1 egg, beaten
fresh breadcrumbs for coating
oil for deep frying

Blend the butter with the parsley, garlic, salt and pepper and divide into 4 rolls. Wrap in foil and chill until hard.

Flatten the breasts slightly with a rolling pin, then put a roll of butter in the centre of each breast. Roll up the chicken meat, completely enclosing the butter. Sew up, leaving a length of thread at one end.

Toss in seasoned flour, then dip in beaten egg and then breadcrumbs. Repeat the egg-and-breadcrumbing. Chill before cooking.

To serve at once: Fry the chicken for about 10 minutes in deep oil hot enough to brown a cube of bread in 60 seconds.

To freeze: Place the uncooked crumbed breasts on a baking sheet, cover loosely with foil and open freeze. When frozen interleave with freezer film and pack in a polythene bag.

To thaw: Leave at room temperature for 6 hours. Cook as above.

Serves 4

Chicken parcels

METRIC/IMPERIAL/AMERICAN
1 medium onion, finely chopped
½ small green pepper, deseeded and sliced
25 g/1 oz/2 tablespoons butter
1 tablespoon plain flour
1 (227-g/8-oz/8-oz) can pineapple rings
1 tablespoon concentrated curry sauce
1 tablespoon chopped parsley
salt and pepper
4 chicken quarters

Sauté the onion and pepper in the butter for about 5 minutes. Stir in the flour and cook for 3 minutes.

Strain the juice from the pineapple and gradually stir it into the flour mixture, together with the curry sauce. Bring to the boil, stirring, and cook for 2 minutes. Halve the pineapple rings and add to the sauce with the parsley and seasoning.

Place each chicken quarter in the centre of a piece of foil and spoon the sauce equally over the chicken. Seal the foil to make parcels. Cook in the centre of a moderate oven (180°C, 350°F, Gas Mark 4) for 40–45 minutes.

To serve at once: Unwrap and serve with rice.

To freeze: Cool quickly and freeze, sealed and labelled, in the foil the chicken was cooked in. Overwrap in a polythene bag.

To thaw: Remove the polythene and place the frozen parcels in a moderate oven (180°C, 350°F, Gas Mark 4) for 1 hour. Serve as above.

Serves 4

Chicken cacciatore

METRIC/IMPERIAL/AMERICAN
4 chicken quarters
75 g/3 oz/6 tablespoons butter
1 large onion, chopped
1 medium green pepper, deseeded and chopped
1 clove garlic, crushed
1 (396-g/14-oz/14-oz) can peeled tomatoes
150 ml/¼ pint/⅔ cup chicken stock
salt and pepper
watercress to garnish

Sauté the chicken for 25–30 minutes in 50 g/2 oz/4 tablespoons butter. Meanwhile, gently sauté the onion, green pepper and garlic in the remaining butter for about 10 minutes. Stir in the tomatoes, stock and seasoning. Cover and simmer for 15 minutes.

To serve at once: Spoon the sauce over the chicken on a heated serving dish. Garnish with watercress and serve with rice sprinkled with chopped parsley.

To freeze: Spoon the sauce over the chicken in a foil dish. When cold, seal, label and freeze.

To thaw: In the refrigerator overnight, then place in a moderate oven (180°C, 350°F, Gas Mark 4) for 25–30 minutes.

Serves 4

Chicken lasagne

METRIC/IMPERIAL/AMERICAN
1 medium onion, chopped
75 g/3 oz/6 tablespoons butter
1 clove garlic, crushed
2 tablespoons/2 tablespoons/3 tablespoons plain flour
600 ml/1 pint/2½ cups chicken stock
225 g/8 oz/1⅓ cups cooked chicken, chopped
100 g/4 oz/1 cup mushrooms, washed and chopped
3 tablespoons/3 tablespoons/¼ cup tomato purée
1 teaspoon dried mixed herbs
8 uncooked sheets lasagne
25 g/1 oz/¼ cup flour
300 ml/½ pint/1¼ cups milk
25 g/1 oz/¼ cup Parmesan cheese, grated

Sauté the onion in 50 g/2 oz/¼ cup butter. Stir in the garlic, flour and stock. Bring to the boil, stirring. Off the heat add the chicken, mushrooms, tomato purée and herbs. Season. Arrange a layer of lasagne in a foil-lined ovenproof dish. Spread chicken sauce over. Repeat, finishing with sauce.

To serve at once: Melt remaining butter and stir in flour. Add milk. Cook for 2 minutes. Season, pour over lasagne. Sprinkle with cheese and place in a moderate oven for 45 minutes.

To freeze: Cool. Open freeze, then lift out of the dish, wrap in foil, seal, label and return to the freezer.

To thaw: Unwrap and return to the dish. Place in a moderate oven (180°C, 350°F, Gas Mark 4) for 1–1½ hours.

Serves 4–5

Vegetable dishes

Having a freezer will enable you to freeze down your homegrown produce and take advantage of good seasonal offers in the shops. The recipes in this chapter concentrate on freezing cooked vegetable dishes and serving frozen vegetables in interesting ways.

Stuffed courgettes

METRIC/IMPERIAL/AMERICAN
8 large fresh courgettes
salt and pepper
100 g/4 oz/½ cup bacon, finely chopped
2 cloves garlic, crushed
1 large onion, chopped
2 tablespoons/2 tablespoons/3 tablespoons corn oil
225 g/8 oz/1 cup tomatoes, peeled and chopped
25 g/1 oz/¼ cup dry breadcrumbs
1 tablespoon chopped parsley to garnish

Wash and dry the courgettes, halve lengthways, scoop out the centre flesh, and chop. Cook the courgette boats in boiling salted water for 5 minutes. Drain. Sauté the bacon, garlic and onion in 1 tablespoon oil. Stir in tomatoes, courgette flesh and crumbs. Season and press this mixture into the courgette boats. Place in a foil dish, spoon the remaining oil over, cover with foil and cook in the centre of a moderately hot oven (190°C, 375°F, Gas Mark 5) for 15 minutes.
To serve at once: Serve hot or cold, garnished with parsley.
To freeze: Open freeze when cold, then transfer to a foil dish. Seal, label and return to the freezer.
To thaw: To serve cold, uncover and thaw at room temperature for about 3 hours. To serve hot, heat through from frozen in a moderately hot oven (200°C, 400°F, Gas Mark 6) for 15–20 minutes.

Serves 4–6

Savoury topped broccoli

METRIC/IMPERIAL/AMERICAN
0.5 kg/1 lb/1 lb broccoli, fresh or frozen
1 tablespoon oil
100 g/4 oz/1 cup onion, chopped
1 clove garlic, crushed (optional)
225 g/8 oz/½ lb tomatoes, peeled
1 tablespoon tomato purée
pinch sugar
salt and pepper
100 g/4 oz/½ cup ham, cut into strips
50 g/2 oz/½ cup Cheddar cheese, grated

Cook the broccoli in boiling salted water until just tender. This will take about 15 minutes for fresh broccoli or about half that time for frozen. Drain and keep hot in a serving dish.

Meanwhile, place the oil in a saucepan, add the onion and cook for about 10 minutes, until soft. Add the garlic, tomatoes, purée, sugar, salt and pepper and cook until fairly pulpy – about 10 minutes. Spread this mixture over the broccoli, arrange the ham over the top and sprinkle with cheese. Place under a moderate grill until the cheese has melted and the dish has heated through. Serve with French bread.

Serves 3–4

Asparagus pancakes

METRIC/IMPERIAL/AMERICAN
300 ml/½ pint/1¼ cups pancake batter or 8 frozen pancakes
    (see page 221)
24 asparagus spears, fresh or frozen
40 g/1½ oz/3 tablespoons butter or margarine
25 g/1 oz/¼ cup plain flour
150 ml/¼ pint/⅔ cup milk
salt and pepper
25 g/1 oz/¼ cup Cheddar cheese, grated
parsley sprig to garnish

Make 8 thin pancakes as on page 13 or remove them from the freezer and thaw. Cook the asparagus in boiling salted water for 10–15 minutes. Drain well and place 3 spears in the centre of each pancake. Roll up and place the pancakes in a flameproof dish.

Melt the butter or margarine in a small saucepan and add the flour. Cook, stirring, for 1 minute, then remove from the heat and gradually blend in the milk. Return to the heat and bring to the boil, stirring continuously. Season to taste and pour the sauce over the pancakes. Sprinkle with the grated cheese. Place under a moderate grill to heat through slowly. Garnish with a parsley sprig.

Serves 8 as a starter or 4 as a main course

Vegetable nut loaf

METRIC/IMPERIAL/AMERICAN
1 small onion, finely chopped
2 sticks celery, finely chopped
1 tablespoon oil
2 medium tomatoes, peeled, quartered and deseeded
1 small carrot, chopped
1 small parsnip, chopped
2 large slices brown bread
50 g/2 oz/generous ¼ cup salted peanuts
¼ teaspoon grated nutmeg
¼ teaspoon dried marjoram
salt and pepper
2 eggs, beaten
2 bay leaves
tomato and watercress to garnish

Cook the onion and celery in the oil, without browning, until soft. Mince together with the other vegetables, the bread and peanuts. Add the nutmeg, marjoram, salt, pepper and eggs. Mix well. Place in a well-greased 0.5-kg/1-lb deep foil dish. Smooth the surface and place 2 bay leaves on top. Cover with greased greaseproof paper and bake in the centre of a moderate oven (180°C, 350°F, Gas Mark 4) for 1 hour.
To serve at once: Garnish and serve cold.
To freeze: Allow to become cold, wrap in foil and place in a polythene bag. Seal, label and freeze.
To thaw: Thaw, wrapped, for about 3 hours.

Serves 4–6

Onion tart

METRIC/IMPERIAL/AMERICAN
75 g/3 oz/6 tablespoons butter
0.75 kg/1½ lb/1½ lb Spanish onions, thinly sliced
40 g/1½ oz/3 tablespoons lard
175 g/6 oz/1½ cups plain flour
1–2 tablespoons cold water
3 eggs
150 ml/¼ pint/⅔ cup single cream
5 tablespoons/5 tablespoons/6 tablespoons milk
salt and pepper
chopped parsley to garnish

Melt half the butter in a saucepan, add the onions and place dampened greaseproof paper on top. Cover with a lid and cook very gently until beginning to soften.

Rub the remaining butter and the lard into the flour and add a little cold water to form a dough. Roll out the pastry to line an 18–20-cm/7–8-inch flan ring.

Beat together the eggs, cream, milk and seasoning. Arrange the onions in the flan base and pour in the egg mixture. Cook in a hot oven (220°C, 425°F, Gas Mark 7) for 15–20 minutes, then at 190°C, 375°F, Gas Mark 5 for 20–30 minutes. Garnish.
To freeze: When cold, wrap in foil, seal, label and freeze.
To thaw: To serve cold, thaw at room temperature for about 4 hours. To serve hot, thaw and then place in the centre of a moderate oven (180°C, 350°F, Gas Mark 4) for about 15 minutes.

Serves 4

Desserts and gâteaux

Delicious homemade sorbets and ice creams can be made quickly and easily with the aid of your freezer, and are ideal ways of using up a glut of soft fruit. Attractive party desserts often require time and care so it is a great help to be able to make them at your leisure and then bring them out later as special-occasion surprises.

Satsuma sorbets

METRIC/IMPERIAL/AMERICAN
10 large satsumas
150 g/5 oz/⅔ cup castor sugar
1 lemon
1 small orange
1 egg white
mint leaves to decorate (optional)

Cut the tops off 8 satsumas to make small lids. Using a grapefruit knife, carefully scoop out all the flesh, being careful not to puncture the skins. Remove the pips from the flesh then liquidise the flesh and strain the juice into a saucepan. Add the sugar and heat gently to dissolve. Remove from the heat.

Grate the rind from the lemon and orange. Squeeze the juice from the lemon, orange and the 2 remaining satsumas. Add the rind and juice to the saucepan. Pour the mixture into a polythene container, leave until cold, then freeze until slushy – about 3–4 hours. Keep the 8 skins and lids in a polythene bag. Whisk the egg white until stiff then fold into the slushy juices. Place the satsuma shells in the hollows of 8 tartlet tins and fill with the mixture. Put the lids on top. Freeze until firm, then replace in polythene bags. Seal, label and return to the freezer.
To serve: Place in the refrigerator for 45 minutes–1 hour. Decorate with mint leaves if available.

Serves 8

Raspberry sorbet

METRIC/IMPERIAL/AMERICAN
225 g/8 oz/½ lb raspberries, fresh or frozen
100 g/4 oz/½ cup granulated sugar
300 ml/½ pint/1¼ cups water
2 tablespoons/2 tablespoons/3 tablespoons lemon juice
1 egg white
whole raspberries to decorate

Thaw the raspberries if frozen. Place the sugar and water in a saucepan and heat gently to dissolve the sugar. Bring to the boil then allow to become quite cold.

Sieve or liquidise and then strain the raspberries. Add the resulting purée to the sugar syrup. Stir in the lemon juice and mix well.

Pour into a polythene container, cover and freeze until slushy – about 3–4 hours. Whisk the egg white until stiff and fold into the mixture. Freeze until solid. If not required immediately, seal, label and return to the freezer.

To serve: Place in the refrigerator and thaw for just long enough to enable you to get out spoonfuls – 30 minutes–1 hour. Too much thawing will cause the sorbet to become slushy. Spoon into dishes and decorate with a few fresh or thawed frozen raspberries.

Serves 4

Strawberry ice cream

METRIC/IMPERIAL/AMERICAN
100 g/4 oz/½ cup granulated sugar
300 ml/½ pint/1¼ cups water
0.75 kg/1¾ lb/1¾ lb strawberries
1 egg white
150 ml/¼ pint/⅔ cup double cream
whole strawberries to decorate

Gently heat the sugar and water to dissolve the sugar, then bring to the boil. Boil steadily for 10 minutes then leave until cold. Sieve or liquidise the strawberries to give approximately 300 ml/½ pint/1¼ cups purée. Mix the syrup and strawberry purée together. Pour into a polythene container, cover and freeze until slushy – about 3–4 hours.

Whisk the egg white until stiff, mash down the fruit ice and fold in the egg white until evenly mixed. Freeze again until semi-solid – about 1 hour. Remove from the freezer.

Whip the cream until softly stiff. Mash down the fruit ice, mix in the cream and freeze until solid. If not required immediately, seal, label and return to the freezer.

To serve: Place in the refrigerator for 30 minutes to soften slightly. Spoon into dishes, decorate with a few whole strawberries and serve with fan wafers.

Note: Other fruit purées may be used in place of the strawberry purée.

Serves 6

Chocolate ice cream crunch

METRIC/IMPERIAL/AMERICAN

40 g/1½ oz/3 tablespoons butter
2 tablespoons/2 tablespoons/3 tablespoons castor sugar
100 g/4 oz/1 cup crushed gingernut biscuits
1 tablespoon cocoa powder
2 tablespoons/2 tablespoons/3 tablespoons water
300 ml/½ pint/1¼ cups double cream, whipped
1 tablespoon brandy (optional)
1 large egg white
100 ml/4 fl oz/½ cup double cream, whipped, to decorate

Line a 1-kg/2-lb loaf tin with greaseproof paper. Melt the butter
and sugar in a saucepan. Remove from the heat and stir in the
biscuit crumbs. Allow to cool. Press half the mixture into the
base of the tin. Dissolve the cocoa powder in the water and add
to the cream, straining if there are any lumps. Stir in the brandy,
if used. Whisk the egg white until stiff and fold in. Pour the
mixture on to the biscuits in the tin. Level the surface and
spread the remaining crushed biscuits on top. Put into the
freezer for about 2 hours to become firm. Turn out of the tin. If
not required immediately, pack in a rigid polythene container,
seal, label and return to the freezer.
To serve: Pipe whipped cream along each side to decorate.
Allow to soften for 2–3 hours in the refrigerator if using after
freezing for longer than the 2 hours.

Serves 6–8

Pineapple polls

METRIC/IMPERIAL/AMERICAN

1 frozen Arctic Roll
4 canned pineapple rings
2 egg whites
100 g/4 oz/½ cup castor sugar
angelica to decorate

Cut the Arctic Roll into 4 slices and place on an ovenproof
plate. Drain the pineapple rings and place a ring on each slice of
Arctic Roll.

Whisk the egg whites until stiff. Gradually whisk in half the
sugar and fold in the remainder. Divide the meringue evenly
between the slices, carefully covering the pineapple and Arctic
Roll and piling it up.

Stick pointed pieces of angelica into the tops and sprinkle
with a little extra castor sugar. Place towards the top of a hot
oven (230°C, 450°F, Gas Mark 8) for a few minutes to brown
lightly. Serve at once.
Note: This recipe is for using frozen ingredients, not for
freezing when cooked.

Serves 4

Hazelnut Pavlova

METRIC/IMPERIAL/AMERICAN
3 large egg whites
175 g/6 oz/1⅓ cups icing sugar, sifted
50 g/2 oz/⅓ cup hazelnuts, roasted, skinned and chopped
1 teaspoon malt vinegar
¼ teaspoon vanilla essence
300 ml/½ pint/1¼ cups double cream, lightly whipped
300 ml/½ pint/1¼ cups apricot purée (see page 223)
2 tablespoons/2 tablespoons/3 tablespoons water
40 g/1½ oz/3 tablespoons castor sugar

Whisk the egg whites until stiff, and gradually whisk in half the icing sugar. Fold in the remainder with the hazelnuts, vinegar and vanilla. Spread in a 23-cm/9-inch circle on a sheet of non-stick paper on a baking sheet. Make a slight hollow in the centre. Bake for 1 hour in a very cool oven (120°C, 250°F, Gas Mark ½). Switch off oven and leave meringue for 1 hour.
To serve at once: Pile the cream into the centre. Decorate the edge with piped rosettes of cream, if liked. Gently heat the apricot purée with the water and sugar. Serve hot or cold.
To freeze: Wrap the cooled pavlova in foil, being careful not to squash it. Seal, label and freeze. Freeze the sauce separately.
To thaw: Unwrap the pavlova and leave at room temperature for 1 hour. Finish as before. Thaw the sauce at room temperature for 1–2 hours or heat gently from frozen. Place the rosettes, still frozen, on the pavlova.

Serves 6–8

Apricot linzertorte

METRIC/IMPERIAL/AMERICAN
75 g/3 oz/6 tablespoons granulated sugar
0.5 kg/1 lb/1 lb fresh apricots, halved and stoned
100 g/4 oz/½ cup butter
75 g/3 oz/6 tablespoons castor sugar
1 egg
175 g/6 oz/1½ cups plain flour
50 g/2 oz/½ cup ground hazelnuts
1 teaspoon ground cinnamon
pinch salt
1 tablespoon cornflour

Dissolve sugar in 2 tablespoons/2 tablespoons/3 tablespoons water. Add apricots and simmer for 15–20 minutes. Drain, reserve syrup. Add the butter, sugar and egg to the flour, nuts, cinnamon and salt, and knead. Chill.

Make the apricot syrup up to 150 ml/¼ pint/⅔ cup with water. Blend the cornflour with a little of this, place all in a pan. Heat, stirring, until thickened. Add apricots and cool.

Roll out two-thirds of the pastry to line a 20-cm/8-inch flan tin or foil tart case. Fill with the apricots and glaze. Roll out the remaining pastry, cut into strips and arrange over the top.
To serve at once: Bake at 220°C, 425°F, Gas Mark 7 for 10 minutes, then 180°C, 350°F, Gas Mark 4 for 25 minutes.
To freeze: Uncooked in a polythene bag. Seal, label and freeze.
To thaw: Unwrap and bake from frozen in a hot oven as above, cook for 20 minutes before reducing heat for further 30 minutes.

Serves 6

Pears in ginger syrup

METRIC/IMPERIAL/AMERICAN
0.5 kg/1 lb/1 lb cooking pears
juice of 1 lemon
300 ml/½ pint/1¼ cups water
75 g/3 oz/6 tablespoons demerara sugar
3 tablespoons/3 tablespoons/¼ cup chopped stem ginger

Peel the pears, core and cut into quarters. Sprinkle with lemon juice to prevent discoloration. Place the water and sugar in a saucepan. Heat gently to dissolve the sugar, add the pears and cook gently until just tender — about 10 minutes. Test with a skewer.

Using a slotted spoon, transfer the pears to a serving dish or a container suitable for the freezer. Reduce the syrup a little over high heat and stir in the chopped ginger. Allow the syrup to cool before pouring over the pears.

To serve at once: Chill well and serve with ice cream or cream.
To freeze: Allow to cool, making sure the pears are completely covered by the syrup. Seal, label and freeze.
Thaw: At room temperature for 2–3 hours.

Serves 3–4

Summer pudding

METRIC/IMPERIAL/AMERICAN
50 g/2 oz/¼ cup castor sugar
4 tablespoons/4 tablespoons/⅓ cup water
0.5–0.75 kg/1–1½ lb/1–1½ lb raspberries and blackcurrants
1 small stale loaf, sliced
150 ml/¼ pint/⅔ cup double cream, whipped, to decorate

Gently heat the sugar and water to dissolve the sugar. Add the fruit, reserving a little of each for decoration. Simmer gently for 5 minutes.

Remove the crusts from the bread and use as many slices as necessary to line the base and sides of a 0.5-kg/1-lb foil basin with a sealing lid. Add half the fruit, place a slice of bread in the centre, add the remaining fruit and cover with more bread. Ease on the lid, place a 1-kg/2-lb weight on top and put in the refrigerator overnight.

To serve at once: Turn the pudding out, place the reserved fruit on top and pipe whipped cream around the edge.
To freeze: Leave in the foil basin. Pack in a polythene bag. Seal, label and freeze. Freeze the reserved fruit separately.
To thaw: Leave in the basin and thaw overnight in the refrigerator or for 6 hours at room temperature. Turn out and decorate as above, using the thawed reserved fruit.

Serves 4–5

Apple bread and butter pudding

METRIC/IMPERIAL/AMERICAN

6 large slices bread, crusts removed
40 g/1½ oz/3 tablespoons butter, softened
75 g/3 oz/½ cup raisins
1 large cooking apple, peeled and sliced, or 175 g/6 oz/1½
    cups frozen apple slices, thawed
40 g/1½ oz/3 tablespoons castor sugar
2 large eggs
450 ml/¾ pint/2 cups milk

Spread the bread with the butter and cut each slice into three.
Place a layer of the bread pieces, buttered side up, in a 1.25-
litre/2-pint/2½-pint ovenproof dish which must be freezerproof
if it is to be frozen. Sprinkle with raisins, apple and sugar.
Continue layering until the ingredients are used up.

   Beat the eggs and milk together and strain over the bread.
Allow to stand for 20 minutes then cook towards the bottom of
a moderately hot oven (190°C, 375°F, Gas Mark 5) for 30
minutes.

To serve at once: Serve hot with cream.
To freeze: Cool, wrap in foil, seal, label and freeze.
To thaw: Leave, wrapped, at room temperature for 1 hour then
place uncovered in a moderate oven (180°C, 350°F, Gas Mark 4)
for 30–40 minutes.

Serves 4–6

Pineapple pudding

METRIC/IMPERIAL/AMERICAN

2 tablespoons/2 tablespoons/3 tablespoons cornflour
1 (376-g/13¼-oz/13¼-oz) can crushed pineapple
3 tablespoons/3 tablespoons/¼ cup marmalade
110 g/4 oz/½ cup soft margarine
110 g/4 oz/½ cup castor sugar
2 large eggs
110 g/4 oz/1 cup self-raising flour
grated rind of 1 orange

Mix the cornflour with a little juice from the pineapple. Heat the
pineapple gently with the marmalade. Add the cornflour and
stir until thickened. Spoon into a 1.25-litre/2-pint/2½-pint
ovenproof dish. Use a foil or other freezerproof dish if the
pudding is to be frozen. Cool.

   Beat together the margarine, sugar, eggs, flour and orange
rind for 2 minutes. Spread over the pineapple.

To serve at once: Cook in the centre of a moderately hot oven
(190°C, 375°F, Gas Mark 5) for 35–40 minutes; cover up with
foil, if necessary, to prevent overbrowning. Turn out and serve
hot or cold.

To freeze: Place the uncooked pudding in the freezer. When
frozen, cover with a lid or foil. Seal, label and return to the
freezer.

To thaw: Remove lid but cover loosely with foil. Place, still
frozen, in a moderate oven (180°C, 350°F, Gas Mark 4) for 1¾
hours. Remove foil for the last 15 minutes.

Serves 6–8

Raspberry gâteau

METRIC/IMPERIAL/AMERICAN

3 eggs
75 g/3 oz/6 tablespoons castor sugar
75 g/3 oz/¾ cup plain flour, sifted
¼ teaspoon salt
2 tablespoons/2 tablespoons/3 tablespoons raspberry jam
300 ml/½ pint/1¼ cups double cream, whipped
0.5 kg/1 lb/1 lb fresh or frozen raspberries
2 tablespoons/2 tablespoons/3 tablespoons sherry
3 tablespoons/3 tablespoons/¼ cup redcurrant jelly

Line the base of a 20-cm/8-inch round cake tin with greaseproof paper and lightly oil.

Whisk together the eggs and sugar in a bowl over a pan of boiling water until the whisk leaves a trail. Remove the bowl and whisk until cool.

Using a metal spoon quickly fold in the flour and salt. Pour into the tin and cook in the centre of a moderate oven (180°C, 350°F, Gas Mark 4) for 25–30 minutes. Cool on a wire rack.

To serve at once: Cut in half and spread the base with the raspberry jam, a third of the cream and then half the raspberries. Cover with the top sponge and sprinkle with sherry. Decorate with the remaining cream and raspberries. Brush warmed redcurrant jelly over the raspberries.

To freeze: Place the undecorated sponge in a polythene bag or wrap in foil. Seal, label and freeze.

To thaw: Leave, wrapped, at room temperature for 1 hour.

Makes 1 (20-cm/8-inch) gâteau

Orange and lemon pudding

METRIC/IMPERIAL/AMERICAN

100 g/4 oz/½ cup granulated sugar
50 g/2 oz/½ cup plain flour
25 g/1 oz/2 tablespoons butter or margarine
1 orange
1 lemon
3 eggs, separated
450 ml/¾ pint/2 cups milk

Mix together the sugar, flour and butter or margarine in a bowl. Add the grated rinds and juice from the orange and lemon. Beat well. Add the egg yolks to the bowl, stir in the milk and mix well together. Whisk the egg whites until stiff and fold into the mixture.

Pour into a 1-litre/1½-pint/2-pint foil dish. Place in a roasting tin half filled with water and bake in the centre of a moderate oven (180°C, 350°F, Gas Mark 4) for 45 minutes until risen and brown.

To serve at once: Serve hot.

To freeze: Allow to cool then cover, seal, label and freeze.

To thaw: Uncover and place, still frozen, in a cool oven (150°C, 300°F, Gas Mark 2) for 20 minutes.

Serves 6

Picnics and packed lunches

Now, instead of having to prepare packed lunches when you are busy trying to cook the breakfast and get everybody out of the house on time, you can just take the required number of portions from the freezer, knowing they will thaw during the morning. And with supplies of picnic fare all ready, the whole family can go off for the day whenever the sun shines.

Sandwich fillings for the freezer

Avoid freezing sandwiches with fillings which discolour or go limp and watery, or tough and dry, for example lettuce, cress, tomatoes, cucumber, hard-boiled eggs and bananas.

Freeze the sandwiches with the crusts on, and remove them on thawing. Always use fresh bread. Wrap quickly so they do not dry out in the atmosphere.

FILLINGS FOR CHILDREN

These are proven favourites with children:

Grated cheese and pickle
Grated cheese with a little chopped skinned tomato
  mixed with tomato ketchup
Mashed tuna with cottage cheese and 1 or 2 drops
  vinegar (illustrated)
Minced ham with sandwich spread

ADULT FILLINGS

Cottage cheese with chopped olives and gherkins
  (illustrated)
Sliced beef with horseradish
Sliced tongue with pickle

To freeze: Make up the sandwiches in the usual way, buttering them well to stop the filling going through. Interleave the sandwiches with freezer layer tissue and place in polythene bags. Seal, label very clearly and freeze. Fillings containing cottage cheese should not be stored for longer than 2–4 weeks.

To thaw: Take the required number of sandwiches from the freezer in the morning and wrap in foil. The sandwiches will be thawed by lunchtime but still be nice and fresh.

Cheese flan

METRIC/IMPERIAL/AMERICAN
50 g/2 oz/¼ cup lard
100 g/4 oz/1 cup plain flour
pinch salt
1 tablespoon cold water
FILLING:
2 tablespoons/2 tablespoons/3 tablespoons sweet pickle
175 g/6 oz/1½ cups Cheddar cheese, grated
2 eggs
150 ml/¼ pint/⅔ cup milk

Place an 18-cm/7-inch flan ring on a baking sheet.

Rub the fat into the flour and add the salt and enough cold water to make a dough. Roll out and use to line the flan ring.

Mix the pickle, cheese, eggs and milk together and pour into the prepared flan case. Bake in the centre of a moderate oven (190°C, 375°F, Gas Mark 5) for 40 minutes or until set and firm.

Remove the flan ring and allow the flan to cool on the baking sheet.

To serve at once: Serve cold with salad or wrap individual portions in foil for a packed lunch.

To freeze: Loosen the flan from the baking sheet, cut into portions and open freeze. When solid, wrap the portions in foil, seal, label and return to the freezer.

To thaw: Remove the required number of pieces from the freezer and leave in the foil at room temperature for 1 hour.

Serves 4–6

Baps and bangerburgers

METRIC/IMPERIAL/AMERICAN
225 g/8 oz/1 cup pork and beef sausagemeat
½ teaspoon dried mixed herbs
3 teaspoons tomato ketchup
3 rashers streaky bacon, derinded and chopped
flour for coating
salt and pepper
3 tablespoons/3 tablespoons/¼ cup oil
3 baps
butter for spreading
1 tablespoon pickle (optional)

Mix the sausagemeat with the herbs, ketchup and bacon.

Divide the mixture into 3 cakes, each about 2 cm/¾ inch thick. Coat with seasoned flour. Fry the cakes in the oil for about 6 minutes on each side.

Remove and drain on kitchen paper. Allow to become cold.

To serve at once: Cut the baps in half, spread with butter, and pickle if liked. Place a bangerburger on each bottom half and cover with the top half. Wrap each filled bap in cling film to keep fresh.

To freeze: Wrap the bangerburgers and baps separately in foil or interleave with freezer layer tissue and pack in polythene bags. Seal, label and freeze.

To thaw: Leave, wrapped, at room temperature for 1 hour, then finish as before, wrapping in cling film to keep them fresh and easy to pack.

Serves 3

Cheese scones

METRIC/IMPERIAL/AMERICAN
100 g/4 oz/1 cup self-raising flour
salt and pepper
½ teaspoon dry mustard
40 g/1½ oz/3 tablespoons soft margarine
50 g/2 oz/½ cup Cheddar cheese, grated
1 tablespoon chopped parsley
3 tablespoons/3 tablespoons/4 tablespoons milk
extra milk for brushing

Sift the flour into a bowl with the salt, pepper and mustard. Rub in the margarine until the mixture is like fine breadcrumbs. Add the cheese and parsley. Make a well in the centre, add the milk and mix with a fork. Knead gently on a lightly floured board and roll out to a circle about 2 cm/¾ inch thick. Brush with a little milk and mark with a knife into 6 wedges.

Place on a lightly floured baking sheet and cook towards the top of a hot oven (220°C, 425°F, Gas Mark 7) for 10–15 minutes. Cool on a wire tray. Cut into the wedges.
To serve at once: Pack individual portions into polythene bags and take on a picnic to eat with a salad.
To freeze: Place in a plastic bag. Seal, label and freeze.
To thaw: Pack, still wrapped, in with the picnic fare. They will thaw in 30 minutes at room temperature.

Serves 6

Sponge and apple squares

METRIC/IMPERIAL/AMERICAN
150 g/5 oz/⅔ cup soft margarine
175 g/6 oz/¾ cup castor sugar
1 egg
grated rind of 1 lemon
225 g/8 oz/2 cups self-raising flour
0.75 kg/1½ lb/1½ lb cooking apples
75 g/3 oz/½ cup sultanas

Cream the margarine with 75 g/3 oz/6 tablespoons sugar, until light and fluffy.

Beat in the egg and lemon rind. Gradually stir in the flour. Transfer half the mixture to an oiled 18 × 28-cm/7 × 11-inch tin. Level the surface.

Peel the apples, slice thinly and spread over the mixture in the tin. Sprinkle with the sultanas and 50 g/2 oz/¼ cup sugar. Cover with the remaining creamed mixture and level the surface. Cook in the centre of a moderate oven (180°C, 350°F, Gas Mark 4) for 1 hour.
To serve at once: Sprinkle with the remaining sugar and serve with custard. Alternatively, sprinkle with sugar, leave to become cold, cut into squares and wrap in greaseproof paper to take as part of a packed lunch.
To freeze: Sprinkle with the remaining sugar. When cold, cut into squares and wrap in foil. Seal, label and freeze.
To thaw: In wrapped portions at room temperature for 1 hour.

Serves 12

Cakes, biscuits and bread

Baked goods freeze very well. Cakes can be frozen plain, and iced after thawing or they can be finished completely and then frozen packed in rigid polythene containers to give protection during storage. When freezing decorated cakes without a rigid container, remember to open freeze before wrapping closely and to unwrap while the icing is still solid.

Chocolate sandwich cake

METRIC/IMPERIAL/AMERICAN
110 g/4 oz/½ cup castor sugar
110 g/4 oz/½ cup soft margarine
110 g/4 oz/1 cup self-raising flour, sifted
1 teaspoon baking powder
1 tablespoon cocoa powder
2 large eggs
ICING:
225 g/8 oz/1¾ cups icing sugar, sifted
75 g/3 oz/6 tablespoons soft margarine
2 tablespoons/2 tablespoons/3 tablespoons hot water
1½ tablespoons/1½ tablespoons/2 tablespoons cocoa
chocolate vermicelli to decorate

Line the bases of two 18-cm/7-inch sandwich tins and brush with oil. Place all the cake ingredients in a bowl and beat well. Divide the mixture between the tins. Place in the centre of a moderate oven (160°C, 325°F, Gas Mark 3) for 25–30 minutes. Turn out and cool. Place the icing sugar and margarine in a bowl and beat in the hot water blended with cocoa.
To serve at once: Sandwich the cakes together with a third of the icing. Spread most of the remainder all over the cake and decorate as illustrated.
To freeze: Separate the layers with greaseproof paper, wrap in foil, seal, label and freeze. Freeze icing separately.
To thaw: Unwrap the cake and thaw cake and icing for 2 hours at room temperature. Finish as above.

Makes 1 (18-cm/7-inch) round sandwich cake

Raisin and ginger cake

METRIC/IMPERIAL/AMERICAN
100 g/4 oz/¾ cup ginger preserved in syrup, chopped
225 g/8 oz/2 cups self-raising flour, sifted
50 g/2 oz/⅓ cup seedless raisins
150 g/5 oz/½ cup plus 2 tablespoons butter
100 g/4 oz/½ cup soft brown sugar
2 large eggs
¼ teaspoon salt
1 teaspoon ground ginger
50 g/2 oz/⅓ cup mixed peel
4 sugar lumps
castor sugar to decorate

Line and grease a 20-cm/8-inch round cake tin. Drain the ginger on kitchen paper and toss lightly in a little flour. Add raisins.

Cream the butter with the sugar, beat in the eggs and gradually stir in the flour, salt, ground ginger, fruit and peel. Turn into the tin. Crush the sugar lumps and sprinkle over the top. Bake in the centre of a moderate oven (160°C, 325°F, Gas Mark 3) for 1¼–1½ hours, or until a skewer inserted into the centre of the cake comes out clean. Allow to stand for 5 minutes. Turn out on to a cake rack.

To serve at once: Sprinkle with castor sugar and, if liked, tie a yellow ribbon around the cake.

To freeze: Open freeze, then wrap in foil and a polythene bag. Seal, label and return to the freezer.

To thaw: Unwrap and thaw for 4 hours at room temperature.

Makes 1 (20-cm/8-inch) round cake

Coffee walnut cake

METRIC/IMPERIAL/AMERICAN
3 eggs
75 g/3 oz/6 tablespoons castor sugar
75 g/3 oz/¾ cup plain flour
¼ teaspoon salt
2 tablespoons/2 tablespoons/3 tablespoons apricot jam
150 g/5 oz/½ cup plus 2 tablespoons unsalted butter
100 g/4 oz/scant cup icing sugar, sifted
1 tablespoon instant coffee dissolved in 3 teaspoons boiling water
75 g/3 oz/¾ cup shelled walnuts

Line and grease two 20-cm/8-inch sandwich tins. Whisk the eggs and sugar in a mixing bowl over hot water until the whisk leaves a trail. Using a metal spoon, fold in the flour and salt. Divide the mixture between the tins. Bake in a hot oven (220°C, 425°F, Gas Mark 7) for 10–15 minutes. Cool.

To serve at once: Spread one sponge with apricot jam. Cream the butter and icing sugar, then beat in the coffee. Spread a little cream over the jam and sandwich the cakes. Coat the cake with most of the cream. Halve 8 walnuts and reserve. Chop the remainder and press on to the sides. Mark a pattern on the top. Decorate as illustrated.

To freeze: Place on foil instead of cake stand. Finish as above except for sprinkling the icing sugar. Open freeze, then pack in a rigid polythene container. Seal, label and return to the freezer.

To thaw: Unpacked for 4 hours. Sprinkle with icing sugar.

Makes 1 (20-cm/8-inch) round cake

Tuilles

METRIC/IMPERIAL/AMERICAN
50 g/2 oz/½ cup almonds, blanched or flaked
65 g/2½ oz/5 tablespoons butter
65 g/2½ oz/5 tablespoons castor sugar
40 g/1½ oz/6 tablespoons plain flour

Chop the almonds roughly. Cream the butter and sugar together until light and fluffy, add the flour and almonds and mix well. Place small heaps of the mixture, about the size of a walnut, well apart on 2 greased baking sheets. Flatten each with a wet fork.

Bake one sheet at a time in the centre of a moderately hot oven (200°C, 400°F, Gas Mark 6) for about 5–8 minutes. Leave to cool for a few seconds before removing with a palette knife and gently curve round a rolling pin. Leave until cool.

Cook the second batch and continue in this way until all the mixture has been used up.

To serve at once: Serve immediately or keep for a short time in an airtight container.

To freeze: Place carefully in a rigid polythene container. Seal, label and freeze.

To thaw: Unpack and arrange on a plate just before serving.

Makes about 20 biscuits

Chocolate and vanilla pinwheels

METRIC/IMPERIAL/AMERICAN
110 g/4 oz/½ cup castor sugar
110 g/4 oz/½ cup butter, softened
1 large egg
225 g/8 oz/2 cups self-raising flour
1 tablespoon cocoa powder, sifted
½ teaspoon vanilla essence
1 egg white

Mix the sugar into the softened butter and beat in the egg. Stir in the flour, knead lightly and divide in half. Knead the cocoa into one-half and the vanilla into the other. Roll out the chocolate dough between 2 sheets of lightly floured greaseproof paper to a rectangle 20 × 28 cm/8 × 11 inches. Repeat with the vanilla dough. Remove both top sheets of greaseproof and brush the chocolate dough with egg white. Place the vanilla dough on the chocolate, remove the greaseproof on top and roll the doughs like a Swiss roll, using the remaining greaseproof to aid rolling. Wrap in foil and chill.

To serve at once: Cut into 5-mm/¼-inch slices. Bake for 10–15 minutes on a greased baking sheet in a moderately hot oven (190°C, 375°F, Gas Mark 5). Cool on a wire rack.

To freeze: Freeze the uncooked dough wrapped in foil or pack the cold cooked pinwheels in a rigid polythene container.

To thaw: Leave wrapped at room temperature for 3–4 hours.

Makes about 34 biscuits

White bread

METRIC/IMPERIAL/AMERICAN
50 g/2 oz/¼ cup margarine or lard
0.75 kg/1½ lb/6 cups strong white flour
2 teaspoons salt
1 teaspoon sugar
15 g/½ oz/½ cake fresh yeast
450 ml/¾ pint/2 cups lukewarm water

Rub the margarine or lard into the flour and salt. Add the sugar and then the yeast blended with the water. Mix to a soft dough. Knead well for 10 minutes, then place in a lightly oiled polythene bag. Tie loosely. Leave to rise until doubled in size – 40–45 minutes in a warm place or about 2 hours at room temperature. Knead well for 2 minutes.

Using half the dough, roll out into a straight piece and tie loosely in a single knot. Place on a greased and floured baking tray in an oiled polythene bag and leave to rise for 30–40 minutes in a warm place. Remove from the bag and bake in a hot oven (220°C, 425°F, Gas Mark 7) for 25 minutes.

Divide the remaining dough into 36 balls and press them together in threes on a greased and floured baking sheet. Cover with oiled polythene and leave until doubled in size. Remove polythene and bake as above for 15–20 minutes.
To freeze: Wrap the cold loaf in foil. Open freeze the rolls, then pack in a polythene bag. Seal, label and freeze.
To thaw: Defrost the loaf, unwrapped, at room temperature for about 4 hours; the rolls for 1½ hours.

Makes 1 (0.5-kg/1-lb) loaf and 12 rolls

Brown bread

METRIC/IMPERIAL/AMERICAN
25 g/1 oz/2 tablespoons lard or margarine
0.75 kg/1½ lb/6 cups plain wholemeal flour
225 g/8 oz/2 cups strong white flour
2 teaspoons salt
2 teaspoons sugar
2 teaspoons black treacle
25 g/1 oz/1 cake fresh yeast
600 ml/1 pint/2½ cups warm water

Rub the lard or margarine into the flours and salt.

Add the sugar, the treacle and the yeast blended with the water. Mix to make a soft dough. Knead well for 10 minutes on a lightly floured surface. Divide the dough into two-thirds and one-third. Arrange the larger piece in a greased 18-cm/7-inch round cake tin and the smaller piece in a greased 0.5-kg/1-lb loaf tin.

Place the tins in lightly oiled polythene bags. Tie loosely. Leave to rise until doubled in size – about 40–45 minutes in a warm place or 1½–2 hours at room temperature. Remove the bags and dust the bread with flour, if liked. Place in a hot oven (220°C, 425°F, Gas Mark 7) and bake the large loaf for 35 minutes and the small one for 25 minutes, or until they shrink slightly in the tins. Turn on to a wire rack to cool.
To serve at once: Store in a bread container until needed.
To freeze: When cold, pack in a large polythene bag.
To thaw: Leave unwrapped at room temperature for 4 hours.

Makes 1 (1-kg/2-lb) round loaf and 1 (0.5-kg/1-lb) loaf

Gingerbread

METRIC/IMPERIAL/AMERICAN
100 g/4 oz/½ cup margarine
75 g/3 oz/6 tablespoons soft brown sugar
175 g/6 oz/½ cup black treacle
100 g/4 oz/⅓ cup golden syrup
1 teaspoon ground ginger
½ teaspoon ground cloves
½ teaspoon ground nutmeg
100 ml/4 fl oz/½ cup milk
2 eggs
225 g/8 oz/2 cups plain flour, sifted
3 tablespoons/3 tablespoons/¼ cup ginger marmalade
½ teaspoon bicarbonate of soda
1 tablespoon hot water
crystallised ginger to decorate

Line and grease a 20-cm/8-inch square cake tin. Heat the margarine with the sugar, treacle, syrup and spices. Add milk.

Beat the eggs together in a large bowl and add the warmed ingredients, flour, marmalade and bicarbonate of soda dissolved in the hot water. Pour into the cake tin and bake in the centre of a moderate oven (160°C, 325°F, Gas Mark 3) for 1½ hours. Cool. Cut into squares and decorate with slices of ginger.

To freeze: Wrap the cold uncut cake in foil and then place in a polythene bag. Seal, label and freeze.

To thaw: Leave wrapped only in foil for 3–4 hours at room temperature. Unwrap and finish as above.

Makes 1 (20-cm/8-inch) square cake

Cherry loaf

METRIC/IMPERIAL/AMERICAN
225 g/8 oz/2 cups glacé cherries
225 g/8 oz/2 cups self-raising flour
175 g/6 oz/¾ cup soft margarine
175 g/6 oz/¾ cup castor sugar
3 standard eggs
¼ teaspoon vanilla essence
6 sugar lumps, crushed

Wash and dry the cherries and toss in a little of the flour. Line and grease a 1-kg/2-lb loaf tin.

Beat together the margarine, sugar, flour, eggs and vanilla essence for 2 minutes. Add the cherries.

Put the mixture into the prepared tin and level the surface. Scatter the crushed sugar over the top and bake in the centre of a moderate oven (160°C, 325°F, Gas Mark 3) for 1¾ hours. The loaf is cooked when a skewer inserted into the centre comes out clean. Turn out on to a wire rack to cool, then remove the paper.

To serve at once: Cut into the required number of slices.

To freeze: When the loaf is cold, wrap in foil and put in a polythene bag. Seal, label and freeze. If liked, the loaf could be cut into slices and frozen with each slice individually wrapped in foil.

To thaw: Leave wrapped in the foil only for about 4 hours at room temperature.

Makes 1 (1-kg/2-lb) loaf

Index